Clinton Walker calls himself a Sydney writer, though he was born in Bendigo, Victoria and raised in Melbourne and Brisbane. He began writing about music in the late seventies, and since then has contributed to Australian publications from the *Age*, the *Australian* and the *Bulletin* to *Rolling Stone*, *RAM*, *Playboy*, *New Woman* and *Inside Sport*. He has previously edited two books on Australian rock'n'roll, *Inner city sound* and *The next thing*.

He was one of the first critics to chronicle emerging Aboriginal rock, and wrote a documentary on the subject for ABC-TV in 1987, called 'Sing it in the music'. He has appeared at the Tamworth Country Music Festival as a member of hillbilly-grunge band the Killer Sheep, who released the single 'Wild down home' on Au-Go-Go Records. He is a republican, and supports the Sydney Swans. He lives near Burwood with his wife, new baby and several animals.

HIGHWAY To HELL

The LIFE & TIMES of AC/DC LEGEND ~ BON SCOTT

by CLINTON WALKER

SIDGWICK & JACKSON

First published 1994 by Pan Macmillan Publishers Australia

First published in Great Britain 1995 by Sidgwick & Jackson
an imprint of Macmillan General Books
Cavaye Place London SW10 9PG
and Basingstoke

Associated companies throughout the world

ISBN 0 283 06263 0

1 3 5 7 9 8 6 4 2

A CIP catalogue record for this book is available from
the British Library

Printed and bound in Great Britain by
Mackays of Chatham PLC, Chatham, Kent

contents

acknowledgements

this book started life as a film proposal. It was my friend Tim
Ferrier's idea, and he's the first person to whom I owe thanks.
Tim was already in the film business, and as an old AC/DC
fan, he could see the potential in Bon's story. He asked me, as
a writer, to help him, and I shared his enthusiasm for the idea.

I remember the summer we spent writing a treatment. After
only a cursory amount of research, Tim and I got it right enough
to arouse terrific enthusiasm on the part of a producer and
potential investors. The project went no further than that.

The reason was that Alberts Productions, which owns the
rights to AC/DC's songs, and with whom we had initially had
agreeable meetings, simply stopped taking our calls. We
could only assume they weren't going to grant us permission
to use AC/DC's music, which effectively killed the film. So
with great disappointment, Tim and I shelved the thing. I still
believe Bon's story would make a great film.

Nevertheless, I refused to let go of the idea. Bon's story was
such a good one and, I believed, an important one, that I
remained determined to tell it somehow. This book is the result.

My intention was only ever to portray Bon through the eyes

of the people that knew him best, and so I had to seek all these people out. I consequently met and got to know a great many people I otherwise wouldn't have; this was an experience I mostly enjoyed and learned a lot from. I figure I would have liked Bon myself, because I found I liked so many of his old friends. I have relied on these people, and I can only extend to them all my sincere gratitude for the faith and trust they extended me, for their time and emotion, and the precious memories and mementos they so generously shared.

Of course, I went to Bon's family first, his mother and father, Isa and Chick, in Perth. 'Ron would have loved this,' Isa kept saying, rolling her r's in a still strong Scots brogue. She and Chick both gave me every assistance they could, and to them I extend my special thanks.

I went back to Alberts in the hope that they might now come to the party, but my hopes were in vain. I still don't know why — they won't tell me — they simply refuse to talk about their fallen comrade. Even after we agreed it was in no one's interest I get the facts wrong, they would not help me check facts. They denied permission to quote from Bon's lyrics. Their lack of grace is astonishing.

Curiously, it was, indeed, only people who had a purely professional relationship with Bon who were reluctant to talk to me. Plenty of them were keen, but just as many weren't. Is this book authorised? they all asked. And knowing what they were really getting at — whether or not Alberts approved of it — I would reply, Well, it depends what you mean by authorised. I would think, I would go on, that it's only Bon's family who have the right to authorise a book about him, and indeed, I have their blessing. And then they would all say, No, no, is Alberts going along with it? and I would say, No — and then they would back off. Alberts seems to generate an atmosphere of fear almost.

Almost without exception though, Bon's personal friends were delighted that an appropriate tribute was at last being paid to him, and were unequivocal in their enthusiasm to help.

I am indebted, then, to Vince Lovegrove, first and foremost, who not only opened quite a few doors for me — to people, like himself, who were Bon's oldest friends — but also encouraged and inspired me all the way along the line. That he did so during a time of such great personal duress is all the more humbling.

Mary Renshaw and Irene Thornton, Bon's wife, let me into their lives, and if a man can be measured by the women in his life, Mary and Irene prove Bon was a fine man. Great thanks also to Mark Evans, Michael Browning, Bruce Howe, and Silver Smith. All these people I kept going back to with questions, and to use as sounding-boards, and their patience never flagged.

I am also indebted to Pat Pickett, Pam Swain, Chris Gilbey, Anthony O'Grady, Christie Eliezer, *Juke*, *Rolling Stone*, Mick Cocks, Joe Furey, Peter Head and Mouse, Uncle John Ayers, John Freeman, Helen Carter, Dave Jarrett, Molly Meldrum, Wyn Milson, John Darcy, Doris Howe, Peter Noble, Adrian Driscoll, Terry Serio, Sam See, Maria and Jim Short, Rob Bailey, Hamish Henry, Dennis Laughlin, Anna Baba, Graeme Scott, Keith Glass, Ian MacFarlane, Richard Griffiths, Perry Cooper, Coral Browning, Paul Stewart, Chris Sturt and Dave Baxter. And to the photographers Philip Morris, Bob King, Peter Carrette, Roger Gould and Graeme Webber. And to a few people who preferred to remain nameless — they know who they are.

Without Pan Macmillan, of course, we wouldn't be here, and thanks to everyone there, especially my editor Julia Stiles, whose empathy has put her in very real danger of becoming a rock chick!

I am indebted to other writers whose research I have plundered, particularly Glenn A Baker, who seems to be the only journalist ever to have 'penetrated' Alberts. For months, I went back and forward to the Mitchell Library in Sydney and the Victorian State Library to rifle through old issues of *Go-Set*, *RAM*, *Juke*, *Rolling Stone* and *Digger*, and I salute their creators and often nameless contributors. I also referred continuously to Noel McGrath's *Australian encyclopaedia of rock & pop*, Peter Beilby and Michael Roberts' *Australian music directory*, Chris Spencer's *Who's who of Australian rock*, and David Day and Tim Parker's *It's our music*. It is a sad fact that Australian popular music still wants for a general narrative history, but I have tried myself to get one up, and still can't.

Naturally, I read the two previously published biographies of AC/DC — *Hell ain't no bad place to be* by Richard Bunton, and *Shock to the system* by Mark Putterford — and I only hope I'm not found out repeating any of their mistakes!

In general, quotes presented oral history style I obtained myself through first-hand interviews; those presented otherwise were derived from other sources, usually cited.

Of course, there are also my own friends and associates who have helped in different ways, among them Tony Hayes and all the people we met in Scotland, David McClymont, everyone in Adelaide (the Herzs, the Norwoods, the Harrises), Bleddyn Butcher and Jude Toohey in London, Richard Guilliatt and Susan Bogle in New York, Ken West, Bruce Milne, Robert Forster and Karin, Dave Graney and Clare Moore, Steve and Helen, Matthew and Dianne, Peter Blakeley, and Stuart Coupe and Julie Ogden. Thanks also to my family, especially my mother. And last but most of all, my wife Debbie, who means more to me than words can express.

No thanks, finally, to the people who have actively discouraged me over the years. The old *Rolling Stone* mob (Ed, Toby, Annette, David and John) I always enjoyed spirited debate with. But I have always wanted to try to find a broader forum, in the mainstream media, and so often I have met with nothing but condescension because I deal not in high culture, not even 'acceptable' polite popular culture like film or even television, but in rock'n'roll. It's ironic that the ostensibly liberated curators of Australian culture are guilty of a rare remaining instance of the old cultural cringe. Imported exotica like jazz, blues and world music seem to be acceptable, but for some reason local pop–rock performers, who say as much about Australia today as our artists in the other fields, and posit Australia as the third-largest producer of pop–rock music in the world, get short shrift. The arts pages seem to think revived Broadway musicals are more relevant. As Peter Wilmoth points out in his recent book *Glad all over*, a great many of the early episodes of 'Countdown' have been junked. Australian rock'n'roll — so meaningful to so many people, not just in Australia but all around the world — deserves better than that. Hopefully this book will be only the beginning.

Special thanks to Penguin Books Australia Ltd for permission to reproduce passages from William Dick's *A bunch of ratbags*; the *Boston Globe* for permission to quote from an October 7, 1970 column by George Frazier; Anthony O'Grady for permission to reprint in full his *RAM* obituary to Bon.

Every effort has been made to reach copyright holders of quoted passages by Lester Bangs (from the essay 'James Taylor marked for death', originally published in *Who put the bomp*, 1971) and Ian Hunter (from *Diary of a rock'n'roll star*), but all efforts proved unsuccessful.

PHOTOGRAPHIC CREDITS

Back cover: Bon's last ever appearance with AC/DC, performing 'Touch too much' on 'Top of the Pops', February, 1980. Picture — LFI. pii — Graeme Webber/Australian Rock Folio; xii — Graeme Webber/Australian Rock Folio; p14 — courtesy John Freeman; 28 — courtesy the Scott family; 40 — picture by Graeme Scott; 54 — courtesy Vince Lovegrove; 76 — courtesy John Freeman; 90 — courtesy the Scotts; 114 — picture by Philip Morris; 134 — courtesy Mary Renshaw; 162 — picture by Philip Morris; 184 — courtesy Mark Evans; 212 — courtesy the *Herald & Weekly Times*; 232 — courtesy Perry Cooper; 256 — picture by Gary Turner/*Juke*; 276 — picture by Philip Morris; 286 — picture by Frank Peters/*Juke*; 312 — picture by Roger Gould/*Juke*.

BLACK & WHITE PLATES: p1 — courtesy the Scott family; 2 — courtesy the Scotts; 3 — courtesy the Scotts (top)/Irene Thornton (bottom); 4 — courtesy Doris Howe (top)/picture by Philip Morris (bottom); 5 — courtesy John Freeman; 6 — courtesy Herm Kovac; 7 — picture by Philip Morris; 8 — picture by Philip Morris (top)/courtesy Matt Dickson (bottom).

COLOUR PLATES: p1 — courtesy Vince Lovegrove; 2 — From the Glenn A Baker Archives (top)/courtesy the Scott family (bottom); 3 — courtesy David Frith; 4 — pictures by Trudy Worme (top)/courtesy the Scotts (left)/Irene Thornton (right)/courtesy the ABC; 5 — courtesy the Scotts; 6 — courtesy Mary Renshaw (top right)/courtesy the Scotts; 7 — picture by the author (top)/courtesy the Scotts (bottom left)/picture by Tim Ferrier (bottom right); 8 — courtesy Mary Renshaw.

Overleaf: Bon on the AC/DC tour bus, Australia, July 1975.

introduction

When Bon Scott died in London on February 19, 1980, AC/DC was on the verge of the breakthrough that established them as one of the most popular rock'n'roll bands of all time.

AC/DC was then a new band on the world stage, as spotty young guitarist Angus Young's schoolboy get-up emphasised. But Bon himself was a veteran, the self-confessed old man of the band, a 33-year-old who had already been around the block twice since the sixties. Pronounced dead on arrival at the Kings College Hospital in South London, the accumulated ardour, the grind of nearly 20 years on the road, had finally caught up with him.

Bon Scott was a man who lived for the moment. When those moments ran out, his reputation solidified into legend: this was indeed one of the last true wild men of rock. The graffiti — BON LIVES! — is still visible scrawled on walls all around the world.

Dead rock stars are often deified on the basis of martyrdom alone, however senseless. But Bon Scott was a working-class hero in life, and he became an icon in death.

AC/DC carried on after Bon died — just as he would have wanted it — yet even as the new line-up of the band, with singer Brian Johnson, has enjoyed the greatest success, it is impossible to shake the feeling that it ain't what it used to be. The Young brothers, Malcolm and Angus, who formed the band and still run it, have acknowledged that it was Bon who set them on their path; and the earthiness, humour and honesty he invested the band with, it today only echoes.

AC/DC's back catalogue has never been out of print, and is still selling. By now the band has sold some 60 million albums world-wide, of which, maybe eight million are the seven albums Bon cut with the band. But more than the timeless appeal Bon exerts on successive generations, and more than his musical legacy, Bon has an iconographic status which is intangible, a presence, a given in our popular cultural heritage. As an Australian musical icon, he has a reach greater than Melba, Johnny O'Keefe, Nick Cave, even Slim Dusty. Appellations like 'an Australian Jim Morrison' are simply degrading, as Bon is the world's one and only Bon and nothing less.

Bon embodies the tearaway spirit, and no one he's touched, even as they might 'grow up' and leave rock'n'roll behind, shearing their greasy locks, trading their denim jacket for coveralls or a shirt and tie, will ever forget his example, the mischievous glint in his eye and the screeching call to arms.

Bon's image was not so emblematic he might now be mass produced like a Ned Kelly or a Kiss or Elvis doll, or even an Angus Young doll; nor does he exist in our collective memory as faded black-and-white newsreel footage, like, say, that of Bradman cutting an English field to pieces. Nor is he a static, still photograph, even for all the movement, the storm it might capture — as several indelible images of JO'K, and many of Elvis do. No, we are more likely to remember Bon fleetingly, flashlike, mercurial. He will be performing, on 'Countdown' maybe, or at a show you went to but can't fully remember after all those years and the rush and haze it was at the time anyway. He will be a splay of elbows and skin and tattoos, grinning with evil intent, grabbing at the microphone, screeching in his inimitable fashion, the eye of a driving storm of volume, rhythm and blues that enveloped everything, that simply lodged itself in the atmosphere as part of the air you breathed and so to which reaction was involuntary, the body jerking in tandem motion. This was rebellion and release superior to any other available in spiritually bereft suburbia. And Bon was its advocate, a denim-clad Pied Piper with a bottle in his hand, a lady in waiting and the hellhounds on his trail...

Bon updated the Australian larrikin archetype. He was 'the original currency lad', as Sidney J Baker defined him in *The Australian language*: 'tough, defiant, reckless', plugged into the urban, electric twentieth century. Part of Bon's appeal was vicarious, it always is with rock stars — they live out our fantasies for us, and Bon very much lived the life of excess his audience could only dream about. But his immortality is not the result of nostalgic yearning. Even after his death Bon remains potent, the brute poet of the inarticulate underclass, a spokesman for not a generation but a class, a class with little influence or barely even so much as a voice. Railing against conformity, mediocrity and hypocrisy, Bon's rebellion, however, was blessedly not nihilistic, but rather the opposite — a lust for life that knew no bounds. With a disregard for all the niceties — even though, ironically, an impeccable politeness was one of Bon's endearing personal traits — he might have been saying nothing more than, Believe nothing they tell you! Break free! Find out for yourself! Live life!

Bon regarded AC/DC's 1976 number five single 'Jailbreak' as one of his best songs, and indeed it might well stand as his most succinct autobiographical statement — jail being a blunt metaphor for the straight life.

It's true that Bon himself grew up hard, even served time, but Bon had no chips on his shoulders. Nor was he motivated by the short man's syndrome which seems to at least partially drive an Iggy Pop or a James Brown. Like Elvis, Bon loved and respected his parents; it was just that he rejected their way of life, as he saw it, the slow quiet suburban death of stolid conformity and insincere gesture. No gesture was ever so sincere as the finger Bon gave to all of this — to polite society, the silent majority, which, with its blinkeredness and apathy, was to Bon the antithesis of what life was all about.

Bon surmounted the odds to become a rock'n'roll star, a singer and songwriter. He wasn't so much a singer as he was a screamer. He could play drums, as he did with his father in the Fremantle Pipe Band. But leaving school at 15, he hardly had any grand plans. It would probably have been enough that he stayed out of trouble. But it's testimony to Bon's strength of character, his pure desire, that after his stint behind bars he never went back there.

What Bon was was the personification of the old adage, 'it's the singer, not the song'. Bon was never more at home than on stage, and perhaps more than his abilities as a singer and songwriter, he was great as a performer. His brilliance was that you believed in him; that, as they say, he could sell a song. Maybe it was his refusal to take anything, himself especially, too seriously — maybe it was just his impishness — but there was something conspiratorial in his grin that encouraged people who otherwise might never have stepped out of line to join in with him, in giving everything dull the finger.

Something touched a nerve, made a connection. Journalist George Frazier, on the occasion of Janis Joplin's death in 1970, wrote a eulogy to her in the *Boston Globe* which uncannily evokes Bon: '... an unkempt, vulgar, obscene girl (though never malicious and with a certain sweetness) who, given a microphone and an audience of her peers, became a wild child. She really couldn't sing very well and she was far more gamin than graceful, and yet the young, as is their way these days, responded to her because of her shortcomings, because of her desecration of discipline. She was marvellous because she was so dreadful, so much animal energy and so little art.'

That Bon too was, and still is, reviled almost as equally as he's adored only confirms his potency. There is perhaps a little bit of Bon in everyone, only some people don't want to admit it — the same people who don't like getting their hands dirty.

Bon's old friends like to say his life was a success story because, it would appear, he got exactly what he wanted. He was initially driven not so much by the need to express himself as the desire, simply, to become a rock'n'roll star, to escape that monstrous suburban straitjacket — and he achieved precisely that.

Vince Lovegrove, who was covocalist with Bon in the Valentines in the sixties, wrote in an obituary to his old friend: 'To Bon, success meant one thing — more — more booze, more women, more dope, more energy, more rock'n'roll... more life!'

They say that being in a rock'n'roll band is a sure way of prolonging adolescence, putting off growing up — and it is — but by the time AC/DC started getting really successful, Bon had been around so long, it only served to illustrate to him what was really important. Fame and riches, in themselves, are empty. The tragedy of Bon's death — symbiotic with the fact that he died, in so many ways, alone in the world — was that he was only just starting to come to terms with a life that had to be lived, which he found he needed to live, beyond, or outside rock'n'roll. Off the road. So busy had he always been chasing his dream he never stopped running. His only refuge was alcohol and sex. When late in the piece he did find the space and time to glance over his shoulder, or fully stop at a byway and look at his life, life in general, he realised what he was missing: a home. It doesn't matter who you are, you need a home to go to.

Bon was a wild man of rock, it's true; but at the same time, the Bon Scott behind the image, as is so often the case, was a different person.

'I encountered Bon Scott a number of times during the seventies,' wrote Australian Rock Brain of the Universe Glenn A Baker, 'and each meeting served to increase my incredulity that a performer's public image could be so at odds with his real personality. Bon really was a sweet man. He was warm, friendly and uncommonly funny. He did not breathe fire, pluck wings off flies or eat children whole. And while his daunting stage persona was by no means fraudulent, it was most certainly a professional cloak that could be worn at convenient moments.'

Nobody who knew Bon can find a bad word for him. He had a generosity of spirit which was perhaps to a fault. But even as Bon was, as everyone who worked with him testifies, a consummate professional, he always leant heavily on the bottle. Monotonous, tedious life on the road ensured it was so. Alcoholic death crept up on him.

Being in a rock'n'roll band is also akin to adopting, or being adopted by a surrogate family, and to Bon, 'The Band', whichever band he happened to be in at any given time — from the Valentines in the sixties, through Fraternity in the early seventies, to AC/DC — was always the closest thing he had to a home.

Bon got married during the heady early seventies. But just as the hippie dream went up in smoke, Bon's marriage too fell apart. Bon was torn during those days, to a point where, literally, he almost killed himself. It was only AC/DC that saved him.

AC/DC provided Bon with a new purpose, a new family. With Malcolm and Angus' big brother, former Easybeat George, presiding over AC/DC from his studio lair, the Youngs were a tightly-knit Scots clan that worked on an all-or-nothing, us-against-them basis; Bon, who had the talent they needed, and happily also happened to be a Scot, was accepted as one of them, a blood brother, and that was that.

Bon, however, was a quite different type of person to any of the Youngs; outgoing, good-humoured, and trusting, where the Youngs were a closed shop, uniformly suspicious, paranoid almost, possessed of the virtual opposite of Bon's generosity of spirit, prone to sullenness. Just as nobody can find a bad word for Bon, few of the people who have had dealings with the Youngs can find a good word for them. But Bon was united with Malcolm, Angus and George because they let him in, as they did so few others, and they shared a common goal — the music — and if nothing else, a ribald sense of humour.

But gradually, as the band became more successful, the mood within it more businesslike, if not downright venal — and everyone had cultivated their own individual personal lives anyway — Bon found himself more alone than ever. In the end, he really had nowhere to go.

The other tragedy in Bon's death was not so much that he didn't live to make it — because *Highway to hell*, his last album with the band, was big enough; after a certain point, the magnitude of success becomes academic — but rather that as a writer, he was really only just hitting his stride.

AC/DC never received their critical due during Bon's lifetime.

Bon was contemptuous of the critics that didn't even try to understand AC/DC, and even while there's few artists that don't crave success on both critical and commercial fronts, what was most important, and satisfying to Bon was simply that people 'got off on it'.

But if it's true as Matisse contended that an artist's greatness is measured by the number of new signs he introduces to the language, then there's no doubt that AC/DC are one of the great rock'n'roll bands.

There's something about listening to old AC/DC albums now, as if, even with all the vitality they still exude, they're preserved in amber. At the time the band was making those records, however, there was nothing else that sounded like them; that so much sounds like them now is testimony to their greatness.

The crosscut riffing which became AC/DC's trademark early on — possibly due to the telepathic empathy between the two guitarist brothers — had a seminal influence on rock as it lurched into the eighties. The metal/grunge axis which represents the cutting edge of rock today, owes as much of a debt to AC/DC as it does Led Zeppelin, the Stooges, the New York Dolls, the Velvet Underground, the Sex Pistols, Neil Young, the Ramones and Black Sabbath.

Critics were slow to acknowledge the fact. It's ironic though perhaps understandable, that Brian Johnson, as an outsider who joined AC/DC at a time when they were fully-realised, has become a spokesman for the band who is actually capable of self-analysis. As he told *RAM* in 1981, '... with AC/DC it's so easy and simple, critics can't get into it and therefore they can't describe it'. What he's saying is that AC/DC have none of the identifiable elements that critics like to latch onto, whether they be literary — lyrics that beg analysis — or the obvious signs of traditions inherited, sources updated.

The wordy Bob Dylan is the orthodox rock critic's yardstick against which all else is measured. Dylan invested rock with meaning, made it something 'serious' (like it's not serious when Elvis declares, 'You ain't nothin' but a hound-dog', and turns the entire Western world upside down!). But too many critics suffer an inferiority complex in the face of their 'high art' brethren who look down on rock'n'roll; they seem to think rock'n'roll needs elevation. What they fail to realise is that rock'n'roll was born of base instincts, of disposability and banality — the commercial imperative — and it's still at its glorious best when it revels in these qualities, accepts them only to transcend them, becomes like the brilliant implosion of a dark star which in itself dies but burns an indelible mark on its beholden.

It's pretension, not intelligence or sensitivity, but pretension that is rock'n'roll's worst enemy. A pretension that would be shamed at its gutter origins.

Music, by definition, transcends the literal, and rock'n'roll is at its best when it springs purely from instinct, uncluttered by intellect. Simple and direct, it can have an immediate power that doesn't have to preclude resonance. If Bon fails to fit the orthodox Dylanesque measure of a great rock lyricist, then more power to him. The real point is a matter of attitude, tone, and honesty. Bon was a storyteller who had a terrific eye for detail yet liked to get straight to the moral of the story, and who also, importantly, rejected self-censorship (he was aware, for instance, of the inflammatory nature of a song like 'She's got the jack' even when he wrote it, but he still went ahead with it).

In a way, AC/DC never fitted in. Clearly, they're not heavy metal, as they're commonly described. Few heavy metal bands have a sense of humour, to start with. AC/DC developed in isolation, in Australia in the midseventies, citing only pure, classic fifties rock'n'roll as a source — Little Richard, Chuck Berry — and it's perhaps because they sprang so directly from this untainted well that, whilst their sound might have seemed generic, it was actually because it was so original that it defied description.

Even Britain's *New Musical Express*, AC/DC's erstwhile arch-critical enemy, had to admit upon the release of *Highway to hell*, 'By taking all the unfashionable cliches and metaphors of heavy rock, discarding every ounce of the genre's attendant flab, and fusing those ingredients with gall, simplicity and deceptive facility into a dynamic whole, they have created an aesthetic of their own'.

There is something uniquely Australian about this. AC/DC's down-to-earth, no-frills style — a sense of modesty almost, even in their arrogance; a passion more appropriate to amateurs, and disdain for self-indulgence — coupled with a spirit of belligerent independence, a devout work ethic, and a profound sense of irreverence, has provided a model, one way or another, for practically every other Australian rock'n-'roll band who's subsequently succeeded overseas.

Bon was colour to the band's movement. As such, as a rock'n'roll star, he was granted licence to exercise a total lack of restraint, in both his life and art. His fans admired him because he wasn't afraid of anything; it seemed that he never stopped to think, just leapt straight in — he gave. He drew his art from life, the rampant fornicator stripped bare. The classic bluesmen addressed many of the same issues, only with more finesse — as does a contemporary black artist like Prince — but Bon, free of all artifice and pretension, talked plain to such a point that it went under the heads of many.

But even if Bon did have better writing ahead of him, that he left us with such classics as 'High voltage', 'Long way to the top', 'Jailbreak', 'Live wire', 'She's got balls', 'Ride on', 'Let there be rock', 'Whole lotta Rosie' and 'Highway to hell', is enough. Certainly, AC/DC has produced little of equal stature since.

By 1979, AC/DC was an altogether different entity to what it once was. Cut asunder by ambition, paranoia and betrayal, it had become big business. Bon's de facto family had left home. Both Malcolm and Angus were buying houses and had girlfriends, whom they would eventually marry. Bon, on a return trip to Australia, bought a motorcycle. With customary bravado, he joked that he wasn't ready yet to settle down. But in reality, unimpressed by all the glittery excess and phoniness of stardom, and, if nothing else, just plain tired — or maybe, just finally starting to become a little jaded — he was determinedly trying to remain in touch with his grass roots, the old friends he had who he knew were true friends. That he lacked the soul mate he so desired ate away at him. The bottle, and rock'n'roll — always the music — was all that sustained him meantime. He was working on new material for an album he knew would be as huge as *Back in black* turned out. He was excited at the prospects. But then, suddenly, surprisingly, his life, his body, demanded its own back.

For too long, Bon had pushed himself too hard. He could give no more.

'The trouble with eulogizing a Janis Joplin,' concluded George Frazier, 'is that, in doing so, we are eulogizing not achievement or artistry but a lifestyle that did no one any good, neither her nor those who idolised her. To try to pass off as art what was merely drunk and disorderly is to mislead the young. There are times when to speak ill of the dead is not to do a disservice, but to endow a wastrel existence with a certain significance — a cautionary memento mori to would-be disciples. In other words, what comfort is Southern Comfort when it contributes to the early end of a foolish little girl? Sometimes the young are very stupid.'

'Jailbreak' became a self-fulfilling prophecy. Like the song's hero, Bon broke his shackles — but only to be shot down in flight.

obituary
vale bon scott

as the most renowned, roughest, toughest, brawlingest rock singer Australia has produced, I always found Bon Scott one of the most genuinely gentle and considerate people I'd ever met. He always had a lewd story, an account of some sordid backstreet aggro to relate, but somehow, when Bon talked about groping groupies and having his face smashed in, it never came across lewdly or sordidly. He related his adventures impishly — with a certain amount of innocent pride and wonder. He was not an innocent of course, but no way was he a degenerate either.

Pain or humiliation were not things he would dish out to anyone, or suffer having dished out to him. With Bon, you were either a friend for life, or someone who didn't deserve to be spoken to. His excesses staggered me, but I could never condemn him — how could you condemn anyone who was so boyishly, naively delighted at being able to fit in yet another drink, another smoke, another groupie grope?

He wasn't a wastrel either. You only had to see him work on

stage to realise the sweat, the effort and monumental stage skill in each and every show. And above all, he took the writing of AC/DC's lyrics seriously, and responsibly. It wasn't a matter of dashing off hard rock, rhyming cliche couplets; he really sweated over the words. Every song told a story, and every story was imbued with the gritty realism of rock'n'roll roadlife.

When the news of his death came through on Wednesday, February 20, they said he'd been found in a parked car where he'd been left by friends the night before. No harm in leaving him there, they thought. It was a familiar routine. Bon often slept it off in a car.

And that's when the impact hit me. Because, in 1976, just before AC/DC tried England for the first time, I'd gone on the road with them for a weekend and ended up in a parked car with Bon Scott — him sick and drunk and asleep, breathing unsteadily, me zonked with exhaustion after trotting around with AC/DC from gig to gig.

There are people who'll tell you Bon Scott had been drunk 24-hours a day since approximately March, 1978, and people who knew that beyond and beside all those steamy-thighed groupies (becoming ever more classy as AC/DC neared the upper reaches of the American charts and concert circuit), there had been a tumultuous and traumatic real love affair in his life since 1976.

And there was the pressure. Bon Scott died as AC/DC were preparing songs for the follow-up album to *Highway to hell*. Once again it was a matter of Bon having to earn his place in the group by producing another series of dirty stories, stated succinctly.

There were people who'll tell you he finally couldn't take the strain anymore, and his death was no surprise. But me, I always believed that somehow, he'd just float to the top, giggling, and ready to do it all over again. He always had before.

Except, this time, he just floated away.

Anthony O'Grady
RAM, March 21, 1980

one
adelaide,
1974

Well, I feel like a shirt that ain't been worn
Feel like a sheep that ain't been shorn
Feel like a baby that ain't been born
Feel like a rip that ain't been torn
   Wish I'd done something so I could boast
But I've had one less than the Holy Ghost
And I hear that he's had less than most
I been up in the hills too long
   That old sow's gettin' too old now
I been up in the hills too long
Ain't a thing on the farm that's safe from harm
I been up in the hills too long
   Well, I feel like a song that ain't been sung
I feel like a phone that ain't been rung
I feel like a barrel that ain't been brung
Feel like a murderer that ain't been hung
   Wish I'd done something so I could brag
I feel like a squirrel that ain't been bagged

25 years and I ain't been shagged
Been up in the hills too long
   Well, I feel like an egg that ain't been laid
I feel like a bill that ain't been paid
I feel like a giant that ain't been slayed
I feel like a sayin' that ain't been sayed
   Well, I don't think things can get much worse
I feel my life is in reverse
One more fuck it'll be my first
I been up in the hills too long.

'Been up in the hills too long'
Bon, 1974

He was working on the weighbridge at the Wallaroo fertiliser plant, down by the docks at Port Adelaide. Loading trucks. Unloading trucks. It was backbreaking work, but Bon had never been afraid of work. He was a Scot, after all, and the Scots virtually invented the Protestant work ethic.

He sweated it out in the heat and grime, listening to a transistor radio. Bon was a small man — 173 centimetres (5' 5") — but somehow he was imposing. He had an implacable sort of frame. It took punishment well. The tattoos completed the picture.

No, Bon wasn't afraid of hard work — Bon Scott wasn't afraid of anything — it was just that he preferred not to have to do it. That, after all, was why he got into rock'n'roll in the first place. It wasn't even so much for the chicks, because Bon could always score — women just seemed to like Bon, and Bon loved women. It was work Bon wanted to avoid, the daily, nine-to-five grind of selling that too-large a piece of your soul in return for what? A nagging wife, an interminable mortgage, screaming hungry mouths to feed? The last thing Bon ever wanted was to feel a yoke around his neck.

Bon wanted to be able to wake up when he felt like it, wherever he found himself. He wanted to do as he pleased, see the world, try everything. He wanted to be able to get up

Left: Up in the hills: Bon helps prepare the site for the Myponga Pop Festival, outside Adelaide; January, 1971.

on stage and strut his stuff and feel like people appreciated it. He wanted to be able to believe in himself.

But Bon's rock'n'roll dream had recently gone wrong. It was February, 1974. He'd just returned from England with, or rather without, Fraternity, the band he'd joined after the Valentines broke up. A wastrel tribe of spoilt hippies, Fraternity had gone overseas expecting success to land in their lap. When that didn't happen, they were stumped. Eventually, they straggled home, embittered and in disarray.

With his young marriage also in tatters, Bon was altogether without a rudder. Not since before he joined his first band, the Spektors, in 1964 had he not been a member of a band; and it was being in a rock'n'roll band that was going somewhere, or at least entertained the hope of going somewhere, that justified Bon's life. Not since the Spektors turned pro had Bon worked a day job. But he didn't even have his wife Irene to support him now.

Bon was crashing at a tiny place former Fraternity leader Bruce Howe had in Semaphore. He was getting around on the new bike he'd bought — a Triumph, which everyone told him was just too big — and seeing Irene and squabbling with her.

To keep himself out of any more trouble, and just to keep his hand in, Bon was mucking around with an outfit called the Mount Lofty Rangers, and it was at this time that he wrote 'Been up in the hills too long'. A bluegrass stomp, it referred, nominally, to the farm in the Adelaide hills that had once been Fraternity's communal home. But maybe, with its sense of discontent, it was rather less literal than prophetic.

One Friday night near the end of February, the Rangers were rehearsing at the Old Lion Hotel in North Adelaide. Bon arrived on his bike, late, and a bit pissed. There was nothing unusual in that. Bon was always running late, and he always carried a flask of Johnnie Walker or Southern Comfort in his pocket. The heady days of tripping were over, but the scene had now become a pretty heavy drinking one.

Bon was upset and angry. He'd had a blue with Irene. That wasn't unusual either — Bon and Irene fought all the time — but this time Bon had been tipped over the edge. Bon's fuse was by any standards a long one; but that night, with all the energy that usually found vent on stage pent up inside him, he snapped.

Bon got drunker and more agitated, and took it out on the musicians. The musicians responded in kind. Absolutely blind, Bon stormed off, telling everyone to get fucked. This was his dark side, when he didn't care even for his own safety, when his recklessness became purely self-destructive. Everyone told him, Don't get on your bike, Bon, you're too pissed to ride. Bon told them to fuck off. He furiously threw an empty bottle on the ground, and, amid smashed glass, roared off.

The hospital rang Irene in the early hours of Saturday morning. Irene rang Vince Lovegrove, one of Bon's oldest friends, who lived just around the corner. Calls from Bon at all hours, Vince later remembered in an obituary to him, were not unusual, but this time Vince knew something was wrong as soon as the phone woke him. He too had watched Bon ride off into the night.

'I went and picked up Irene and we went down to the hospital,' Lovegrove said. 'Bon was a mess. All his teeth were wired up, he was on a respirator, and he was abusing the nurses, abusing them through this respirator!'

A report ran the following day in the *News* under the headline SINGER INJURED: TOLL 145. 'Well-known Adelaide pop singer Bon Scott has been seriously injured in a motorcycle accident,' it read. 'Scott, who suffered a broken arm, broken leg, broken nose and concussion in the accident at Croydon, is in a serious condition at the Queen Elizabeth Hospital intensive care ward.'

After three days in and out of consciousness, and then four weeks in traction, Irene finally took Bon home. He had almost died; but maybe, as things so often are, the accident was meant to happen. Bon was certainly one to believe in fate. Mobility was central to Bon's philosophy of life: it was just, keep moving. And here he was laid up with his leg in a cast, with wires through his jaw, resenting the hell out of his condition, but finally being forced to stop and think.

He decided that he had to leave Fraternity, Adelaide, even Irene. He didn't want to give up on his marriage, but he had to. His calling was somewhere out there on the road, and Irene just wanted to settle down. And while he appreciated the fact that Fraternity had opened his musical horizons after the shallow Valentines, he realised he'd had enough of this serious shit. He wanted to rock'n'roll, pure and simple.

Bon had to find a ticket out.

When he got back on his feet, Vince gave him some odd jobs to do — putting up posters, driving around visiting bands, painting Vince's office. In August, Vince brought a virtually unknown band by the name of AC/DC to town.

It was the answer to all Bon's prayers.

Vince kept telling Bon how good these kids were, and urging him to come down and have a look at them. They wanted a new singer and Vince had the idea of putting them and Bon together. Bon was sceptical, but he went along to see them one night anyway.

Hobbling into the Pooraka Hotel, Bon had no idea he was staring his future in the face. But AC/DC was everything he could have asked for — a gung-ho young rock'n'roll band in need of a front man. If Bon had any doubts about himself — that he wasn't fully recovered from the accident, or that at 28 he was getting on a bit — they were swept aside. AC/DC and Bon were made for each other.

Within weeks, Bon was playing his debut performance with the band in Sydney. The Youngs had found the link they were after. AC/DC were on their way.

Inspired though he was, Bon knew it was still going to be a long way to the top, but he was prepared to give everything he had. For the old man, as his new young cohorts called him, it would be third time lucky.

two
scotland

I t's an Arctic wind that whips across the Roods, on the upper side of the small Scottish town of Kirriemuir, where Bon Scott spent the first six years of his life.

Kirriemuir nestles in the foothills of the Cairngorms, low in the highlands in the county of Angus, in Scotland's southeast. 'Gateway to the glens', it is a town today of barely 5,000 inhabitants; a quaint, rustic, tiny network of narrow streets and lanes onto which red-stone buildings crowd for frontage.

Kirriemuir grew up around its sole industry, jute-spinning (jute is a flaxlike fibre used in canvas manufacture). In the eighteenth century, with the arrival of the loom, the town was thriving. But by now, Kirriemuir has outlived its usefulness. It is notable only as the birthplace of JM Barrie, author of *Peter Pan*. Bon doesn't get a look in.

It's a little more sheltered down in town, on Bank Street,

High Street, Kirriemuir, after the war.

where Bon's father Chick worked in the bakery owned by his father, Alec, with his brother, George. Alexander Scott had started the business in 1920, two years after Charles, to give Chick his proper name, was born.

It was warm in the floury air of the bakehouse, where the men worked long and hard. But the days seem short when you get up in the middle of the night to start baking for dawn, when dawn itself is late and sunset early, and you are a young man who likes a bit of a lark. Chick had wanted to go to sea with his friend Angus, but his parents wouldn't allow it. Instead, he served an apprenticeship at the bakery, and joined the local territorial Citizen Military Forces (CMF).

When the Second World War broke out in 1939, Chick was one of the first to go. He was 22. He served in the army as a baker, in France initially and then Ireland, North Africa and Italy.

Before he was sent to France, Chick was stationed in Kirkcaldy, a seaport just across the Firth of Forth from Edinburgh, and it was there that he met Bon's mother, Isa. Isobelle Cunningham Mitchell was one of the four daughters of George Mitchell. Her family was, as she put it, just 'ordinary folk, workin' folk'. She was lean and small, a pretty girl with strong bones and sharp eyes. Chick was a bit of a wag, with tattoos on his forearms and a gaunt handsomeness.

Isa and Chick both enjoyed music. 'I met him at the dancing,' she remembers fondly.

Music has always been common ground in Scotland, a country otherwise almost schizophrenic. With the sort of puritanical religious heritage that can only be divisive, Scotland is governed by tensions. The tension between arrogance and modesty, material poverty and cultural wealth; between dependence and a rebel streak, stoicism and wild release; between those who drink too much and those who don't touch a drop — and worst of all, between getting drunk and getting sober. Scotland still has more deaths due to drinking than just about anywhere else in the Western world — and just as many wowsers to shake a finger at the fact.

Chick and Isa Scott maintain their own balance. Isa, who disapproves of drink, buzzes with nervous energy, chattering incessantly. Chick is more reserved, laconic. As a youngster, he admits, 'I just liked to get out and have a good time, be a bit of a delinquent'.

Music ran through life in Scotland after radio and before TV, and so it did through both Chick and Isa's families. Chick's father used to do a bit of singing, and his mother, Jayne Belford Nielson, encouraged musical activity. Five years Chick's senior, his brother George played piano in local bands, and George's children would go on to play various instruments as well. Chick had had lessons on piano and fiddle, but he never stuck at it.

Isa's family was musical too: 'We just loved music. Mum would play the piano. Dad played the piano, and the organ, had a lovely operatic voice.'

Scotland was hardly touched by the war and life for Isa went on as usual in Kirkcaldy. 'Just no lights at night time.' And the fact that her man was away fighting.

Chick and Isa married in 1941 on one of his leaves from Ireland. Chick's mother didn't exactly approve of the marriage — she felt Isa's social station was beneath the Scotts' — but Chick was determined. In 1943, Isa gave birth to a son, Sandy. He died nine months later. Chick never saw him.

Chick was demobbed on the very last day of 1945 and he and Isa moved to Kirriemuir. Chick's father bought the couple the house in the Roods, which Isa named Raymondscraig after a park she used to visit in Kirkcaldy. It was a small house, a terrace, but it was plenty enough for frugal people.

Chick and Isa would go out to the dancing. Isa would go to church on Sundays. Chick was a member of the local amateur light opera company (Gilbert and Sullivan), and played drums in the Kirriemuir Pipe Band.

ISA: 'There was a pipe band nearly every week, every Saturday night, marching through the square.'

The world, then, that Bon entered as Ronald Belford Scott, on July 9, 1946, was a happy one. The war was over and, as Chick recalls, 'I was in business with my father, and my brother, so we hadnae money troubles or anything'.

The young Bon, or Ron, as his mother still calls him, was a typical tyke: 'He was into everything. A mind of his own. He went walking himself, I never had to do anything, he just walked in one day.'

By the time Bon started school he was already displaying errant traits.

ISA: 'He used to never come home from school. He'd just go off with some of his little mates, and never think of comin' up the hill. I used to have to go chase him. So it started young!'

'He was mischievous, I would say more than anything. Not naughty. He just had a mind of his own and if he wanted to do something, that was it.'

He had also started displaying a primal musical bent.

ISA: 'Mad on drums, he was, mad on drums. Played on a biscuit tin. Or the bread board, he could practise on a bread board. He loved it. People heard him practising, and they knew.'

And so when the pipe band marched through the town square every Saturday night, the peeling of the pipes rising into the Scottish sky, silver in the summer's twilight, 'Ron,' Isa still huffs exasperatedly, 'had to get and march up and down with them'.

Life was steady for the Scotts. Isa had given birth to another son, Derek, in 1949. But, as Chick says, 'You get a bit unsettled after six years in the army'.

Scotland has long watched its sons and daughters migrate to greener climes, and never more so than in the fifties and sixties. If there was a postwar boom going on, it certainly wasn't happening in Scotland. It was happening in places like America, Canada, New Zealand and Australia. This was a time when the New World was encouraging migrants from its British forebear, when it needed people to build a future. Australia was offering assisted passages, which meant British families could travel, by boat, for a mere ten pounds. And Scotland was never going to get any warmer.

ISA: 'My sister lived in Melbourne; they migrated about a year before us, her with her husband and her little girl, June, and that put us on edge then. We thought, Oh, I'd love to go out there too.'

Australia was a new frontier in the 1950s, a huge underpopulated continent bursting with potential wealth. Escaping the war relatively unscathed, the imperative then was not so much to rebuild as it was to build, period. But even before the war, as the then prime minister Billy Hughes put it, Australia believed it must populate or perish in the face of Asia's teeming millions. So in 1947, Australia embarked on an immigration program of a scale almost unequalled this century.

Of course, it was all based on the so-called White Australia Policy. Clinging to Mother England's apron strings, Australia's ideal migrant was exclusively European, and preferably British. Australia offered a fresh start, a sunny, open vista for those prepared to take the plunge — and thousands of Britons were, happy to leave their grey, wartorn homeland behind.

But the number of British migrants fell short of expectations — mainly because there weren't enough ships to transport them — and Australia, still in need of people and without any other alternative, opened up to refugees from camps in Southern Europe. By 1951, these displaced people comprised half of the migrant intake.

By 1955, Australia — a country with a prewar population of barely seven million — welcomed its millionth migrant. If 'welcomed' is the right word. Wogs and dagoes were openly resented. Not even the English were unreservedly accepted; Australians could never quite shake their suspicion of whingeing Poms. But if we liked to pour scorn on the Irish, as is common all over the world, it was the Scots we embraced unqualifiedly.

Australia and the Celts generally have much in common. Australia's roots, as a British penal colony, are as Irish as they are English, after all. And just as Ireland and Scotland have long been downtrodden by England, so too has Australia. Australia shares with the Celts a rebel streak and a wry, laconic sense of humour, not to mention a terrific thirst. But if Australians felt threatened by the Irish and their Catholicism, we could readily identify with the Scots and their Protestant heritage.

It's unlikely, then, that the young Ronald Scott ever suffered racial taunts in Australia. And if he did, well, he was a tough little nut, who could always stand up for himself with a belligerence that belied his small stature.

The Scotts arrived in Australia in 1952. Bon was six.

ISA: 'Coming out on the boat I used to sing to Ron, I used to learn him tunes, all the words. Just singing them over. He picked them up good.'

They landed in Melbourne, and moved in with Isa's sister, who lived in Sunshine, a suburb in Melbourne's industrial west. Then they got their own house at the bottom of the street. Sunshine is situated next door to Footscray, helping to form the wrong-side-of-the-tracks enclave that is western Melbourne. In the early fifties, the area was a haven for migrants — Italian and Greek as well as British — who lived in rows of terraced houses and worked in local industry.

Life in Sunshine was rough and tumble, but at a time of full employment, few went without the necessities. Chick got a job as window-framer. The future was wide-open.

Bon was enrolled in Sunshine Primary School.

ISA: 'He even played on little drums when he went to the first school at Sunshine. The kids used to march to school and Ron was at the end of the line playing the drums. It kept everybody in step.

'I used to go to church on a pushbike in Sunshine. Ron used to like going to church. Not that there was anything in it, he just liked the singing. But that was as far as it went. Oh, they all went to Sunday school when we first came out here, until they got old enough to say, Oh, I'm not going back there.'

In 1953, a fourth son, Graeme, was born, a baby brother for Bon and Derek. The red-haired, freckle-faced Bon was in grade one at the time.

ISA: 'Ron loved music. He started off in school with a recorder. He wanted to learn piano, we had a beautiful piano, he was seven years old at the time, but he wouldnae go to the lessons. So after a while, he wanted an accordion. So what did we do, we sold the piano and bought an accordion, and he went to lessons for that. That lasted a while. Ah, but he wanted to play the drums. We sold the accordion and he got his first drum set. Of course, he picked that up himself then. You never had to tell him to do that, it was just natural to him.'

At the same time, Bon's tearaway spirit was starting to take flight.

ISA: 'He used to go to Footscray baths, and come home and tell me he'd been jumping from the highest diving board. That's just the kind of person he was. You wouldnae have to dare him to do it.'

When Bon learnt to swim, he was extremely pleased with himself. He liked the feeling of weightlessness, of drive, as if he could break away from all the earthly bonds. But of course, that wasn't enough. He had to scale the high-diving board. He would properly fly now.

Everybody would be watching, all the girls as well as the boys, and they would have to be impressed by anyone so brave. So Bon climbed the tower, and standing up there, on the end of the board where it's springy and slippery, he might have felt a twinge of fear if he wasn't already consumed by his own performance, aware that all eyes were upon him. From way up above, he could see the other kids standing around the pool's edge, teeth chattering in the cold, but transfixed by him. And then the lifeguard noticed, and shouted, Hey, come on now, you come down from there this instant; and that was all the encouragement Bon needed. It was then and only then that he commenced his descent. He paused for the beat — the incipient mark of his natural sense of timing — and then he leapt. And as he flew through the air, he felt a rush of blood through his small tensile frame and he felt more alive than he ever had in his short life.

He hit the water with a belly-flopping splash. His flapping around as he broke the surface was equalled only by that of the lifeguards at poolside. He climbed out of the water, and now he maybe even felt more alive, as his body reverberated and he was at once chided by the adults and had all the kids wide-eyed and open-mouthed. The boys were full of admiration and envy; the girls, fear and wonder.

Bon had just taken his first curtain call, and he liked it. It was the sort of high he would spend the rest of his life chasing.

In 1956, Graeme was diagnosed as having asthma and the family moved to Perth. The doctors said the hot dry climate of the west would be better for him.

Bon was going on ten. Rock'n'roll had just hit. The world would never be the same again. Bon's world was about to change for that reason too, and for others of his own, to boot.

three
fremantle

Standing at the mouth of the Swan River, some 20 kilometres south of Perth, the port town of Fremantle, like most
of the Western Australian coastline, claims a sandy, wind-
swept beach front.

Playing host to Australia's defence of the America's Cup in
1986, Fremantle was transformed. But when the circus left
town, Fremantle reverted to its former sleepiness.

Established as a port in 1829, Fremantle remained busy
until after the war, when the wharfing tradition, as it was
around the world, began its slow death due to container-
isation. Fremantle was nonetheless still the docklands, the
dangerous, bustling stamping grounds of sailors, spivs,
prostitutes and a general manner of hard men only.

In the fifties, Fremantle was boosted by the construction of
the Kwinana industrial complex some 24 kilometres to the

Scotland's Fife Free Press *reported in 1962, 'One of the side drummers in the* *Fremantle Pipe Band, who played at the opening ceremony of the Empire Games, in* *Perth, was Ronald Scott, son of Mr and Mrs Charles Scott, who formerly resided in* *Roods, Kirriemuir.'*

south. People started to make their homes there, among them the Scotts.

Chick went ahead of the rest of the family. He had a job lined up with the same firm he'd worked for in Melbourne. Chick would find a place for the family to live, while Isa packed up house in Sunshine. He signed a short lease on a house in South Fremantle, before he found one to buy on the other side of the river.

ISA: 'North Fremantle was a nice place when they were growing up, it used to be like a country town.'

The Scotts' home, on Harvest Road, was a big red-brick Federation house that stood on the peak of a rise overlooking the river.

ISA: 'I joined a Scottish club in Fremantle, and my husband joined the Caledonian Society, and that's why we got to know people.'

Chick also joined the Scots pipe band which was a good part of the pride of Fremantle. Bon tagged along with his father, and joined the band too, as a side-drummer.

'Before TV, we used to sit around and listen to the radio,' said Bon's youngest brother Graeme. 'My dad and Ron used to go out to practise for the pipe band, drumming. It was a big occasion when the bands played, the whole family used to go out, put on their kilts, strap the drums on. Me and Derek would follow behind. Those were the big occasions, Scottish things.'

Bon and Derek attended North Fremantle Primary. Bon was never greatly enamoured of school, but he got by, and didn't get into any more trouble than most headstrong boys.

Chick and Isa were dedicated parents who pretty much allowed the three boys the run of the house, but when they did say jump, they meant jump! The boys, in turn, respected their parents' authority, and didn't push them. It was this that taught Bon the good manners that never deserted him.

Outside school, Bon had his musical pursuits, and the river was nearby, and if ever there was a water baby, Bon was it.

ISA: 'You never needed to worry where they were, they were always down the river. All the time. They'd just walk down — didn't need a car, we didn't have a car at that time, it was just two minutes away — so then they'd come home for something to eat, then they'd go down again... Derek was a quiet kid. Ron was more outgoing, he had a lot of friends.'

Bon appeared on stage for the first time at North Fremantle Town Hall, when he played a recorder duet with a friend in a school concert.

In 1959, aged 12, Bon started secondary school at John Curtin High. He also started to get into the more serious sort of mischief that boys of that age will. As his adulthood friend Pat Pickett put it, 'When you're a kid, there's always one guy who did it when he was 12, you know — Bon was that guy'.

Rock'n'roll was also starting to set a bead on Bon's mind.

Australia's first baby-boom teenagers were knocked for six, as they would have put it themselves, when in 1956 they saw *The Blackboard Jungle,* the film that sported Bill Haley's 'Rock around the clock' as its theme. It was the first rock'n'roll song Australia had heard.

Isolated Anglophile Australia could not have even begun to anticipate rock'n'roll. In the United States, rock'n'roll, for the early fifties, was a thundercloud brewing on the horizon, the music and the attitude of the urban black ghetto and rural white trash alike. In Britain, restless kids — tomorrow's teddy boys — were just waiting for something like rock'n'roll to come along.

Australia in the early fifties, however, still clung, culturally, to Mother England's apron strings. Accents and attitudes on the radio assumed British parentage. Australian country music was a unique, indigenous innovation, but it meant little in the cities.

Australian kids at the time, to paraphrase Nik Cohn, 'shared everything with their parents... danced to the same music, sat through the same films, [wore] the same clothes'. Bodgies and widgies were inner city toughs who had emerged during the war in response to visiting American servicemen and all the cultural baggage they carried — the stylish cut of their clothes, the music they liked to dance to, their exotic slang — but even after the war, bodgies were still revelling in archaic swing jazz. There had to be something more than Frank Sinatra.

'Rock around the clock', then, was a revelation. Elvis, not much later, sealed it.

Overnight, a Sydneyside Frank Sinatra/Johnnie Ray imitator, Johnny O'Keefe, became a Bill Haley imitator. Haley himself was nothing more than a second-string hillbilly singer who got lucky on a black R&B trip. And this was the very birth of Australian rock'n'roll — an imitation of an imitation.

Both Britain and Australia produced little first generation rock'n'roll of much worth because neither country had any tradition in the American roots of the music. Britain went on to produce great rock'n'roll in the sixties — as opposed to Australia's very erratic output — because young British musicians sought out those roots and consciously emulated them. Australia, on the other hand, was denied the opportunity to hear the great body of American black music because local record companies, colonial outposts to British head offices, refused to release it.

Johnny O'Keefe couldn't help but be a mere facsimile of rock'n'roll, an entertainer sooner than a singer, who simply changed his stripes. But even if O'Keefe started a long way from the source, and even if he admitted himself he was a limited singer, he became a convincing enough rock'n'roll performer because he found in rock'n'roll something that aligned directly with his own larrikin spirit. O'Keefe became a star for the very reason that Australians identified with him as one of our own — and that was an epochal traversal of the cultural cringe. For perhaps the first time ever, urban Australians embraced a musician because of his Australianness.

In O'Keefe's wake, rock'n'roll stormed the barricades. It was grappling in the dark — guitarists had to build their own instruments, copying designs out of photographs of American bands — but it was naive enough not to become discouraged.

Said Bon himself in the film *Let there be rock*, 'Back in about 1957 or '8, I used to sing in the shower, and my mum used to say, Ron, if you can't sing proper songs, shuttup; don't sing this rock'n'roll garbage.'

Australian kids had got a hold on rock'n'roll, even if it was only a toehold, and they weren't going to let it go.

Bon was absorbed by the drums.

CHICK: 'What was he, novice champion at 12? And then he was under-17 champion for five years.'

GRAEME SCOTT: 'He played on TV one time, he went on and played drums while there was this girl who did the highland dancing, there was a piper there.

'He loved the attention from the girls. He was in the paper one time, in the Scottish get-up, with two highland dancers, about the same age as him, 12 or 13, and he had this big smile on his face.'

But even as Chick and Isa took pride in the lead Bon set, he was courting disaster. Going down to the river now was a less innocent exercise. Boys would be puffing on cigarettes, and sneaking off behind the bushes with girls. School was a meeting place that was only barely neutral. Kids in gangs from surrounding neighbourhoods converged at school, enacting an uneasy truce which would be broken as soon as they were out of their school uniforms.

Growing up working-class in Australia in the fifties was to grow up tough. You had to be able to fight, and if you didn't vigilantly keep your guard up, you would be knocked down. To be knocked down was to be weak, and to be weak was the lowest of the low.

As William Dick wrote in *A bunch of ratbags*, his classic documentary novel of growing up a bodgie in mythical Melbourne suburb Goodwood, a thinly disguised version of Footscray: 'If you didn't belong to a mob, you just didn't belong. The kids in mobs picked on you and you got belted up and made to fear them. But if you belonged to a mob, you were given a certain amount of respect.'

GRAEME: 'Ron and his friends Terry and Moe formed the nucleus of a gang, and once they got their cars, they were full on.'

Bon was drumming, swimming, learning to fuck and learning to fight. School came a poor last and he left as soon as he was legally able, when he turned 15 in 1961. He got a job as a farmhand on a market-garden, driving a tractor. Later his friend Terry got him a job on the crayfishing boats, as hard a way to make a living as any there is.

Being a fisherman proved too much even for Bon though, so he quickly chucked it in and got a job working for Avery Scales, as an apprentice weighing machine mechanic.

Bon was a rocker. Rockers superseded bodgies. Bodgies abandoned Johnnie Ray to jump on the rock'n'roll bandwagon, but the move, to rockers especially, who, as their name suggests, were born of rock'n'roll, was typically transparent. Identified by their slicked-back hair, leather jackets and skintight pants, as opposed to bodgies' preppier predilections (Tony Curtis crew-cuts and cardigans), rockers were into Elvis, Little Richard, Jerry Lee Lewis, Chuck Berry. The likes of Buddy Holly or Fats Domino were considered weak, far too tame, clean cut. It was the bad boys that rockers like Bon were into.

It was perhaps only the details, however, that distinguished one cult from another. Sidney Baker's definition of the archetypal larrikin could equally be applied to bodgies, rockers or mods, and would certainly seem to apply to Bon. 'He dressed with exaggerated precision, he extracted comfort from being a member of a gang, he was alleged to have too much money and to lack parental control, he looked upon refinement in social conduct as a form of weakness ... he was given to spasms of violence ... [he had] contempt for anything effeminate.'

'It was all rock'n'roll, jiving,' said Maureen Henderson, who hung around with Bon and her brother Terry, Bon's best mate. 'Me and Bonnie, we were a couple of the best jivers in Fremantle. He was a good jiver.'

Movies, which Bon went to see at the drive-in, were a primary source of inspiration — *The girl can't help it, Hot rod gang, Jailhouse rock, King Creole.* All things American, like rock'n'roll itself, were exotic and attractive. Everybody was especially into the cars. Befinned and chromed American tanks were a symbol of everything truculent young Australians aspired to — they were flash and fast and dangerous.

Bon was thumbing his nose at authority. Although there was an impishness about his defiance, a bravado that rather innocently asked, who says I can't? when provoked, Bon could turn nasty, striking back with unforgiving viciousness.

He was only small, but he had a fearsome reputation as a street fighter, who could not only tear a bigger man apart, but would himself refuse to be beaten.

MAUREEN HENDERSON: 'They went up to East Perth to get tattoos. Terry got "Death Before Dishonour" on his arm, and Bonnie got that one, just above his hairline, when he pulled his jeans down. Terry was sitting on one side of him, I was on the other side, and tears were just rolling down his face. He couldn't do his jeans up for weeks, he had to stay at home. Because he used to wear these, we used to call them stove-pipes, and his were so tight, he put them on by turning them inside out and rolling them up his legs.'

GRAEME: 'In those days, in Fremantle, it was all gangs. Gangs were pretty hard in those days. There was nothing else to do. Other gangs didn't come into your neighbourhood unless they wanted to fight.'

Said Vince Lovegrove, who would later form the Valentines with Bon, but then lived in the more sedate, semirural Apple-cross: 'I used to play football, when I was about 14 or 15, and we used to be shit scared of going down and playing South Fremantle, because they were the rough team.

'Fremantle was always looked down upon by the rest of Perth. It was a scary place. There was a picture theatre there, and I went to see a movie there one night, I had to get a bus, and I remember my parents giving me this lecture, Come straight home, don't hang around, there's a lot of bodgies and rockers there, just be careful.'

Bon's gang consisted of him and Terry, his best mate, and Moe, Dave, Archie and Dick, plus Maureen and a couple of other girls. Girls were very much second-class citizens. The gang cruised, and hung out. On weekends, they went to dances, which were as good for blues as sheilas. They seldom went to pubs; occasionally, they'd down a couple of bottles, or pass around a flagon of invalid port, but drinking was not a priority. The big thing was just hanging out, in Fremantle, at the Cafe de Wheels. The car park would be packed with Customlines, Ford single-spinners, Chevvys, Dodge Customs, and all the boys would be milling around them. Brawls erupted like flash fires, over nothing — it was merely testing your mettle. At other times, down dead-end back roads or at deserted beaches, there were gang bangs.

It was a lifestyle uncannily similar to that described by William Dick's hero Terry in *A bunch of ratbags.*

> We'd been running with the pack for nine months or so, and were we tough! We had proved this in our many street brawls. I hadn't had so much fun in my whole life since I had become a bodgie and joined the boys. We had plenty of sheilas knocking around with us, and there was always one of them willing to indulge in love play with us. There were also the other real tough widgies, who thought nothing of taking on a dozen or so of our boys in a back-up [gang bang]. I had been in a couple of back-ups since joining up, and I thought they were terrific fun. All the boys reminded me of a lot of dogs chasing after a bitch that was on heat when they were arguing about who was next and worrying about missing out on a turn.

Like they'd seen in the movies, Bon and his mates tested their mettle racing their cars.

MAUREEN: 'There was one time, they had this drag down at Port Beach, Terry had this car, it was a Ford, single-spinner. They were mad on cars. They used to pinch them too, go for a ride. Anyway, there were dragging, and Bonnie hit this FJ, a ute, split it in half. Oh, they used to drag down there all the time.

'They used to go out and knock fuel off. I would have to go look-out while they siphoned it.'

In early 1963 Perth was experiencing what *West Australian* columnist Athol Thomas said, 'appears to be one of Perth's worst outbreaks of larrikinism'. Bodgies 'plagued' the Windmill Tearooms, forcing it to move from the city to Subiaco, and finally to close. Police were called in to break up, as the *West Australian* reported, 'between 150 and 200 youths [who] caused an uproar in a North Fremantle snack bar on Sunday morning'.

Bon and Terry were well known, by the cops and everyone else alike, as two of the toughest kids in Fremantle. When you're boss cocky, someone's always coming along who wants to try and knock you off your perch, so Bon and Terry had to fend off challengers all the time; fight them and beat them. They also had to put up with the constant attention of the police. If anyone was going to get pinched for anything in Fremantle, Bon and Terry were the first suspects. One time, Terry copped a hiding off the police for something someone else did. Things were starting to get serious.

Bon was running wild in the streets and local legend had him responsible for the vicious beating of a copper.

At the height of this war of attrition, Bon moved in around the corner with Terry and his family. Whether he jumped or was pushed is unclear, but even if his parents weren't entirely naive, Bon wouldn't have wanted them to know the worst, and so he may well have left of his own accord. Either way, he wound up with the Hendersons, where he was accepted unquestioningly. Olive and Jim Henderson already had nine kids, and so with a few other extended-family members also floating around their big house, Bon was hardly noticed.

Bon was drawn to danger; it got the adrenalin flowing and attracted attention in the same way that diving off the high board had all those years ago in Sunshine. But even as he ran by night with the boys, by day he was a diligent worker, and he won Avery's Best First Year Apprentice Award.

ISA: 'At that age, you couldn't follow him. He had a mind of his own, that lad. He was mad on pipe bands until he got to 17, and then he wouldn't wear a skirt no more. He went right against the kilt. We just had to go along with him because it was his way. We never said, Don't do that, Ron — if I did say, Don't do that, he would just go out and do it.

'So after he gave up the drums in the pipe band, well, that was all he thought about, music, he wanted to get in a band.'

GRAEME: 'He knew he wanted to do something with music, but I think he just didn't know how to do it.'

Rock'n'roll, by the early sixties, was dead in the water. Elvis was in the army, Buddy Holly was dead, Chuck Berry was in jail, Jerry Lee Lewis was in disgrace and Little Richard was in church. The music business was back in charge. Clean-cut teen idols — all of whom seemed to be named Bobby (Vee, Vinton, Rydell) — were the order of the day.

However, the one new white innovation that did emerge during this period — and hit Australia — was instrumental rock'n'roll. The Shadows inspired young middle-class boys all over Australia to pick up electric guitars. It was a style Australia was better suited to. After all, it was surf music as much as anything, and in the early sixties, beach culture was growing as rapidly and naturally in Australia as it was in California.

Vince Lovegrove was a 14-year-old at Applecross High in 1961, when he joined an outfit called the Dynells. 'They were friends of mine, who had a Shadows-type band, because that was the go then, it was just pre-stomps. But they were still mainly surfies we played to. We used to play all the surf clubs down the coast.

'We used to put our own shows on in the beginning, hire a local hall, buy a couple of crates of soft drink, throw them in a tub of ice, charge double, you know. This was just pre-Beatles. What would happen was, the band would go out and play their instrumentals, and everyone would be up dancing, and then half way through the night, the singer — that was me — would get up to do a few songs. That was when everyone would take a break and go and get a drink!'

CHICK: 'Ron used to go down to Port Beach, they used to have dances down there, and they used to get up and sing there. But he wasn't in a band then.'

The Port Beach dances were run by their star, Johnny Young, who would sing a bracket or two in front of his band, the Nomads.

MAUREEN: 'We all used to go to the stomps down there at Port Beach, but we didn't like Johnny Young, we thought he was a poof or something, so we used to call out, We want Bonnie! We want Bonnie!'

Bon would jump up and have a sing, but he wouldn't do some wimpy ballad, rather a rock'n'roll song, like 'Long tall Sally' or 'Blue suede shoes'.

MAUREEN: 'All the girls used to go wild over him, and I think that caused a bit of trouble. Johnny Young used to get pretty upset.'

The first Beatles single — 'Please, please me' — was released in Australia in February, 1963. It stiffed. It would be almost a year before their second, 'She loves you', went straight to number one.

Bon, meantime, had been to hell and back.

CHICK: 'Evidently, someone assaulted a girl at the dance...'

ISA: 'And he retaliated...'

CHICK: 'And the police came...'

An item ran in the *West Australian* on March 13:

A 16-year-old youth pleaded guilty in the Fremantle Children's Court yesterday to charges of having given a false name and address to the police, having escaped legal custody, having unlawful carnal knowledge and having stolen 12 gallons of petrol.

He was committed to the care of the Child Welfare Department until he was 18 with a recommendation that he be kept in an institution of maximum security.

He was put on a five pound bond to come up for sentence if called on in the next two years on the unlawful carnal knowledge charge.

What happened was that Bon had 'gone for a walk' with this girl, who was under the age of consent, and when they got back to the hall, some other guys wanted a piece of her too. Bon launched into them. When the police showed up, Bon tried to put one over them — and almost succeeded. He took off in Terry's car, only to be apprehended trying to get away with some petrol.

Later, Bon would never much talk about this episode in his life, but he did confide in Silver Smith, a woman with whom he lived for several years. 'Something really worried him personally. He had this thing that he had to make it up to his parents for something that had happened way back when. Part of his drive to be successful was to do it for mum and dad. His grandparents came out from Kirriemuir when he was 15 or 16, and this was a big thing for the family; and Bon got into some sort of trouble, and he ended up in remand at this boys' home, and when his parents went to see him, he wanted more than anything to go home, but he was so ashamed that he refused to see his parents — he just wouldn't face up to it. And so he had a choice of either being remanded into his parents' custody, and it all being forgotten, or going through the legal process, and he made the choice of going through the legal process.

'By the time he got out, the grandparents had gone home, and of course, they subsequently died. So he always wanted to do something to rectify that.'

Fronting his first band, the Spektors, in 1965. Bon: 'I was a drummer in those days and I used to play half the night on drums and spend the other half singing. The singer also played drums — but not as good as me! Then I got an offer from the Valentines as drummer but I wanted to be a singer so I joined as singer. It wasn't because I wanted to be up front — it was because the singer used to get more chicks.'

four
the
valentines

Wake-up was at six a.m. The screws would come by and rouse their charges. Bon jumped to. He quickly made his bed, folding the blankets just so, army-style. His cell was opened and, inspection passed, he joined the other boys as they filed down to the showers. Many of them were already puffing on a fag. Riverbank was a juvenile institution — the youngest inmates were 14 — but they all received a weekly tobacco ration. It was pure horseshit, called Waldon, but it was something to suck on, something to break up the monotony. Butts were saved. The showers were cold.

The day ahead held little brighter promise, maybe dinner if it proved any good, or a sing-along after that. But there were more pitfalls along the way. A cross look, a slip of the tongue,

could get you into all sorts of trouble. At worse, for fighting —
and fighting was par for the course — you could end up in the
box.

Riverbank wasn't any ordinary boys' home; it was a prison
for boys. It was where the really bad boys went. Bon served
nine months there.

Newly built in the early sixties, situated at the base of the
scrubby hills on the northeast edge of Perth, Riverbank was a
modern brick structure which at least allowed for some light
and air and decent facilities. But still, it was a dark, hard place.
Kept under lock and key rather than in open dormitories,
these boys didn't need too much prodding to become violent.
Sexual favours were taken not given.

During the week, the boys worked in craft shops or around
the place in the kitchen or the laundry. Bon would never
forget the hours spent on his hands and knees, scrubbing. He
missed the fresh air. And it was always cold, freezing cold.

In the evening, after dinner, the boys congregated in a
common room. They played cards, listened to the radio. They
were encouraged to read, or sing, or play musical instruments. Any activity, in fact, which didn't result in a blue was
considered fruitful.

Saturday was a lay-day, usually given over to sport. On
Saturday night, maybe there'd be a movie. On Sundays,
chapel was compulsory, and then after lunch, visitors were
allowed. Sometimes a concert was staged for visitors.

Bon decided early in the piece that jail was a mug's game.
Bon was no fool. It was obvious there was no percentage in a
life outside the law. He could see that most of his fellow
inmates were going to spend the rest of their lives in and out
of jail. And that wasn't for Bon. He owed his parents better, if
nothing else. He was going to keep his head down and his
nose clean, just do his time and get out as soon as possible.

The silver lining to Bon's time inside was that it was then he
started to take seriously the idea of getting into a band. He
was hearing the Beatles on the radio; a change was in the air.
He took to spending his recreation periods mucking around
on drums, with a couple of other boys. They learnt a few
songs, and called it a band.

ISA: 'We went up to a concert one day there, and he was playing, and he said then, 'Oh, I'm going to be famous. And I just...Anyway, he was keen, he knew that's what he wanted to do. But as a drummer, not as a front man.'

Bon was released by Christmas 1963. The carnal knowledge charges would not be proceeded upon. It was deemed that Bon had learnt his lesson. As Isa said, it 'mebbe did him the world of good'. Bon moved back in with his family.

CHICK: 'When he came out of Riverbank, his parole officer said, The best thing you can do is get into the CMF, so I took him up, and I don't know what happened, the parole officer went with him, but they just didnae want him.'

Australia was by then involved in the Vietnam War, and so Bon had to register for National Service, but he was never called up. Later, he would claim, 'Ich wurde von Militardienst ausgeschlossen, es hiess, wegen mangelhder Anpassungsfuhigkeit!' — 'I was rejected by the army, because, they said, I was socially maladjusted'.

Bon put his time at Riverbank behind him. That he was able to do so, when most juvenile offenders return to incarceration, is testament to the firmness of his resolve and his strength of character. All he wanted to do now was to get into a band. Being in a band would provide him with a channel for all his energy.

If Bon had ever had a nasty streak, prison scared it out of him. 'Bon didn't have a mean bone in his body,' said Wyn Milson, with whom Bon would shortly form his first real band. 'He never looked for trouble. But if it happened, he wouldn't walk away. The trouble was, that was when girls started going for guys in bands, and the other guys didn't necessarily appreciate that. I was a little guy myself, and if anyone was harassing me, Bon would always step in. So he got branded as a troublemaker, when in fact he was probably the only one standing up.'

Bon got back on the straight and narrow. He got a job as a storeman with the egg board. He was flailing for sweet life at the drum kit he had installed in the bay window of his mother's living room. He met two boys who worked at the Kwinana oil refinery — Wyn Milson, who played guitar, and

John Collins, who was a singer — and roped in his friend Brian Gannon, who played bass, and the Spektors was born.

Born in Wales in 1948, Wyn, who lived in Medina, beyond Kwinana, had picked up a guitar after hearing the Shadows. Then the Beatles hit. And then the Stones. And as Wyn put it: 'The Shadows were square. Even the Beatles were guys in suits. But the Stones...!'

The Spektors were a weekend band that played around on the Perth circuit for a year or so in 1965 before it merged with its top rivals the Winztons, fronted by Vince Lovegrove, to form the Valentines.

In the reflected glow of the Beatles, a beat music scene sprang up in Perth, as it did in practically every other city in the Western world. Its king was Johnny Young. Young was training as a DJ when he started playing dances as singer with the Nomads in 1962. In 1965, he was made host of a new local TV show called 'Club 17'.

The Spektors played their first performances at the Medina Youth Club in early 1965. This gig was momentous not only for that reason, but also because it was how Bon met a pretty 17-year-old blonde called Maria Van Vlijman, with whom he became infatuated, and spent the next four years in an on-again-off-again relationship. Bon had had girlfriends before — he had had plenty of girls, period — but none was like Maria.

MARIA: 'I think it was one of those police club dances, on a Friday night; there would have been about a dozen people there. Anyway, out through the back door comes this guy, small, with tattoos. Well, I didn't know anybody with tattoos. And his mother was in tow, being really quite bossy. It turned out it was Bon, and she had to drive him there with his drums, because he'd lost his licence or something. I became secretary, or president, or whatever, of their fan club.'

Maria was from the right side of the tracks, a good Catholic girl of solid Dutch parentage. To Bon, she was a cut above all the slack molls and dirty scrags he used for what he could get, and he courted her and wooed her with all his best worldly wiles.

MARIA: 'He was going to marry me; he wanted to marry a

virgin, and I was going to be it. But I knew for a fact, behind my back — I learnt later on — there was those gang bangs. But I never saw anything like that. Maybe I was just naive. Bon was very experienced, but to me, he was this nice boy. You couldn't swear around me. And there was no drinking.'

Apart from the fact that the rampantly lascivious Bon managed to keep his hands off Maria, their relationship was also bizarre because at the same time Maria was also seeing Brian Gannon, unaware that he was barely over 15. As Maria herself put it, she was 17 going on 12; Brian Gannon was 15 going on 21. It was a ménage-à-trois which existed with its participants' full knowledge, and which they all somehow managed to cope with. Just.

MARIA: 'If we were going out to a gig, I would be holding Bon's hand, with the rug over my knees, and holding Brian's hand as well. I kissed both of them, but didn't go to bed with either of them. It was a wonderful time for all of us.'

Through 1965, the Spektors played weekly gigs, or stomps, held in halls and surf clubs, like the Cave, the Shakeway, the Big Beat, the Z-Club and the Rendezvous. They would get 20 minutes or so in the middle of the bill with half a dozen other bands, like the Johnny Young-less Nomads, the Dimensions, the Triffids, Russ and the Little Wheels, and the Winztons. The Spektors' set consisted of Stones' songs, 'Gloria', and the Beatles' 'Yesterday'. Stomps were dry, though the boys in the band always had a bottle of ale or two stashed out the back.

WYN MILSON: 'The whole problem with being a band in Perth back then was the search for material. It was a consuming process, because you just couldn't get anything, no blues, or anything like that. You used to have to dig for it.'

Bon would borrow his father's new Falcon station wagon to lug his drums around. That lasted until he fell asleep at the wheel one night. The paper reported that Ronald Scott (19) 'was taken to hospital with facial injuries after the car he was driving hit a light-pole on Stirling Highway, Claremont'. It added that Brian Gannon (15), 'a passenger in Scott's car', suffered 'concussion and cuts'. It was the first of many injuries Bon would inflict on himself.

The band was back on deck the following weekend. Bon

was a hard man to keep down. An appearance on 'Club 17' in October was tangible evidence that the Spektors were indeed as the *West Australian* put it, 'one of Perth's top five rock groups'.

The band continued playing into 1966 without making much greater headway, though they could hardly have had any complaints. The Spektors had started out as a fun thing, and they were having the time of their lives. The band was often billed as John Collins and the Spektors, though Bon would occasionally step up to the mike to sing a song or two. He was learning to like the applause, learning to like being a centre of attention. He didn't find it difficult.

Bon won out over Brian Gannon for Maria and the couple revelled in the throes of puppy love. Maria got a job in the pay office at the Fremantle docks, and since her parents had moved further away into the country, she took a lease on a flat in east Fremantle with her brother Joe, despite her tender years. This meant that Bon, who only lived across the way in north Fremantle, was able to spend all the more time with her. He had by then tossed in his job at the egg board and was working as a postman.

He reserved all his most gentlemanly charms for Maria. He would dress up just to have lunch with her every day, then return to work. Bon and Maria's families mutually disapproved of the relationship. To Maria's parents, Bon was an undesirable, a larrikin; to Chick and Isa, Maria was stuck-up, snooty.

MARIA: 'Every night, we'd do something, even if it was just watch TV. I would be out with Bon till three or four o'clock every night, and then have to get up at seven to go to work. I was always late.

'It was a ritual every Saturday to go to a place called Musgrove, where all the new bands would play. We used to go to church on Sundays.

'Oh, we'd go down to the wharf, and Bon would buy fish'n'chips, and we'd watch the waves.'

Maria would attend Spektors' gigs and rehearsals alike.

ISA: 'They used to practise in my house. The band, in my lounge! We all had to clear out and go into the kitchen when they practised.'

The scene was still growing. Johnny Young joined new local independent label Clarion Records, and released the single 'Step back', an Easybeats song. It went to number one nationally in June, 1966.

When Johnny Young predictably set out for the brighter lights of Melbourne, he left a big gap behind in Perth. Neither the Winztons nor the Spektors, the next two best acts in town, were quite equipped to fill it, and they may well have cancelled each other out in the attempt. But if they joined forces, there would be nothing stopping them.

The idea to form the Valentines was hatched by Vince Lovegrove in cahoots with 6KY DJ and music director, Allan Robertson. Robertson, who named the band, could see potential in an act that had two lead singers. After all, it had worked for the Twilights, Sam & Dave, the Righteous Brothers.

Vince had known Bon for a while. Vince had left school to take up a journalism cadetship at the *West Australian*, but threw that in to concentrate on music. After the Dynells, he fronted the Dimensions, before forming the Winztons. In the obituary to Bon that Vince wrote for *RAM*, he recalled, 'Bon was the cute little drummer with cute little eyes, pixie-like ears, a cute, turned-up nose, a cute little Scottish accent, and about four very obvious cute little tattoos. In rock'n'roll in those days, you could go a long way being cute. We became friends.'

The Winztons hit a peak when they played at the Capitol Theatre with Billy Thorpe and the Aztecs, who were then riding high on hits like 'Mashed potato' and 'Poison ivy'. There was a party afterwards.

VINCE LOVEGROVE: 'We got invited to this party, up in Dalkeith, it was our first real rock'n'roll party like we thought they must have had all the time in the eastern States. Bon and I went, and I remember being really intimidated by Billy Thorpe, afraid to talk to him, and he was only a year older than we were. But we just thought, Right, well, this is it, this is what it's all about, this is for us!'

Vince was then working as a sales assistant at Pellew's men's wear in Fremantle, and Bon would drop in on him away from his postie rounds. '[We] realised our ambitions were the same. To go to Melbourne and be the best band in the country,' Vince wrote. 'Bon didn't want to drum anymore, and as I was the singer in my band, we decided to be democratic and have two singers.'

ISA: 'Ron liked being up front. I don't think it suited him being behind the drums.'

The formation of the Valentines sorted the men from the boys, or at least those that had steady girlfriends from those that didn't. The Valentines' plan was to turn pro and it's near impossible to combine a career in rock'n'roll and marriage. John Collins and Brian Gannon gave up music altogether and both soon settled happily down to married life. But Bon — Maria or no Maria — was going to do what he was going to do. He insisted on bringing Wyn Milson into the band with him, which suited everyone fine, as Wyn was quite serious about his music.

From the Winztons came guitarist Ted Ward and bassist John Cooksey, whilst drummer Warwick Findlay was recruited from Russ and the Little Wheels. Cooksey, however, was shortly replaced by Bruce Abbott.

The band was driven by a calculated careerism. Bon and Vince had together seen their future — their names in lights in the eastern States — and they were prepared to do anything to get it.

They were turned on in the first place by the Beatles and the Stones, but it was Australian acts that really inspired them to give it a serious go. They'd seen the success enjoyed not only by the Easybeats, who were their godhead, but also Ray Brown and the Whispers, Billy Thorpe and the Aztecs, and then the Masters Apprentices and the Twilights. And if Johnny Young could do it too, then surely so could they.

A hierarchy evolved within the Valentines that saw Vince emerge as the band's leader and premier sex symbol. Bon, for the time being at least, deferred to Vince, because he knew Vince could get them what they wanted. Vince was a smooth operator. His experience at the *West Australian* had taught him a useful media savvy, and his charm and cleverness made him a natural at public relations, and promotion, self or otherwise.

At any rate, Bon always had Wyn's ear, and it was Wyn who emerged as the band's musical director, for what that was worth — the whole band was still grappling in the dark for a real musical sign.

But even if Bon was prepared to hand the reins over to Vince — and he didn't want to know about administration or money — the pair's rivalry coloured the Valentines' personal dynamic, and certainly affected their own relationship, though they remained friends, till the day Bon died.

One of the first edicts brought down in the new regime was that girlfriends at gigs were a no-no. This meant that Bon had to tell Maria she couldn't come to the band's debut at Broadway. Maria was horrified, not least of all by the fact that Bon was prepared to pass on Vince's demand, and even while she conspired with Bon to buck Vince, appearing at every subsequent show (there was no love lost between Maria and Vince either), she was plotting to get her own back on Bon. She wanted to see him squirm, make him beg.

The Valentines took over all the same gigs and fans that the Winztons and Spektors had previously divided, and that immediately made them top dogs in Perth. They were heavily rotated on the 6KY 'Big K' dance circuit — it helped that they were nominally managed by Allan Robertson. They also played licensed discos like the Top Hat, North Side and Trend Setter, which were raking it in thanks largely to the Western Australian mining boom.

The Valentines' repertoire consisted mainly of soul covers — Sam & Dave, Wilson Pickett (the roots of the Rolling Stones) — plus songs by mod staples the Who, the Small Faces and Spencer Davis.

WYN: 'We used to sneak into the 6KY record library late at night and go through the old stuff looking for singles that had the big hole in the middle. You'd find something and say, Who's this?'

Garbed in matching blue sharkskin suits, the band was also developing a sensational stage act which would even soon incorporate flashbombs.

In January, 1967, the Valentines played before their biggest ever crowd — over 3,000 teenagers — at a concert for

Torchbearers for Legacy in Perth's Supreme Court Gardens. The *Sunday Times* praised the band: 'with lead singers Bon and Vince clearly demonstrated [sic] their vibrant personality'.

Life, then, for the band was good. They'd all quit their day jobs. There were always parties, and everyone was young and pretty. Bon and Maria made a handsome couple, even if they squabbled a lot. Maria liked to play cat and mouse with Bon. But when the games became too much to bear, Bon took up overtly with a go-go dancer by the name of Lyn. Maria soon lured him back though.

'Now established as one of the star attractions on the Perth scene', as a 6KY fan club flyer put it, it was inevitable that the Valentines would link up with Clarion Records. Headed by Martin Clarke and distributed by Festival, Clarion was one of the many independent labels that sprang up and fostered local talent in Australia in the sixties. The Valentines thus went into a primitive studio off Hay Street in the centre of Perth very late one night, and emerged the following morning clutching a one-take, two-track tape of two simple tunes.

'Everyday I have to cry' was a rolling, melodic song originally cut by black US country–soul singer Arthur Alexander; while 'Can't dance with you' was a B-side for the Small Faces, a prime slice of proto-funk/rock. As a debut single by a band from the backwoods of Perth, it wasn't bad, and when it was released in May, 1967, it duly climbed the Western Australian charts to a top five position.

The Vallies, as they were affectionately known, were on a roll. When the all-conquering Easybeats played two shows at His Majesty's on June 12 on their return tour from England, the Valentines supported. The Easys took a real shine to them. It was likely on this occasion that songwriter–guitarist and fellow Scot, George Young, first noticed Bon, how redolent he was of his own band's front man, 'Little' Stevie Wright. Of course, of all the Easybeats, Bon idolised Little Stevie particularly, to the point of consciously aping his moves.

The Valentines partied with the Easybeats back at their hotel, as hordes of screaming teenage girls littered the footpath below. The two bands swapped shirts like opposing Grand Final football teams, and the Easys even knocked up a song on the spot for Vallies. Not much of a song, it's true, but one that would constitute the Valentines' second single.

'She said' was the first of three songs the Easybeats would give to the Valentines, and it was the start of the lifelong relationship George Young would have with Bon.

Bon and Maria had kissed — at most! — and made up, but just as soon, Maria was taking off for the big smoke, Melbourne. There had to be something more there than working in the pay office at the Fremantle docks.

MARIA: 'I was ready to go, but I don't think I would have gone if I didn't know that somewhere down the track, Bon was going to come too.'

Wyn Milson, by this time, had effectively moved in to the Scotts' North Fremantle home, rather than having to commute all the way to Medina all the time. 'Bon just said, Come and stay at my place; didn't ask his parents, and basically, they just accepted me. When I think about it now, if someone lobbed at my house, and was coming in at three every morning making hot chocolate, leaving burnt milk in the saucepan, and then went to bed in the lounge room so you couldn't go in there till one in the afternoon, I would throw them out. But they never said a word.'

'She said' was released in July, backed with a lame version of Phil Spector's 'To know you is to love you'. It was a step back for the Valentines, probably only recorded because it was penned by the Easybeats. Bon blew a recorder, presumably just because he could. Not even all the Valentines' hometown hero status could save 'She said'. It stiffed.

The irony is that even as the single couldn't get out of the blocks, the band won the State final of the Hoadley's Battle of the Sounds. The Valentines flew to Melbourne to compete in the national final, and though they were beaten to first place by the Groop, they made a good impression. Tastemakers Ian Meldrum of *Go-Set* and DJ Stan 'The Man' Rofe both gave them the nod. Vince, of course, got in some serious networking during the visit; and so, flying home, the Valentines had no second thoughts as to where their future lay.

The band's plan was to get together the money to pay for

the move to Melbourne. They got onto a winner in an all-day every-day gig at the Royal Show, with Ronnie Burns.

WYN: 'You'd do a half hour on stage, then go out the back so they could throw everybody out, and then you'd go up and do it again.'

Bassist Bruce Abbott fell victim to the dreaded fiancée disease, and decided to stay behind in Perth and get married. He was replaced by John Cooksey. Bon wrote to Maria just a week before the band was due to leave for Melbourne.

> We have had no end of complications with our trip. It looked almost as though we would have to call it off till we got more money. Vin and I are going to Perth tomorrow to sell everything we can lay our hands on...
>
> I guess that you're having a great time going to all the new places. I hope we can both have a good time together when I arrive. I hope that it works out this time. If it doesn't I don't know what I'll do. I'll be so flippin' lonely.

VINCE: 'No one in Perth could understand why we wanted to leave. They said, It's paradise here, it's sunny, we've got all these beautiful beaches. What could you say?'

The band finally got it together and they all met at the station to catch the train. The scene was like something out of Exodus. Mothers were sobbing, fathers standing stoic. The boys were beside themselves.

They felt like explorers or crusaders. The trip across the Nullarbor Plain was all of four days — somehow they would have to contain their excitement — and at the other end, Melbourne was still very much an unknown quantity. But they were blessed with the hope of the age, the confidence of their youth and their innocence.

If and when they returned to Perth, it would be as stars, conquering heroes. And so it would be.

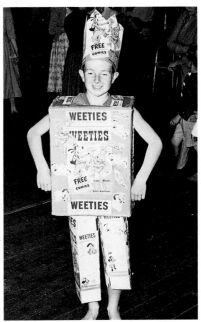

ABOVE LEFT: A year old – Kirriemuir, July 1947 – with Isa. Chick in the background.

ABOVE RIGHT: Isa: 'He was into everything. A mind of his own.'

BELOW LEFT: Harvest Road, Fremantle, 1956. Isa: 'You never needed to worry where they were, they were always down the river. All the time.' Bon never lost his love of the water. 'Our gang': Bon (right), younger brother Derek (centre).

BELOW RIGHT: In fancy dress. Graeme Scott: 'He loved the attention'.

ABOVE: 'Old Year's Night', 1957; Bon and Chick dressed up to play. Isa: 'He was mad on pipe bands until he got to 17, and then he went right against the kilt. He wouldnae wear a skirt no more.'

BELOW: Bon listed as his previous occupations, 'weighing machine mechanic, crayfisher, postie, farmhand'. As a postman, 1965.

ABOVE LEFT: Bon met his first serious girlfriend, Maria Van Vlijman, in 1965. He always carried this photograph with him.

ABOVE RIGHT: Bon and Maria in their best mod finery, 1966.

BELOW: Bon and Irene marry, Adelaide, January 24, 1972. Graeme: 'It was a surprise to me, because not long before, Ron was telling me, You don't ever want to get married!'

ABOVE: Adelaide's Clefs in Melbourne, 1966, before Barrie McAskill took over the band and it became the Levi Smith Clefs. Left to right: drummer Gil Matthews (who later joined Billy Thorpe and the Aztecs), singer McAskill, bassist Bruce Howe, guitarist Les Tanner (kneeling) and erstwhile leader, organist 'Tweed' Harris.

BELOW: Bon and Bruce Howe at Jersey Road, Paddington; early Fraternity days, August 1970.

ABOVE: Vince Lovegrove: 'They wanted to be the Band'. Fraternity as a six-piece; winter 1971. Left to right: Mick Jurd, John Freeman, 'Uncle' John Ayers, Bruce Howe, Bon, John Bisset.
BELOW: Fraternity on stage in England, an outdoor show in South London supporting Mungo Jerry; June/July 1973. Left to right: Bon, John Freeman, Uncle.

Malcolm Young's first real band, the unapologetically named Velvet Underground, circa 1972. Left to right: Herm Kovac, Malcolm, Andy Imlah, Michael Szchefswick, Les Hall. Both Kovac and Hall went on to play in AC/DC's Alberts stablemates, the Ted Mulry Gang.

Bon in the studio – Alberts – in March 1976, during the recording of *Dirty deeds done dirt cheap*. Uncle: 'Within that dynamic range that was Bon's voice, he was just incredibly loud, had amazing presence'.

ABOVE: Bassist Mark Evans joined AC/DC in March 1975, completing the band's classic line-up. Left to right: Malcolm, Bon, Angus, Phil Rudd, Evans.
BELOW: 1979 AC/DC promo shot featuring bassist Cliff Williams, second from left, who replaced Mark Evans after he was sacked in May 1977.

five melbourne

the Valentines arrived in Melbourne on Friday, October 13, drawn inextricably to the city which, in 1967, was Australia's indisputable pop capital.

The rivalry between Melbourne and Sydney is one of Australia's oldest. Sydney, city of water, speed and light, is the New World to Melbourne's Old, with its long winters, its sombre, more rarefied air. The two cities' rock'n'roll scenes have always been distinctly different, and have always vied for supremacy.

In the very early sixties, both cities played host to thriving teenage dance circuits. The music was almost entirely instrumental rock'n'roll, which even then evinced differences. However, when the Beatles exploded and every instrumental band in the land scrambled to find a singer — not to mention grow their hair — it was Sydney, for some reason, that

Be Our Valentine in '69

The Valentines go bubblegum. Left to right: Vince Lovegrove, Doug Lavery, Bon, Wyn Milson, Ted Ward, John Cooksey. Vince: 'Melbourne was a lot more teeny bopper orientated, which we foolishly catered to because it was good for the ego. But it wasn't really doing us much good musically.'

produced the first rush of hits. But Sydney's dominance wouldn't last long. By the end of 1965, the emphasis had swung to Melbourne. It would not return to Sydney till the start of the eighties.

Success in rock'n'roll, like most fields, takes more than talent, and Melbourne had more than just bands. It had the look, the mod image that Sydney seemed to lack. And it had a new breed of entrepreneurs who were important facilitators. Melbourne's live circuit was second to none, with its trendy, if unlicensed discos, like Berties, the Thumpin' Tum and Sebastians, in addition to countless suburban dances.

A second wave of acts, including the Loved Ones, Bobby & Laurie, the Groop, Normie Rowe and Ronnie Burns broke through, leaving all but the Easybeats eating dust. The Masters Apprentices and the Twilights moved over from Adelaide, and then, Johnny Young from Perth. Melbourne was also home to TV's 'Go!!' show, and then 'Kommotion' and 'Uptight', and to the scene's bible *Go-Set* magazine.

Little of the music itself was actually any good — Australian musicians, without any background in blues-based rock'n'roll, were still just trying to get a handle on it — but the seeds of something greater were being sown.

When the Valentines pulled into Flinders Street Station on that Black Friday morning late in 1967, they had no tangible plans.

VINCE: 'We had Ronnie Burns's phone number. We called him from the station. He came and picked us up and took us to a Chinese restaurant. We stayed at a hotel that night.'

The *West Australian* had reported on the eve of the band's departure, 'The Valentines are willing to start at the bottom and work hard and these qualities have proven to be most necessary'. Indeed The Valentines would struggle for some time yet.

Within a week of arriving in Melbourne, the band was being managed by former Loved Ones singer Gerry Humphries, in partnership with Johnny Young's drummer Don Pryor — for what it was worth. The pair threw a generous reception to launch the band along with 'She said', but then — nothing.

Humphries and Pryor's interest dropped off. The band did, however, sign on with AMBO, the Australian Management Booking Agency, which farmed out the talent to a large proportion of Melbourne's discos and dances. But with 'She said' going nowhere, getting gigs wasn't going to be easy.

As if by way of a rude baptism, the Valentines were sent bush, on a tour of rural Victoria. They got around, gear and all, in a Kombi they'd bought and daubed in psychedelic hues.

Renting a house in far eastern Melbourne suburb Burwood, the band almost literally starved, earning barely enough to cover costs from unattended midweek gigs. They would go into supermarkets and eat in the aisles, or steal milk money on the way home late at night. In their early twenties though most of them were, the Valentines were still boys who had barely broken away from their mothers' apron strings, and they had no idea how to look after themselves. Female fans helped.

Vince wrote: 'Bon was the only guy in the band unruffled by our seemingly hopeless situation. He was a great positive inspiration in those days when we needed it most.'

Bon would occasionally stay with Maria, who had a flat in the same block as Humphries and Pryor, in swish South Yarra. But their relationship would always be problematic. Bon had chosen his path in life, but Maria seemed unwilling to accept the reality that it entailed — that he would be away a lot, on the road; that he would attract a lot of attention, particularly female; and that he would make no money, at least not initially. They were always arguing. The rest of the band, in turn, resented Maria for the hold she had on Bon. However, even with her taunting, Bon was hopelessly romantically in love. Whenever he was away, he would write her love letters, sometimes several times a day.

MARIA: 'He used to talk about how when the group was successful and it would be on the road in Australia, and America, it would have a tour bus, and on the back would be a little caravan attached for he and I!'

Bon was possibly a little intimidated by the sophisticated, cliquey Melbourne scene, and so was happy to put his faith in Vince, who seemed capable of scoring the necessary social points. It suited Vince's ego to be making decisions for the band. Strangely, there was a streak in Bon that was quite subservient. It was not so much that he craved acceptance, rather that he wanted to please people, and at best he could be quite unselfish. So for the meantime at least, he was bowing to both Maria and Vince.

VINCE: 'It was a confusing time anyway, for guys. Bon always seemed troubled by something, whether it was his creative desire as opposed to feelings of inadequacy due to his working-class origins, or lack of education, I don't know. But there was some sort of conflict there, where he was unsure of himself. He had a lot of bravado, but really he was a softie underneath.'

Vince pulled off a coup when he managed to sell the band to Ivan Dayman. Dayman was the man behind Sunshine Records and Normie Rowe, and he controlled a circuit of venues all over Australia.

As Dayman booked the band into Adelaide for a week in February, Clarion released a third Valentines single, 'I can hear the raindrops/Why me?'. These were the first two original songs cut by the band — written by Vince and Ted Ward — but both were eminently forgettable, and the disc, again, died a death.

In March, the band ventured for the first time to Brisbane, and then to Sydney and then back to Melbourne. It was an experience that taught them just how gruelling life on the road could be. They lived, collectively, on a bare $300 or so a week, which was what Dayman paid them. They travelled by bus, train, car — however they could. They lugged all their own gear; they stayed in boarding houses and seedy hotels, and they played dives. But they wouldn't have changed things for quids. This was the life they'd wanted.

By the middle of April, they were back in Sydney for an extended eight-week stay. This was a turning point for the band and for Bon.

Staying at the shabby Americana Hotel in red-light district Kings Cross — which was then buzzing like a boom town, due to the influx of American servicemen on R&R leave from Vietnam — the band was still strapped for cash, pooling funds to eat fish'n'chips. But they were getting somewhere at last. *Go-Set* stringer David Elfick proclaimed that the band's 'performances at Sydney's Op-Pop disco justified their rating as Perth's number one group ... They have a distinctive sound ... they play Pickett, Redding type numbers, straight top 40 and comedy ("Would you like to swing on a bra?").' No band, at that time, played its own material on stage, unless those songs were already hits.

Bon wrote to Maria that posters for the band were plastered all over Sydney, and that while they were going down well — had even 'drew the biggest crowd in six weeks at Op-Pop' — it 'could be a lot better', and so were 'going to have a meeting to try to find out how we can best improve ourselves'. The band was geed up in anticipation of going into Festival's Pyrmont studios with ace producer Pat Aulton. Bon wanted to try out some Dusty Springfield songs.

The Valentines were a bit like babes in the woods in Sin City, Sydney, but they quickly took to it all.

MARIA: 'In his letters, he would say, Don't worry, I'll be faithful. What a liar he was!'

Drugs were a new dimension altogether.

VINCE: 'We met this piano player called Bobby Gebert, who turned Bon and I onto our first joint. We didn't know it then either, but these guys were gay. We were so naive, we just thought they were in fancy dress. They had licorice papers, to roll joints — it was the whole thing. We were sitting there looking at each other, giggling like two little kids, saying, Has it affected you yet? Then we realised, we were just these two guys sitting in the corner at this party, we were stoned, and so we panicked and ran out of the place. We got back to the hotel and the other guys said, You guys have had drugs, you're out of the band — because we had a rule, no drugs — and so we said, yeah, well, okay...'

At the end of April, Maria paid Bon a visit in Sydney. Long-distance love affairs are inevitably hard to handle, and Bon and Maria's was starting to show the strain. But the couple spent a happy weekend together. As soon as Maria got home, however, the push and pull started all over again. The band had gone up to Brisbane. Bon spent all his time and money on phone calls. Maria was jack of Bon's absence — she knew there were other women — and she was talking about going back to Perth. Bon began to fear that Maria might have taken up with someone else herself. When the band returned to Sydney, Maria came up again. It was as plain as day to both of them then that it wasn't going to work. They were each other's first love, but as young lovers do, they'd grown apart.

For the second time in just over a year, Bon saw Maria off on the train — but this time, there would be no reunion down the line. Maria would always occupy a special place in Bon's heart, and he would remain in touch with her right up until he died. More immediately though, there was too much going on to waste time moping and any number of willing young women to help take the pain away.

The band finally got into the studio in late May and cut their next single, 'Peculiar hole in the sky', another Easybeats song. This they did with a session player on drums, as Warwick Findlay had buckled under the financial pressure, having a wife to support, and had left the band to find a real job.

The Valentines were over the moon about 'Peculiar hole in the sky', and fairly enough. It was a quantum leap for them, a good song done justice, cut in an almost modern studio with a capable producer, invested with all the appropriate psyche-delic overtones. It was released in July. *Go-Set*, strangely, was not terribly impressed and it didn't sell.

When the band pleaded in an ad for the single, 'Please buy a copy — we're starving', they were only marginally stretching the truth. They had by then moved back to Melbourne and recruited a new drummer in Doug Lavery, and though they were starting to get ahead playing the Ivan Dayman circuit, Vince was still looking for a stronger connection.

They moved into a two-storey terraced house in seedy St Kilda, in Dalgety Street, just off the notorious Fitzroy Street sleaze strip. Bon, now a legitimate bachelor again, had the attic bedroom, which he painted fire-engine red, whence he reigned as a gay blade supreme.

It was around this time he met a girl called Mary Wasylyk, who would become a lifelong friend. Born of Ukrainian parents in 1950, Mary grew up in Melbourne's industrial western suburbs, and after school went into fashion design. She saw the Valentines for the first time at a Sunday afternoon show at the Bowl, a disco in Melbourne. 'You used to have arguments, you know, who was better, the Valentines or the Zoot? I used to make these hippie beads, and the band all really liked them, so I got to know them, and I stayed friends with Bon ever since.

'They were just trying to copy the English bands, sort of like an extension of the Easybeats but not as good. I mean, looking at them, none of them seemed talented, really!'

It was at Dalgety Street that the Valentines started to run really wild. They became the premier party animals in a scene that aspired to complete psychedelic degeneracy. It was 1968. *Sergeant Pepper* had changed everything. Hendrix and the Doors had hits. Bon's brother Graeme, then 15, came over on holidays, and had his life changed. 'Women were everywhere, and ganja. Vince gave me my first smoke. They'd go off to a show, and come back with women, sit up all night and smoke, whatever. For someone like me to come straight out of Fremantle, I couldn't go back to that, so the only way out was to jump a ship.' Graeme remained a merchant seaman for many years to come, and he would drop in on Bon whenever he was in port.

Vince sussed an opening for the band at AMBO. Headed by Sri-Lankan–Australian Bill Joseph, the agency had been revitalised by its employment of one of the new breed, Michael Browning. Browning was running Berties and Sebastians, and also managing Doug Parkinson, then the hottest new act in town. Vince figured that if he could parley an AMBO agent into also managing the Valentines, the band might curry some favour in the same way Doug Parkinson seemed to.

The Valentines were well drilled, well established on the live circuit, and even though 'Peculiar hole in the sky' had failed to set the world on fire, its potential, plus Vince's determination, was incentive enough for Bill Joseph himself to take on the band. Ron Tudor, who was then launching his own June Productions company (and would go on to form the Fable Label), also came on board, signing the Valentines to a deal whereby June would record the band, and then lease the tapes to Philips.

Everything was thus in place, finally, for the Valentines to launch a full-scale assault on Australian teenagers.

The Summer of Love took place officially, in San Francisco, and nominally also London, in what was Australia's winter of 1967. Its impact would be superficial in this country. A local pop hit that could be described as psychedelic did not arrive until 1969, in the form of 'The real thing'. Acid rock, as such, hardly happened in Australia.

The reason why Australia missed the first blooming of flower power was essentially because the turnkeys reclaimed control of the asylum. The new order that had pulled the rug out from under the music business establishment in the early to midsixties — independent record companies and young entrepreneurs as well as artists — had by then been absorbed by the mainstream. The big record companies, those that traditionally ran the music game, had had enough time to adjust to the new rules and now they wanted their ball back.

Radio was reluctant to play far-out new acts like Hendrix. Radio was more comfortable with the Monkees. The black soul sounds of Tamla-Motown and Stax, so successful in America and Britain, were hardly heard in racist Australia.

1968 was not a vintage year for Australian pop. Not a single Australian record would go to number one in 1968, as opposed to previous, and proceeding years, which were littered with local chart-toppers. The impetus of 1965 and '66 had been dissipated.

Following in the footsteps of the Monkees, the success of acts like the Ohio Express and the 1910 Fruitgum Company certified bubblegum as the biggest commercial trend of the year. Bubblegum was music that was shamelessly commercial, simplistic and repetitive to the point of inanity. Ultimately disposable, and more than likely manufactured, it particularly impressed Australian record companies.

Australian musicians had only just come to terms with chirpy Beatlesque harmonies, but now they were discouraged from going any further. In America and Britain, sales of albums superseded singles in 1968. Australia wouldn't even get accurate album charts until 1970. The hot new local acts were the Groove, who would go on to win the 1968 Battle of the Sounds, and Johnny Farnham. Both were confectionery.

At the end of 1968, an intense marketing campaign swung into action around the Valentines. In November, they made the unequivocal statement in *Go-Set* that they were a bubble-gum group, 'not afraid about being commercial'. The band had buffed up its image — Bon was dusting down his tattoos with foundation, and straightening his hair with sticky tape — and they wore matching orange frilly shirts, flares and beads. Although they would suffer in comparison with prettier band the Zoot, who exploded onto Melbourne around the same time with their 'Think Pink' campaign, they hit the media all over Australia with a season's greeting card proclaiming, 'The slogan for this year is "BE MY VALENTINE IN '69"'.

Bon filled out a profile in which, shaving three years off his age — claiming to be 19 when he was 22 — he revealed:

Likes — My room (painted red), long blonde hair, sex, showers, swimming
Dislikes — People who hate Crater Critters (ex-Weeties pack), being disturbed whilst thinking, washing and ironing
Loves — Parents, my pet Crater Critter
Favourite Food — Ice cream
Drink — Sand Zombie
Actor — Vince
Actress — Julie Christie, Vanessa Redgrave
Groups — Beatles, Moody Blues
Singer, Male — John Lee Hooker, Otis Redding
Singer, Female — Supremes
Music — Scottish Pipe Band music, soul, worried jazz

The Valentines put down a new single called 'My old man's a groovy old man'. The song was yet another product of the prolific Vanda and Young partnership, which found its way to the band via Ron Tudor. Tudor also proffered an obscure Pretty Things' song, 'Ebeneezer', for the flip-side.

June Music had an office conveniently located just a couple of doors down from the state-of-the-art Armstrong's Studios. *Go-Set* had trumpeted some months earlier, 'People will no longer be able to blame a lack of equipment for poor Australian record production. Last week, Bill Armstrong's studio in Melbourne installed an 8-track Scully recording machine'. 'My old man' was as dynamic as it was vacuous — classic bubblegum.

After sessions for the single were completed, the Valentines hit the road again. Brisbane was something of a stronghold for the band, and they spent the Yuletide there. Vince remembers a remarkable Christmas Day:

VINCE: 'We had this fan up there who was Chinese, and he invited us over for Christmas dinner. But what happened was, we took this mescaline. It was hilarious. Ted thought he was a hippopotamus, he just sat in the pool all day. Bon and I went to this lunch, it was meant to be a traditional Western Christmas — roast turkey and everything, you know. So we get there, and this guy comes to the door, and as soon as we walk in the room, where the parents are there to meet us, Bon just becomes a Chinaman, you know, he's got his arms folded and he's squinting with this stupid grin on his face, and he's bowing and going, Ah so, Ah so. These people didn't know what was going on. Anyway, they serve the food, and I suppose we must have thought this turkey was alive or something, because we just ended up getting out of there, we were virtually running down the road screaming. We started hitching, and of course no one would give us a lift, so we ended up walking all the way back to the motel, it was seven miles or something. We got there, and Ted's virtually turned into a prune, he's still in the pool, he still thinks he's a hippopotamus!'

Returning to Melbourne, the band had to find new digs as the lease on Dalgety Street was up. Bon, Wyn and Ted set up headquarters at a flat in South Yarra, on Toorak Road, at the centre of something of a pop-idol enclave. Johnny Farnham was a neighbour on one side, Johnny Young the other. Vince moved in just around the corner.

Molly interviewed not just Vince but the whole band for

Go-Set in January. What image were the Valentines trying to project? he asked John Cooksey. 'A very happy, sweet, but sexy commercial type image,' Cooksey replied. 'At the same time, we want to be able to entertain the disco crowds.'

'My old man's a groovy old man' was launched on February 14, 1969 — Valentine's Day itself. It took off immediately, although almost inevitably it was overshadowed by the Zoot's contemporaneous first hit, 'One times, two times, three times, four'. But the Valentines were away nonetheless.

When they played the That's Life disco in Prahran that night, 'the audience', as Molly reported in *Go-Set*, 'screamed in unison, We love the Valentines. As soon as they appeared the audience went completely berserk and started to storm the stage. The two lead singers, Vince and Bon, were dragged to the floor and Bon's pants and jacket were completely ripped off him.' Writing on March 1, Molly went on: 'This has been a regular occurrence since that particular day. Last Saturday night the Valentines appeared at another Melbourne dance, Picadilly, and drew a record attendance of over 2,000 teenagers. Cupids (the Valentines' symbol) were thrown out to the audience and in turn the audience threw back bubblegum. The Valentines didn't even get through their first number before the stage was stormed.

'Ripped clothes and accessories was repeated and when Doug, the drummer, got up to sing, he left the stage two minutes later sporting only a pair of red underpants. The group were supposed to appear for 45 minutes but their performance had to be cut down to 20 minutes because the audience became completely uncontrollable.'

On March 10, the Valentines played a free concert before a crowd of 7,000 at the Alexandra Gardens, as part of Melbourne's annual Moomba festival. A 'riot' ensued during which Vince was arrested on charges of assaulting police. Vince was certainly a provocateur — Bon was the passive one of the pair, content to hang back and just sing — but all Vince did was push an overzealous cop from the stage with his bare foot. He was fined $50, and put on a 12-month good-behaviour bond.

With a new drummer, Paddy Beach — Doug Lavery had

left to join Axiom — the Valentines concentrated on gigging around Melbourne, working Beach in and consolidating support. 'My old man' eventually peaked nationally at number 23.

Paddy Beach (nee Veitch) was recruited from a trio called Compulsion, a Maori Hendrix-clone act that Michael Browning had brought to Australia from New Zealand just before it imploded. When Paddy, who was white, joined the Valentines, pint-sized roadie John Darcy came with him. Darcy, as he's known to all, remembers his first meeting with the band, at Toorak Road.

DARCY: 'I meet the guys, and they're checking me out, because of the size of me, you know, because they'd just started to get some of the bigger gear. They said, Do you reckon you'll be able to handle the gear? I said, I'm pretty fit, I've always done a bit of boxing, I go to the gym. So they said, Alright, we'll give it a go. Then Bon says, Hey, you feel like a fuck? Well, that sets me back a bit, but I say, Well, yeah, I could always go a fuck, and so he says, Well, just whip into the front room there, there's a young chick there, she'll give you a go, no worries. So I go into the front room and there's all these chicks there, stark naked, so I figure I'll go for it. So I'm laying on this bed, stark naked, there's this chick going down on me, and Bon comes in and says, How do you think you'll like the job? I go, Well, I suppose I can try and adapt.'

The Valentines' image might have been squeaky clean, but their reputation was easily the worst of any band around. Dope smoking was also constant.

The band played a lot of cards and neighbour Johnny Farnham was a frequent visitor, but Farnham's manager Daryl Sambell wasn't at all keen on his charge being seen to be associating with such degenerates.

DARCY: 'You'd wake up each morning, and look out the little eyepiece in the door, and by 9.30 there'd be maybe three or four young girls there, in the hallway at the top of the stairs. At maybe 10.30, it'd be, Oh, there's seven out there now. They were all like under 12. After lunch they'd start to get a bit older, you'd get the 14-year-olds starting to turn up. Of course, I'd be in and out, I'd have to duck up to the Toorak

Village to get the papers, milk. I'd be stepping over girls. They'd be, Oh, can we come in, can we see the guys, can you get us their autographs? So I'd say, Look, I'll see what I can do for you. So you'd let some in for 15 minutes or so, hand out some autographs. And then later on you'd let the older ones in; they could cook the meals for you, and clean the flat, do the washing and ironing. Then of course there'd be a couple of older ones who'd supply a bit more than that, give you a bit of a work-out before you had to go off to a job. It was unbelievable. Every day of the week it was the same.'

Even in their wildest dreams, the Valentines couldn't have imagined it would be as wild as this. Bon was in his element. He had a little trick he employed to sort out the goers from the prick-teasers among the girls who came backstage. He would let off one of the smoke bombs the band exploded on stage as part of its act, and when the smoke cleared, he would be standing there naked. The girls who didn't run off screaming had to be goers. The band performed indecent acts upon young girls in the back of the bus on fan club picnics, and then dropped them off back into their worried mothers' waiting arms, reassuring these women, as sweet and innocent as you like, that their daughters had been in good hands — as indeed they had — and then laughing at how Bon especially could put it over them with all his boyish charm.

The band went out on the road, touring through Canberra, Newcastle, Queensland and South Australia, but already, cracks were appearing in the facade. Back in Melbourne in early August, they played a reception at That's Life to launch a new Coca-Cola commercial. 'Most surprising thing though,' the *Herald* reported, 'was to hear the Valentines play a bit of rhythm in contrast to their labelled "bubblegum" style. As bass guitarist John said, "We weren't under any pressure tonight, so we decided to prove a point" — that they are versatile.'

The very next night, the Valentines failed to take out the Battle of the Sounds, finishing second to the tied Doug Parkinson and Masters Apprentices; but the band was already set on a new path. Having met with commercial success, the Valentines, predictably, now wanted artistic credibility. Bubblegum, after all, was throwaway pap for little girls.

VINCE: 'The scene was changing, it was starting to get serious, it was getting to the point where you had to be good.'

The novelty of local bands was wearing off. No longer was it enough to merely ape your idols. Australia might have missed out on the Summer of Love, but in mid-1969, with Woodstock just around the corner, it was starting to catch up. New English and American bands that predicted seventies rock, like Led Zeppelin and Santana, had an immediate and profound impact. A schism was drawn deep between dances and discos. The dance circuit catered to teeny boppers, with bubblegum bands; whilst discos, though still unlicensed, became the province of adult-oriented, so-called 'soul artists' like Max Merritt and Billy Thorpe, both on the comeback trail, and Doug Parkinson and the Levi Smith Clefs, who would take Australian rock into the seventies.

'Our aim,' Vince told *Go-Set*, 'will be to present to dance crowds a wild act with a heavy sexual slant and attempt to please disco audiences by playing original free-form music. Just as Doug Parkinson made the transition from discos to dances, we hope to do the reverse.'

The Valentines made the transition that the Zoot, and even the superior Masters Apprentices, couldn't. They would soon become a staple on the disco scene in Melbourne and Sydney alike. Ultimately though, and ironically, the Valentines' musical coming-of-age also proved to be their undoing.

VINCE: 'We found we had too many ideas for one band. We started to fall apart as well as become a better band.'

As the single 'Nick nack paddy whack' was released, the band went out on the road with Russell Morris, Johnny Farnham, Ronnie Burns, the Zoot and the Masters Apprentices as part of the huge Operation Starlift tour. 'Nick nack paddy whack' proved to be something of an embarrassment. An adaptation of the children's nursery rhyme, originally cut as a possible theme for a proposed afternoon TV show, it was never intended for release. But its failure to chart was proof positive that the bubblegum bubble had burst. Further encouragement to get serious came in the better response to the single's B-side, a song called 'Getting better', which marked Bon's first ever writing credit, shared with Wyn. It was a convincingly urgent call to arms.

Bon particularly wanted his due. What credibility the band did have was largely thanks to him — his voice was acknowledged as one of the best in the business — and with an increasing amount of confidence, not to mention experience, he was ready to assume more of the initiative.

Vince was naturally reluctant to relinquish leadership, but he knew what side his bread was buttered on. At the same time, Bon was sensitive to Vince's feelings, and so he still looked to him for the nod. But certainly, the days of Vince's autocratic rule were over. Vince told *Go-Set*: 'Admittedly, I'm more popular than Bon, but he's a far better singer than I'll ever be. In fact, I think he's the most underrated singer in Australia.'

The Valentines were chuffed when 'real musicians' like Billy Thorpe and Wendy Saddington started showing up at their gigs. They were invited to Billy's pad in East Melbourne for spaghetti or a curry, and in doing so joined a quite exclusive little club. The Levi Smith Clefs came around and hung out at Toorak Road.

But still the Valentines clung to their original teenage female fan base, playing dances as much as discos, if for financial reasons as much as any other. They would work every week from Tuesday or Wednesday through to Sunday, building up on Friday to Saturday night, which often entailed three or four gigs. They would get around in the Ford Thames van that Darcy drove, lugging increasingly large amounts of equipment. The aesthetic progression rock was making was directly related to the advancements in its technology, its gear. Bon even wrote an essay for *Go-Set* at the time, admonishing bands who might be cheating their fans by settling for second-rate PA systems.

VINCE: 'On a Saturday night, you'd do three shows: an early dance, a late dance, and then you'd do a club. Racing around all night, and you did it carrying all your own gear, so the thing was, you couldn't possibly do all that without some kind of stimulant.'

DARCY: 'On a Saturday night, you might start off, say, at the Ringwood Town Hall, do the first spot there, about 8.30, and of course, you'd only play for half an hour, and then you'd throw the gear in the van, and tear down to Dandenong. You might do the Dandenong Town Hall in the second spot, then whip the gear out again and race down to the Frankston Mechanics Hall and do the feature spot there. That would finish at about 11.30 or so. We'd stay straight for those gigs. Then the last gig would be back in the city, at one of the clubs there, Berties or Sebastians, so on the way there, as soon as we'd loaded out of Frankston, we'd be tearing up the highway, and that's when the joints would start coming out, and we'd get stuck into the cookies. We used to make these hash cookies, it was a real good blast, and we found we could eat them without all the smoke giving the game away, you know. Wyn would come out of his room with this big cookie jar; they looked like butternut snaps!'

WYN: 'We would undergo this transformation at midnight. We would literally change, we would take off our matching outfits and put on jeans. We'd stay straight up until then, if you like, then we'd let our hair down, and go to Berties and do what wasn't the mainstream music — Led Zeppelin, guitar solos, percussion, all that. And that's when Bon really came into his own.'

DARCY: 'We'd get so stoned we'd just be giggling and carrying on, but it was really harmless sort of stuff. Anyway, we'd end up back at Berties, and I'm sure people used to come there just to watch us set up. You'd be off your face, and they had this tiny little triangular stage there in the basement, at the bottom of this really narrow stairway, and you'd have to set up.

'The signal was, they used to flick the light on and off when you were meant to start. Of course, we were always late, so it got so it was like a strobe! They'd have to keep the joint open just so we could play.'

VINCE: 'That's when a lot of the best music came, you know.'

DARCY: 'We'd get home at maybe 3.30 in the morning, and we'd just get home and keep partying on. Barrie McAskill and the Levi Smith Clefs, any band that was around from inter-state, they'd come back and party with you.

'It was like a little world of our own, we could sit up there nice and stoned and just watch the world go by outside. But we were pretty well known by then, the flat was, so anyone who drove by at four in the morning could have looked up and thought, Oh, the Valentines are having another party.'

WYN: 'Then you'd have to be up at 7.00 to go out to Channel 0 at Nunawading to do "Uptight". There'd be some pretty sick-looking people wandering around, wanting to get their make-up done.'

When John Cooksey announced his intention to leave the band in September, the Vallies decided not to replace him, but rather have Ted Ward switch from second guitar to bass. It was in order to rehearse this new line-up that the band took off on September 15 for a two-week sojourn at the Jan Juc Surf Lifesaving Club near Torquay, on the western Victorian coast. And it was here they came a real cropper.

'The pop world rocked last week,' read *Go-Set* on October 4, 'when the police raided the practice hideaway of top pop group, the Valentines, and found them in possession of the drug, marijuana.'

It was the first en masse bust of a band in Australia, and it caused a scandal, although within the rock world, it only enhanced their credibility.

It transpired that the band had been dobbed in by, to quote *Go-Set*, 'a well-known member of one of our top pop groups', who 'informed [on the Valentines] to save his own neck on a similar charge'.

Unbeknownst to the band, they had been under police surveillance for some weeks. The cops followed them down to Jan Juc, where they were dividing their time rehearsing, smoking, listening to Led Zeppelin and smoking. It was too cold even for Bon to go in the water.

Having watched the isolated clubhouse for five days, the cops simply knocked on the door with a search warrant on Saturday night, September 20. The band shat themselves. The cops found a pipe and a quantity of Moroccan powder.

With a court hearing scheduled for October — though they

would not eventually appear until the following February — the band either boldly or foolishly spoke out against drug laws. 'We believe it should be legalised,' Vince told *Go-Set*. They even got onto the subject of police harassment. Bon had always been known as the joker in the band, but he was becoming more serious in his new, more frontal role, and on this occasion, came about as close as he ever would to making a directly political statement.

'They should realise that what we do is right for us,' he protested. 'We respect a lot of things about their job, but they shouldn't persecute whole groups of people just for being different.' In another interview, he said, 'The Australian government deserves a few ripples. They'll be the last to legalise homosexuality, and pot will be the same.'

In the aftermath of the bust, the band instituted a no-smoking rule, but it was doomed to failure, and in fact, all it did was create divisions.

DARCY: 'We made a pact, Okay, no more smoking, we've got to straighten out, for the good of the band. Well, Bon, Paddy and myself just sort of ignored it. Vince went off on his own trip too, I think. Wyn and Ted went along with the letter of the law, and that went on for a few months before they realised what we were doing. They were pretty cut, actually.'

In late October, the band went to Sydney for the first time since the Op-Pop days. Sydney had regained some initiative, since it had taken so readily to the new dawning in rock. Bands like the La De Das, Flying Circus, Jeff St John and Copperwine, Chain, Max Merritt and the Meteors and Levi Smith Clefs boasted firm followings in licensed discos like the Whiskey-A-Go-Go, Caesar's Palace, Here and Chequers, which catered as much to R&R'ing American servicemen as local hipsters. 'Head' bands like Taman Shud and Tully were so far out they ran their own 'stirs', free gigs for freaks.

VINCE: 'Sydney and Melbourne were two totally different places then, in terms of the audience. Melbourne was a lot more teeny-bopper orientated, which we'd foolishly catered to because it was good for the ego. But it wasn't really doing us much good musically.'

The band was rapt to be back in Sydney, where they hadn't

suffered so much from labelling. Playing a residency at Caesar's, as Tony Johnston later reported in the *Herald*, 'They didn't wear their uniforms, because as Vince said, that age group aren't really worried about a group's image, they're just interested in the music'. Bon described what the band was doing as 'trying things, feeling around for a musical direction'.

For two nights at Caesar's, they supported the Easybeats, who, on the verge of folding in England, had been lured to play a final return tour of Australia. Yet though this was the band that had given the Valentines so many pointers, the Vallies were somewhat perplexed, because whilst everyone else in rock was launching off into the smoky stratosphere, the Easybeats had come full circle and gotten back to basics, playing straight-ahead rock'n'roll.

Staying at a big house the promoter provided for them on the edge of the expansive Centennial Park in Sydney's trendy eastern suburbs, the band was hanging loose. Bon and Vince became friendly with a couple of girls who were waitresses at Caesar's, and so they spent much time at their Kings Cross flat, getting friendlier. They would drop acid and go tripping in Centennial Park. Bon was developing a taste for liquor too, becoming something of a bar fly.

The Caesar's gig was so successful that the band was booked back there for a fee reported 'to be the second highest paid an Australian group', whatever that meant.

Although the rot was already setting in, the band's demise would be a drawn-out process, just due to its common bond. Vince, who had just turned down a part in the Australian production of *Hair*, told *Go-Set*: 'We probably have more personality conflicts within the group than anyone else — Bon and I have often come really close to punching the shit out of each other. But with all of us the group is the most important thing — it always comes first, before personal arguments, before chicks, before smoking, everything.'

In December, the band was lured to make its triumphant return to Perth; and, as it happened, this homecoming would appropriately serve as a virtual last hurrah. The band always said they wouldn't go home until they could do it as stars, and certainly, they were welcomed back like prodigal sons. When they arrived at Perth airport, they had to run the gauntlet of a reported 4,000 screaming fans, to be sped away in waiting cars.

The band played a big New Year's Eve show for 6KY back in their old stamping grounds, the Supreme Court Gardens. Staying at Vince's parents' place in Applecross, they enjoyed the run of the Perth clubs.

On the five-hour flight back to Melbourne, they kept up the bratty rock star act, outraging fellow passengers with their obnoxious behaviour, all to the tune of the tape they'd just acquired of the second Led Zeppelin album, blasting from the back of the cabin at full volume.

When they finally appeared in court in Geelong in February, the band pleaded guilty as charged. Counsel William Lennon, however, argued, 'The group have told me that under the influence of marijuana they become more perceptive to musical sounds', and that 'long-haired pop stars weren't automatically louts and drug addicts, and that they had not encouraged other teenagers to follow their example'. The band each received a $150 fine and a good-behaviour bond.

With the dissolution of the Toorak Road flat, the Valentines' end drew nearer. Rumours were rife that they were breaking up. Even Bill Joseph had to ring *Go-Set* to find out what was going on.

DARCY: 'We were like lost souls then. After having something going so strong for a while.'

It was really only a sense of loyalty that was holding the band together now. What would be the band's final single, 'Juliette', was released in April. A dead ringer for 'Dear Prudence', and written by the band collectively, it ran right into the so-called radio ban anyway, and barely scraped into the top 30. The radio ban was a strange episode in Australian pop history, in which the big record companies demanded payment from radio stations for the right to play their product, on the basis that it was providing radio with programming; a demand at which radio naturally scoffed, claiming that it was providing record companies with essential, free promotion.

The result was a stand-off, during which time no major label records, locally-produced or otherwise, were heard on the airwaves. What happened, of course, was that independent labels, who could see the opportunity in refusing to side with their major big brothers, stepped into the breach and filled radio's programming void for free, with a glut of local cover versions of American and English hits, plus even the occasional original Australian track. Yet though June Music boss Ron Tudor's new Fable Label would be a big winner out of the ban, the Valentines, who still came out on Philips, lost in the crossfire.

The failure of 'Juliette', for whatever reason, was the last straw. The Valentines were on the road in Newcastle when the bullet was bit. Talking later to *Go-Set*, Vince said it was because their opinions conflicted so much. 'None of us were really happy in the group any more, but we didn't say anything because we didn't want to hurt the others.'

Bon wrote to Maria, to whom he was speaking again, from Newcastle on June 2:

Got some news for you. Guess what? The Valentines are breaking up on the 1st August. It's been coming about for a while now and it came to a head last week when we found out that Vince was waiting for confirmation from a couple of jobs. Ted, Wyn and I decided we'd dig to split anyway and form a group of our own and run it the way we wanted to, so that was it ... Vince is going to work for *Go-Set* and Paddy will get another group. We're going to add an electric piano and organ and a new drummer and go into hiding for a couple of months. Then we'll record an LP and a single and follow it up with a shit-hot group and make lots of money. The funny thing about it was that there were no arguments or hard feelings as everyone realised that a change was due.

The band returned to Melbourne and played its last show with a distinct lack of fanfare, at Werribee, a desolate, far-flung suburb known only for its sewage treatment plant.

DARCY: 'The last job, it was a funny one, because no one ... it didn't sort of hit home, that we were doing the last job. I was sort of blown out, What, we're doing the last job down at Werribee? It was like, it was a Sunday night, and so we were doing this job, and that was it. It was like, Shit, what are we going to do now?'

But if Bon had plans, they ended up just that, best-laid plans. He was made a better offer. It held great promise.

Fraternity go bush, Aldgate, September, 1971. Left to right: Mick Jurd, John Freeman, 'Uncle' John Ayers, Bon, Bruce Howe, Sam See, John Bisset.

six
fraternity

adelaide was probably the last place Bon would have expected to end up, but within six months of the Valentines' dissolution, it was there that he found himself, living the whole communal hippie trip as a member of the band Fraternity.

Fraternity leader Bruce Howe asked Bon to come up to Sydney to join his band as soon as he heard the Valentines were breaking up. Bon leapt at the chance: Fraternity was the hottest new band in the land.

Fraternity had strong Adelaide connections to begin with. It was, after all, the band that had spun off the hallowed Levi Smith Clefs, an Australian musical institution led by Adelaide legend Barrie McAskill. Bruce Howe himself was an Adelaide boy, as was drummer John Freeman. And the band was already tied to Adelaide-based independent record company, Sweet Peach.

But it was going to Adelaide, removing themselves from the centre of things, that cruelled Fraternity's potential. Such, however, was the naivety and conceit that characterised the times, Fraternity were convinced the world would come to them, and in the process establish Adelaide as an alternative music centre like some sort of antipodean Nashville.

It wouldn't quite happen that way.

Adelaide is a sleepy small town; not a city, many say, but a big country town, if a very sophisticated one. As Australia's first free settlement — as opposed to all the other major cities, which have convict roots — the South Australian capital has always regarded itself as a bastion of liberalism and the arts. The biannual Adelaide Festival remains Australia's premier arts event.

Adelaide also has an extremely significant rock'n'roll tradition. As the city that in the seventies spawned Cold Chisel, the Angels and the Little River Band, it has proved a wellspring of talent. But Adelaide bands have always had to flee Adelaide to make it.

Fraternity flew in the face of convention when they were lured back to Adelaide by an offer of support made by a wealthy patron of the arts. They were immediately elevated to superstar status there, and it was this that blinded them to reality.

But then, in the early seventies, reality was a concept seriously under siege.

Adelaide had produced a disproportionate share of top groups during the sixties as well, among them the Twilights, the Vibrants, the Masters Apprentices, the Groove and the Zoot.

In 1967, South Australia predicted the national sea change when Don Dunstan became premier. Dunstan was a Labor man in a pastel-coloured safari suit, who set a pace even Gough Whitlam was hard pressed to equal. South Australia was the first state to legalise homosexuality, to decriminalise pot, and to recognise women's rights.

When South Australian licensing laws were amended to allow late-night closing, rock'n'roll moved into pubs. The climate was thus perfect for a band that believed it could rewrite all the rules.

Bruce Howe had only ever reluctantly left Adelaide in the past. Growing up in the rough and tumble docklands of Port Adelaide, Howe became a professional musician almost as soon as he left high school in 1964. He joined an outfit called the Clefs, a rock'n'roll revue led by Englishman Tweed (nee Winston) Harris. Gigs were plentiful; the scene was exploding.

When Scotsman Barrie McAskill joined the Clefs later in 1964, he was already something of a godfather of the Adelaide scene. With his band the Drifters, he helped pioneer rock 'n'roll in South Australia. The Clefs provided McAskill with a more contemporary vehicle, and gradually he took over the band from Harris. Moving to Melbourne, the Clefs established a reputation on the circuit there, cutting a couple of singles. But it wasn't long before the young Bruce Howe had returned to the warm bosom of hometown Adelaide. Tweed Harris himself would also eventually leave the Clefs, as the band became a virtual game of musical chairs going on around McAskill.

By May, 1969, however, Howe was back in the fold, as the wild and sometimes outrageous McAskill assembled a new incarnation of what was now known as the Levi Smith Clefs. The old one had left en masse to form Tully, one of the very first Australian 'heavy' bands. This new version of the Clefs met with the greatest success. Its line-up was completed by guitarist Mick Jurd, keyboardist John Bisset, and drummer Tony Buettel. Jurd was a few years older than Bruce, a Sydneysider who had played since the early days of rock 'n'roll; Bisset was a Kiwi who had come over to Australia with a band called the Action; Buettel had been in Brisbane's seminal blues crusaders, the Bay City Union.

The Levi Smith Clefs were a disco band without peer, save perhaps for Max Merritt and the Meteors. They learnt their chops playing four sets a night, six nights a week, at the Whiskey. 'They constantly draw huge crowds,' read one newspaper report. 'Many American negro R&R men who come to Sydney on leave speak highly of the Clefs' gutsy sound.'

It was a measure, however, of the lack of initiative of major Australian record companies that the Clefs' success as a live band didn't translate onto record. It took maverick new Adelaide-based independent label Sweet Peach to try to achieve that.

Sweet Peach was a forerunner of indies like Havoc, Sparmac and Mushroom, which rose, with the music, in the early seventies. It was the result of a partnership between American emigree Pam Coleman, who wanted to buy into the thriving music scene she saw in Australia, and expatriate English producer Jimmy Stewart, who had set Australia on its ear when he created the huge 1968 hit 'Love machine' out of an anonymous studio band called Pastoral Symphony. Sweet Peach's first album release was 1969's *In the quiet corners of my mind* by Kevin Johnson, who is today best remembered for his redoubtable 1973 hit, 'Rock 'n' roll (I gave you the best years of my life)'.

The Levi Smith Clefs visited Adelaide in June 1969 to play a season at the 20 Plus Club. Sweet Peach put them into the studio at that time; after a matter of mere hours, they emerged with a finished album. At around the same time, Doug Ashdown, a folkie who had recorded for CBS during the sixties, was back in hometown Adelaide at a loose end. Joining forces with Jimmy Stewart, he set to work on an album for Sweet Peach, for which, taking a leaf out of Dylan's book, the Clefs were recruited 'to provide some rhythm'.

The Clefs' album, *Empty monkey*, was released in March, 1970, following a single, lacklustre reworking of Junior Walker's 'Shotgun'. Complete with a laminated, stiff-card gatefold sleeve and esoteric artwork, it looked for all the world like an American record. Appropriately, it was greeted with unbridled zeal. *Go-Set*'s review opened with the line, 'THIS IS THE BEST ROCK ALBUM EVER PRODUCED IN AUSTRALIA'.

In retrospect, *Empty monkey* is ponderous and overwrought, but at the time it was groundbreaking simply because it was an album, and so few other Australian bands had actually cut albums. Even so, it wouldn't sell.

Meantime, MCA in America had heard the Doug Ashdown

album — a double-set no less (Australia's first) called *Age of mouse* — and expressed interest in releasing it. All this went to the Clefs' heads. Didn't backing Australia's answer to Dylan on a double-album make them the Australian equivalent of the Band? The Clefs became convinced they were leading Australian rock's charge into a new age of seriousness. So, like Tully before them, they split from Barrie McAskill. Christening themselves Fraternity, they headed for Sydney, leaving McAskill high and dry in Melbourne. They set up house in a two-storey terrace in Jersey Road, Paddington, near Centennial Park, and Sweet Peach put them straight into the studio to cut a single to capitalise on the radio ban.

With two tracks in the can — one a Doug Ashdown song 'Why did it have to be me?', the other a Moody Blues album track, 'Questions' — Fraternity signed on with the dominant Nova agency to look for work.

The Valentines' decision to break up had been announced by then, and so Bruce got in touch with Bon. But even before Bon could make it up to Sydney, Fraternity scored the resident spot at Jonathans, a disco on Broadway in south central Sydney. Junior partner in the residency was a young band from the Sydney suburbs called Sherbet.

With Bruce and John Bisset sharing singing duties as they had on the single, the band played Doug Ashdown songs, Band songs, a few songs left over from the Clefs, and a few standards like 'Little Queenie'. Other musicians would sit in, among them Maori vocalist extraordinaire Leo de Castro, 'Uncle' John Ayers a harmonica player who regularly sat in with Copperwine, and an erstwhile singer by the name of Dennis Laughlin, who himself had recently left Sherbet to be replaced by Daryl Braithwaite, and was then working for Nova. Fraternity was promising the arrival of a great new singer.

Meanwhile, in Melbourne, as Barrie McAskill assembled yet another Clefs, Bon played the last few Valentines shows. By the time he arrived in Sydney, he had sprouted a goblin-like beard. He slotted straight in. 'The last time we saw Bon Scott was at a teeny-bopper concert in Melbourne, with the Valentines,' read one Sydney paper. 'We thought he was wasting his voice then. We know he was now. A distinctive, heavy voice... and the group is very, very professional.'

Fraternity was hot. The band boasted that MCA in America, after hearing the single, now wanted an album from them. Sweet Peach started hustling studio time. The Sydney *Sunday Mirror* ran a full page pin-up of them, proclaiming them as 'rapidly on the way to becoming Australia's greatest hard rock group'.

Bon wrote to Maria on July 15:

Well, everything up here is peaches and cream. If the writing is worse than usual it's because I'm sloshed. I've been sitting out on the patio in the beautiful warm sun writing for about two hours drinking brandy and coke. I've managed to become quite an alcoholic in two weeks. The disco we play in is licensed + we get spirits real cheap so...

The group is gas. I'd go so far as to say world class. We'd shit over anything in Australia as overall sound goes. We've had offers to go to Adelaide and Perth already but we're not going on the road until our LP is released. We start recording next week. It will be all original, most of the stuff written by Doug Ashdown who you may have heard of. We signed overseas contracts yesterday for America and we should be going in about three or four months. I'd love to go to the States and make it without ever appearing anywhere in Australia except Sydney and without any bullshit.

Sydney, with its licensed disco circuit, was booming, so much so that it momentarily overshadowed Melbourne. Copperwine had had a hit album. The Flying Circus was in line to win the Battle of the Sounds. Fraternity led a pack of newer bands, which included Chain, with Wendy Saddington on vocals, Blackfeather and Leo de Castro's King Harvest.

Woodstock's effect had been felt. The sheer musical naivety of the sixties had been outgrown. As far back as 1968, Australian musicians had begun searching for something — a sense of where the music had come from, so as to know where it might now go. When the radio ban was lifted after six months in October, 1970, a new mood dawned. 'It was an explosion of creativity, not all of it for the best, but everyone was having a go, trying to forge a new path,' said Sam See, a founding member of Sherbet, who would go on to join the Flying Circus, and then later Fraternity, and then later still, rejoin the Circus.

SAM SEE: 'I got to know Fraternity by being a late-night drinker at the Whiskey. The thing I really liked about them was that they were trying to approach an Australian sound. Later on it happened. They weren't really popular, but musicians, the hip cognoscenti liked them. We would have heated arguments at Jersey Road — Bruce and I used to argue at great length and great volume — where I'd say, Well, we blew you guys off stage tonight, in terms of the audience, and he'd say, Yeah, but we're doing something of our own.'

'There were a lot of folk singers around then too, and so we all got into songs, words that meant something,' said Peter Head, who had much in common with Fraternity as a member of Adelaide allies, Headband. 'It was the first time anyone used Australian place names in songs. I remember having arguments with people who said you can't use Australian names in a song, they sound daggy, they've got to be American.'

When Barrie McAskill and a new Levi Smith Clefs arrived back in Sydney to resume their Whiskey gig, Bruce Howe immediately swooped on them to poach drummer John Freeman, another old Adelaide boy, to replace Tony Buettel.

When Bon moved into Jersey Road, the first thing he did, again, was paint his room fire-engine red. The house was a regular meeting place. Sam See lived just around the corner. Virtuoso Blackfeather guitarist John Robinson often slept on the couch. Robinson had almost completed a song called 'Seasons of change' which Fraternity helped him finish, and so he gave it to them.

The turntable hit in the house was the recently-released debut album, *In the court of the crimson king* by Robert Fripp's prototype English artrock outfit King Crimson. Bon would sit crosslegged on the floor in front of the stereo, stoned, soaking it up. Other favourites included Deep Purple, Procol Harem

('Whiter shade of pale' had been a hugely influential record), Poco, the Band, Rod Stewart, Van Morrison. Mick Jurd was the band's resident musicologist, and he named artists like Wes Montgomery, Barney Kessel and BB King as his heroes. The mood of the times was such that the more esoteric your taste, the more 'progressive' you must be.

Fraternity were trying to get a start on recording the album the Americans apparently wanted. Bon wrote to Maria in September.

Being Saturday it's our last night for the week. We will be leaving Jonathans soon and going to greener pastures for more money. It's been gas working there because it helped the group improve over three months what would have normally taken six. We're doing about 70 per cent original songs now and by the time you see us we'll be doing about 150 per cent or something.

Wendy Saddington and Jeff St John (name dropping again) came down to hear us on Thursday night and sat in with us on a couple of songs. They reckon we would probably be the best in Australia. Coming from them it's a real compliment.

Our record called 'Why did it have to be me', is released this week. Unfortunately it was recorded before I made it up here and I'm not singing on it. But it don't matter as long as it gets airplay for the group. It will be released in the States next week and with a lot of luck, well, who knows. We start the LP again soon as we have to have it out for Christmas and this time all the songs on it will be our own. I haven't contributed anything worthwhile yet but once again it don't matter. The only thing that counts is the group.

The single failed to do any business. By then though, the band was able to fob it off as a premature and already redundant artifact. They were only thinking about the album. But the single was never released in America, and the album they would eventually finish, after a few false starts, would be shelved even in Australia.

Livestock, as the album was called when it was finally released by Sweet Peach over a year later, was a mishmash. Often featuring Bon on recorder, songs like 'Jupiter's landscape', 'Raglan's folly', 'You have a god' and 'It' were pompous, ponderous pieces of artrock; 'Grand Canyon suite' was would-be Aaron Copeland; only the title track, 'Sommerville', and 'Cool spot' still stand up as tight, sharp little exercises in sophisticated songwriting and arrangement.

The hype, however, was still running hot. Fraternity appeared live on super-groovy new ABC-TV show 'GTK'. New national magazine *Sound Blast* put Bon on the cover, wearing war-paint and an expression to match.

After playing a few shows late in September on the belated Australian tour by the 1910 Fruitgum Company, the band played the support spot on a tour by Jerry Lee Lewis. They 'did some nice instrumental things,' Greg Quill reported in *Go-Set*, 'and Bon, all painted and cheeky, managed to make people laugh a little.'

The Killer tour took Fraternity to Adelaide, where they supported Lewis at the Apollo Stadium, and played a couple of gigs of their own at a disco called Headquarters. It was this visit which would alter the course of their career.

Anticipation surrounding Fraternity naturally ran high in Adelaide. It was further pumped up because Vince Lovegrove, ironically, had also landed in Adelaide, and was in a position to hype his old mate's new band vigorously.

In addition to his gig as *Go-Set*'s Adelaide correspondent, Vince was writing a music column for the *News*, and had managed to get a local TV show up and running on Channel 9. The show, called 'Move' like his newspaper column, was essentially an expanded, weekly variation on 'GTK'. Its premiere episode of October 17 featured Fraternity, 'Australia's only group with a completely original repertoire'.

'They came — they played — they CONQUERED!' Vince wrote in *Go-Set* of the Headquarters gig. Never had prodigal sons been made to feel more welcome. But if the band had been progressing quite nicely, the course of its career was about to alter with the intervention of one Hamish Henry. Henry was the man behind the Grape Organisation, a booking agency that promoted Headquarters, among other Adelaide gigs. But Hamish Henry was much, much more than the average rock entrepreneur.

Henry was a rich kid with a vision, a patron of the arts who had been swept up in the euphoria of the Age of Aquarius. Born into old Adelaide money, he held down a day job with the family business, State City Motors, whilst he also ran a successful North Adelaide art gallery as well as Grape. But what Henry really wanted was a band he could cultivate himself. When he saw Fraternity at Headquarters he knew he'd found what he was looking for. He made them an offer: he'd set them up in Adelaide, house them, equip them, manage them, pay them a wage.

It was, of course, an offer Fraternity couldn't refuse. They left Adelaide set to return there for good in January.

The band swung through Melbourne on the way back to Sydney, to play two nights at the Thumpin' Tum. Bon caught up with Darcy there. In Sydney at the start of December, he wrote to Maria, whom he'd missed in Melbourne.

> We went over real well at the Tum both nights although I must admit it looked like a Valentines' Fan Club outing. I was really knocked out at the old faces who hadn't forgotten me.
>
> Adelaide was too much. It was the best trip I have ever done anywhere ever. We were treated like Kings. We were given a Valiant station wagon to drive around in and a van and roadie for our gear. We didn't carry a single item the whole time we were there. We absolutely killed the crowds at Headquarters where we played and we even had four days' holiday at John (drummer) Freeman's beach house. Toooo much.
>
> Saw my pal Vince. We did his TV show. It's really good and when it goes national he should be on top of the world again. I don't know if Graeme told you but we're going to Adelaide to live on Jan 4. I'll tell you all the reasons next time I see you as it's too detailed to write about.

On December 19, Vince broke the news in *Go-Set* that Fraternity were about to take the radical step of moving to Adelaide. The talk was still of going to America by the following June or July.

The band played the Odyssey festival outside Sydney, between Christmas and New Year, before heading for Adelaide where it would play Myponga, which would serve as a virtual homecoming.

Neither Myponga nor Odyssey was the first Australian outdoor rock festival — that distinction belongs to Ourimbah — but they all predated Sunbury, which, inaugurated in 1972, is the Oz rock festival most commonly remembered.

Allowing six months for the idea of Woodstock to reach Australia, Ourimbah was still premature. While its bill boasted the cream of Australia's progressive bands, virtually none of them actually had a record out. A year later, when Myponga took place, it was a different story. 1971 can still be considered a golden era for Australian rock'n'roll, a time when it came of age in so many ways. By the early part of '71, with at least a couple of the major record companies now confident enough to get down among the grass roots, a new wave of credible, creative post-San-Francisco Australian bands dominated the music scene at every level. Having worked their way up on the live circuit, bands like Billy Thorpe's born-again Aztecs, Spectrum, Chain, Blackfeather and Daddy Cool — nearly all of them from Melbourne — straddled the singles and newly-instituted albums charts alike, and filled houses all over the country.

The timing was apposite. Australia in general was on the eve of something of a social revolution. After more than 20 years' conservative Liberal government, the Labor Party would storm to power in 1972, led by the great reformer Gough Whitlam.

With a bill boasting an exclusive appearance by Black Sabbath as well as the cream of Australia's progressive bands, Myponga — bankrolled, almost inevitably, by Hamish Henry — was the biggest thing to hit Adelaide since the Beatles attracted a record crowd of 300,000 to a civic reception there in 1964.

'The age of historic high cultures is at an end,' said Adrian Rawlins, the Meher Baba disciple who compered Myponga. '[It is] an age when rhythm brings a new and real spiritual uplift to the young. The kids are responding to vibrations within themselves, rather than to conventional standards imposed from without.' This sort of psychobabble went down a treat.

However, for Fraternity, even though Myponga received them rapturously, it was ultimately more akin to a death knell than a homecoming. The revolution in Australian music didn't emanate from Adelaide, and Fraternity was too far removed from the centre of it to benefit at all.

Sydney enjoyed a place in the sun around the turn of the decade, but that momentum just as quickly dissipated. Everybody just seemed to skip town. As the Americans withdrew, the disco circuit degenerated into a province of showbands. Melbourne, again, regained the initiative, and it was Melbourne that played host to 1971's extraordinary surge of creativity.

The act that epitomised the era was Billy Thorpe and the Aztecs. After Thorpie was declared bankrupt in 1967, he repaired to Melbourne to start over. By 1969 he had assembled a new incarnation of the Aztecs, featuring guitar hero Lobby Loyde, and had gained an ambitious manager in Michael Browning. Thus commenced an ascent which would see Thorpie reign unassailably as the king of Oz rock during the early seventies, and the Aztecs a band which would change the face of Australian rock'n'roll.

Chain and Leo de Castro set up shop in Melbourne, Chain now in its classic form with erstwhile Bay City Union singer Matt Taylor out front. Ross Wilson was also exerting his patriarchy — the break-up in 1969 of his Party Machine spawned not only Daddy Cool but also Spectrum.

The other legacy of the repressed late sixties was that there were not only musicians, but also entrepreneurs who were all the more determined to break through. The power structures that would form the basis of those which still exist today were then being built. It was during this period that future mogul Michael Gudinski emerged. After serving an apprenticeship at Bill Joseph's AMBO agency, Gudinski corralled Joseph and fellow former AMBO agent Michael Browning to form Consolidated Rock when AMBO folded in 1970.

The generic guidelines for Australian rock were being set. Bands like Spectrum, Daddy Cool and Company Caine might have taken individualistic tangents, but together bands like the Aztecs, Chain, and Carson constituted a unified push. These bands were trying to connect with the roots of rock — the blues, basically — in which Australian music had so little tradition and for which reason it had always lacked body, not to mention soul. And even if the Aztecs' recordings have not stood the test of time — today sounding sludgy and bloated at best — their grinding, guttural base established the foundations for a monstrous mutation of the blues which was unique to Australia.

Thorpie's sole ambition at that time, many testify, was simply to be the loudest band in the world, and with his trademark massive stacks of Strauss amplifiers, designed by Lobby Loyde (who had by then left the band), he came pretty close. Former Valentine Wyn Milson was then serving as Thorpie's sound mixer: 'It was a rougher, boozier sort of thing. The start of headbanging. The audience didn't so much want to listen to the music as be flattened by it.'

Fraternity had more than a little in common with both the blues and arty strains, but they were in no position to capitalise on it, stuck away in Adelaide, seemingly reluctant to get out on the road, and tied to a record company whose reach was severely limited.

After playing Myponga, the band went into the studio to put down 'Seasons of change', the first single featuring Bon. On April 8, they played a support spot on the Adelaide leg of the Deep Purple/Free/Manfred Mann Australian tour. At the end of April, as the single was released, they moved en masse onto the farm up in the hills.

It was perhaps the first sign of things to come when 'Seasons of change' was beaten to the punch nationally by the version released by Blackfeather, whose John Robinson was the song's author after all. But Adelaide was an idyll which lulled Fraternity into a false sense of superiority, and as 'Seasons of change' climbed the South Australian charts, they chose to deny the signs.

Bon and Irene on their wedding day, January 24, 1972, just prior to leaving for England.

seven
london, 1973

'**f**raternity live like no other band in Australia,' Vince wrote in *Go-Set*, 'in a house in the hills 17 miles from Adelaide. Surrounded by seven acres of bushland, they're secluded from everything but nature. What a buzz!'

Fraternity had noted the Band's example — the Band set up a communal base on a Woodstock farm called Big Pink — and Hemming's Farm, as Fraternity's Aldgate property was known, became their own Big Pink.

In May, Uncle (John Ayers) came to town with Copperwine and stayed behind. Bruce asked him to join Fraternity and he moved straight onto Aldgate.

'Fraternity are into a trip of their own,' Vince went on. 'Sure they know they're good. Why else are they playing music professionally? But they've passed the ego scene years ago. They don't need ego trips, because they see too many good things in life, and they don't want to lose them.'

Of course, this idea was farcical as Fraternity was a strictly hierarchical, very volatile band. Bruce Howe was the boss — there were no two ways about that — and Mick Jurd was his senior partner. John Bisset, who wrote more material than any other single member of the band, was a brilliant but troubled man; he and Mick Jurd did not get on. Both Bon and Uncle simply managed to go with the flow. Uncle was out of it, even by the standards of the day.

HAMISH HENRY: 'Bon was just a gregarious, very nice guy. I used to swim with him; he was a very good swimmer. To Bruce and Mick and John Bisset, a singer was probably something of a necessary evil, and so Bon revolved around them, rather than vice versa. Bon was always late, for rehearsals or gigs or whatever, and Bruce and Mick probably did discuss sacking him, but they couldn't have done it. I think the band was appropriately named, because it was very much like a family, and Bon belonged to the family.'

'Fraternity was a shitter for Bon, because all those other guys were educated, and he started to feel like he was inferior,' said Pat Pickett, who became friends with Bon after encountering Fraternity in Melbourne around this time. 'They wouldn't let him write any lyrics. A lot of the early AC/DC stuff was written during those days.'

JOHN FREEMAN: 'Bon joined Fraternity to learn about music really, I think. Whatever else, he could sing, and he had what most singers would give their eyeteeth for — a distinctive voice. He joined Fraternity so he could learn about music, so he could go off and be a rock'n'roll star.'

Bon and Bruce were like chalk and cheese, but they shared a bond, and Bon readily deferred to Bruce. With his portly stature and prematurely thinning hair, Bruce looked almost Buddhistic, and indeed, he had a sort of an aura about him, and a hold over the entire band. Bon and Bruce remained close even after Bon effectively deserted Fraternity. Bruce was perhaps the only man Bon ever really confided in, whose advice Bon always sought out and respected.

If Bon's own musical input was lesser than it might have been, well, he felt privileged just to be working with musicians he held in awe. Not that a real lot of work can have been done. A couple of gigs a week, at most? In their entire three-year, two-album career, Fraternity produced barely a dozen original songs.

PETER HEAD: 'Fraternity spent most of their time on magic mushrooms. Everybody smoked dope, everybody. Everybody took mushrooms. Plus, Fraternity were all heavy drinkers as well.'

The days and nights at Aldgate passed in one long, slow, lazy, hazy stoned-immaculate flow. There was no call to do anything especially. If food was required, a big, brown, sloppy pseudomacro stew was concocted. 'Hamburgers hurt,' muttered Uncle. Every weekend, tribes of beautiful people from Adelaide would descend upon the place, tripping out, soaking up the good vibes generally, and fucking each other silly.

Bon was almost 25. He had not a care in the world. He acquired the nickname Ronnie Roadtest due to his willingness to try anything. Vince described him as, 'constantly in a dream world of his own ... but he's having a ball'.

Late in May, Fraternity went out on the road, first to Perth, then Queensland. Response in Perth was ecstatic — the band upstaged Chain, then riding high on the back of 'Black and Blue' — although in Queensland, it was mixed. A *Go-Set* review of a Brisbane gig described them as 'loud, too loud sometimes'. Sheer volume was part of Fraternity's arrogance.

This, of course, was a time when the Sunshine State's fabled hillbilly dictator Joh Bjelke-Petersen was at the height of his powers, and Fraternity ran afoul of the law. Playing on the Gold Coast, the cops showed up and told them to turn down. Which they did, but with qualifications.

BRUCE HOWE: 'Bon made this speech, on stage, about the Queensland cops, you know, and the promoter was standing there, just shaking his head. Bon was quite naive about political things. He was very street smart, he had this ability to assess people on the spot, their character, and generally his gut feelings were pretty good. But when it came to politics, that sort of knowledge, he was absolutely fucking hopeless.

Of course, it went over really well with the crowd, because he'd stood up.

'The cops stopped the show; we had to get off. I said to Bon, you dickhead. Because I used to be like that with him, when he'd do things like that, when he'd be at his most naive. I said, I told you what it was like up here. We started to talk about politics. Bon didn't understand the technicalities. Like, listening to politicians talk on the TV, or reading about it in the paper, used to bore the shit out of him, but we might be just sitting on the bus, out of it, nobody else around, and Bon would say, Well, why is it? Why is that allowed to happen in Queensland, and yet if I said that in Adelaide nobody would give a fuck?'

UNCLE: 'Bon was really perceptive in some ways. Blind in others. In some ways he had his feet firmly on the ground. He was so down to earth, there were some areas where Bon could see the wood for the trees where others couldn't. Yet there was that other side that was out to lunch.'

Back in Adelaide, the band resumed its comfortable lifestyle. Talk around the rest of the country was that Fraternity had become complacent in its spoilt domain. They countered that they were preparing to go to America.

JOHN FREEMAN: 'Hamish should have made us work a lot harder, we should have done much more work on the east coast. But we always thought we were above that.'

At home, Fraternity could do no wrong. Routinely playing at least once a week at the Largs Pier Hotel, they established themselves as an Adelaide legend.

Melbourne is usually cited as the birthplace of pub rock, yet while it may have been the cradle, it was in Adelaide that Australia's first real regular pub gigs sprang up — and the first of those was the Largs Pier. At the height of Melbourne's renaissance in 1971, its live circuit still consisted largely of dances and discos. Pubs wouldn't open up to rock'n'roll for a few years yet. Adelaide pubs, however, embraced this new trade.

The Largs was down by the beach at Semaphore, opposite the pier of the same name. After all the taboo-breaking of the sixties, kids were growing-up a lot quicker, and nothing made them feel more grown-up than going into pubs. This meant that the crowds at the Largs ranged from 15-year-olds, who were able to get away with getting in, to sixties survivors — all determined to write themselves off to the tune of roaring rock'n'roll.

Bands that regularly went over to Adelaide — the Aztecs, Daddy Cool, Max Merritt and the Meteors, the La De Das — loved playing there. But Fraternity were the hometown heroes who had baptised the place, its veritable house band.

Fraternity changed with its audience. The Largs was as rough as guts and Bon felt right at home there. He would prop up the bar, a hard-up hero wallowing in Scotch and adulation. Occasionally he would catch some flak. After all, as a tall poppy he was asking to be cut down. Besides, he would flirt with all the wrong girls. Bad girls. Who had bad boyfriends. Brawling was commonplace. Regular audience members included Jimmy Barnes and his half-brother John Swann.

JIMMY BARNES: 'We used to go into Adelaide, and we'd go in a gang to fight, you know. It was, hey, let's go into Adelaide — and wreck it!'

JOHN FREEMAN: 'At that stage, because it was the only gig of its type, it used to draw a much wider audience than just the locals, and I think there might have been an element of the locals versus everybody else. The thing was, it was just so crowded — we used to play on this tiny stage in the corner — and so how 700 people could possibly spend four hours in an environment designed for four, without some sort of aggravation, well, it just couldn't happen.'

SAM SEE: 'Bon was always into a bit of a scrap. I was never partial to it. But he'd go out to the bar, have a drink with this guy, fight that guy...'

UNCLE: 'I remember Bon and JB [John Bisset] at the Largs Pier once, both totally blind drunk, trying to find the biggest cargo-ologist in the room to fight him. He had to be at least nine foot six! I saw Bon jump off the stage a couple of times, because he saw it actually happening in the crowd. But I never saw him set on anybody, or set them up.'

The Largs crowd had no truck with anything poofy, or cerebral. Rapidly disappearing, then, were Fraternity's artrock tendencies, replaced by a harder, rockier edge. The band's own claim that they single-handedly spawned pub rock is overstating the case, but considering their evolving style and the seminal influence they exerted on Cold Chisel, the zenith of the genre, it's a claim containing more than a grain of truth.

BRUCE: 'You had this young audience that would come and see you, and the more quad boxes and horns you stuck up, the louder you were, the more they liked it. They could tell what you were trying to do.'

In August, Fraternity took out the national Battle of the Sounds. Sherbet were the only other group to come near them, as *Go-Set* reported. But again, this only had the adverse effect of enforcing Fraternity's belief that all was well.

The sheen had worn off the Battle by then — it no longer carried the same prestige it once had, and the crowd at Melbourne's Festival Hall, where the final was held, was quite thin — but still it meant that Fraternity went home with much booty under their arms, including air fares overseas, and free studio time at Armstrong's.

'They won the Battle,' remembered John Brewster, a friend of Bon's who was a roadie, 'and there was all these prizes, so they divvied them up among everybody, and there was this stereo left over, after everyone had got their equal share. So they decided what they'd do was, whoever did the grossest deed, got it. So they're on their way back to Adelaide and Gus — they used to have this bus driver called Gus — all of a sudden, he pulls up the bus on the side of the road, and jumps out. He leaps the fence, grabs a sheep, humps it, and he goes, Howzat! He got the stereo. Bon told me that.'

Sam See, home from Canada with the Flying Circus, was at the Battle show. Bruce asked him to join Fraternity. He leapt at the chance.

With the Battle win in the bag, Channel Nine in Adelaide, which had produced 'Move', made a special on Fraternity. The show portrayed the band at work and play up on the farm. Of course, there's no show without Punch, and so Bon had to put on a performance. Attempting a party trick riding one of the company trail bikes, he left the dirt road and came off into a briar patch. He emerged wearing a sheepish grin and a number of cuts and bruises.

Bon's trail bike stunts were legendary. He is variously said to have taken off on one from a party in the nude, and rode one up a flight of stairs into a crowded gig. On another occasion he impulsively rode over to Melbourne from Adelaide one weekend for a birthday party. Ill-prepared, wearing only a T-shirt, he got sun- and wind-burnt by day; and by night, kipping in a ditch by the side of the road, he froze.

In September, *Go-Set* ran a cover story which proclaimed, 'Fraternity: The Next Big Band?'. The band journeyed to Sydney to play a short season at Chequers. A backstage scuffle ensured the season was even shorter — the band was sacked as a result. Fraternity's petulance had a way of turning in on itself. The question mark *Go-Set* had qualified its headline with was prophetic.

Back in Adelaide, Bon moved off the farm and back down to town. Along with Bruce and John Bisset — and Bisset's wife Cheryl and son Brent, not to mention dog Clutch — they found a place on Norwood Parade, within spitting distance of the city.

BRUCE: 'Me and Bon and John didn't take too kindly to the house in the hills. All these people would go up on the weekends, and just sit around and look at the trees and say how lovely everything was. Me and Bon, if there was a prospective fuck or a wild time in the offing, we'd go back down to town. The problem was getting from the hills down to town. So we shifted back down.'

Bruce was running amok because his girlfriend Anne was in England. Bon was raging as ever. At first Bon took up with a girl called Fi who was one of the Valentines' foremost Adelaide fans. She'd returned to Adelaide after Bon saw her in Melbourne, where she was working for, of all people, Mary Wasylyk, now Walton, who had opened a boutique on trendy Chapel Street in Prahran. Bon hadn't seen much of his old friend Mary since she got married, until he walked into the In Shop to see Fi. He was surprised, and delighted, to encounter Mary there too and their friendship was renewed.

The relationship with Fi was short-lived, as she was looking for a man who was husband material. Bon was lots of things, but he wasn't that. On the rebound, he met a woman called Clarissa, a dancer with the Adelaide Festival Theatre, but that too was a brief fling. Before long, he was having an affair with a married woman called Margaret Smith. With her doctor husband, the petite, attractive dark-haired Margaret was a regular visitor to the farm. Her marriage was crumbling, and though her relationship with Bon was doomed in the short term, she would reappear later in his life.

PETER HEAD: 'She was a rock'n'roll groupie made good. As soon as I saw her, I thought, She belongs with Bon. She was that same sort of wild woman.'

BRUCE: 'Bon loved his girls, but he didn't give them a lot. Sex. And things. Like, he'd come home with a bunch of flowers, or he'd cook a meal. But he wouldn't talk intimately to them, or share secrets, about his past life, whatever. He could commit to the boys, because boys are boys, and so when you have to go off and fight another war, and everyone pats you on the back. But when it came to women, a family, that was very scary to Bon.'

There was something about Bon that set him apart. Maybe the tattoos he'd become so ashamed of symbolised indelible blue watermarks of a wasted, cruel youth.

JOHN FREEMAN: 'I don't think anybody ever saw the real Bon, I don't think Bon ever knew the real Bon, that was his trouble.'

UNCLE: 'He was always willing to look for it!'

JOHN FREEMAN: 'That was running away from it. He had such charisma it was difficult for him not to be on stage 24-hours a day.

'You know, he could walk into a room at a party and sit down in the corner, and he would be instantly surrounded by a crowd of women, who would put down their lives for him. My mother said he could put his slippers under her bed anytime, and my mother's a very conservative old woman.'

UNCLE: 'My mum too. Bon had this thing about him, he really touched people when he met them, in a way you thought he really cared about you. So many guys considered him their best mate.'

JOHN FREEMAN: 'Life was only ever a transitory thing to Bon. He would drop a trip without worrying if there was anything he had to do that day. I know him to have gone to the dentist, for major surgery, whilst he was tripping. I've never known anyone else that would do anything like that.'

UNCLE: 'Bon lived for the moment. Forward planning, I mean, I don't think that was a part of his life. But I can never remember Bon not trying his hardest. I remember him living for the show, being alive during the show, and everything else being an anticlimax.'

In September, Bon met the woman who would become his wife, Irene Thornton. Irene had just returned from a year-long working holiday in England. She knew Vince's girlfriend Julie, and through her and Vince, met Bon. She decided, as so many women did, that she fancied him. The difference was, she snared him.

Born in Adelaide in 1950, Irene was a nice girl from suburban Prospect. That she had just returned from England made her very cool. That she was also strikingly attractive, quite tall, with long, straight blonde hair and a slender figure, and was very down to earth — she liked a drink, wouldn't say no to a smoke, and enjoyed a joke, dirty or otherwise — made her irresistible to Bon.

Irene went with Vince and Julie to a party up on the farm. It was then that she first encountered Bon. Looking for the toilet, she burst in on him in a bedroom, sucking some woman's toes. The next time they met, at the Largs one night, she was more impressed: 'He was funny. Chatting away, you know, he just came out with comical things. We just hit it off.'

It was a whirlwind, fairytale courtship. For their first date, Bon and Irene went to the drive-in, and both sat bolt upright all night. Such was the effect Irene had on Bon, he was uncharacteristically nervous in her presence. They would go out and hold hands, and Bon would plant a peck on her cheek as he sent her inside at her parents' place at the end of the night. Irene was a princess, just as Maria had been, but unlike Maria, she would extend her golden braids out from the ivory tower.

Irene fell in love with Bon, and she loved him for what he was. She remembers a night they spent together, early in the piece, poring over a copy of the recently released *The adventures of Barry MacKenzie*, both breaking up. 'I suppose we just had the same sort of sense of humour,' she said. Indeed, it's impossible to overestimate the value Bon placed on laughter, and this he shared with Irene.

Irene was amused by his banter, and his hijinks. One time, to shock Irene's teenage sister Faye, he took off all his clothes and bounded past her and a girlfriend watching TV like he was Skippy the Bush Kangaroo. Faye was mortified; Irene, like Bon, was reduced to tears.

Soon enough, Irene was staying over at Norwood, and before long she moved in there.

The headline on Vince's column read, THEY'VE FAITH IN ADELAIDE: TO RECORD IN SA, but the fact of the matter was that Fraternity didn't trust anyone in Australia to produce them. If Adelaide studios were inferior, at least there Fraternity could produce themselves. But the battle was the same Australia over.

SAM SEE: 'I don't think it [the sound] was ever caught on record, as a lot of Australian acts at that time weren't. The bands were victimised by the studios.'

BRUCE: 'The live gigs were the greatest satisfaction. We could not get it down on record. But we had some great live gigs.'

October saw two 'new' Fraternity singles released. The band had by now left Sweet Peach, and so in retaliation the label exhumed a track left over from the *Livestock* album sessions. 'The race' was a lyrically complex Doug Ashdown song described by *Go-Set* as 'not [a single] which will help the group'. The other new slice of vinyl was 'If you got it', which the band cut itself in Adelaide, and put out on its own independent Raven label. A straight boogie, it climbed to number two on the South Australian charts.

The band was now talking about going to America by June or July of the following year, 1972. Meantime, it's not as if they put their heads down at all. It was summertime, and the living was easy.

UNCLE: 'There was this one party, the Three-day Party, I think we'd played these two gigs, the Largs Pier, and the Bridgeway, there was 2,000 people there, it was Christmas or New Year's Eve or something, and so everybody was invited up to our place for a party. It went for three days. There was barbecues, security guys, whole bars full of spirits, bonfires all round the lawn. I had children born in my bed and grand-mothers die; I remember picking up my sheets with a broom-stick and taking them out to the bonfire at the end of the three days, I wasn't going to sleep in them again. I haven't been to a three-day party since. Those days are gone.'

Bon and Irene were getting on swimmingly. Bruce was a lot happier too, because Hamish had flown Anne out from England to be with him. That was the sort of thing Hamish did. He believed, and he put his money where his mouth was. When the band needed a new Hammond organ because this particular song called for that particular sound, he got it for them. He had the foresight to form a publishing company for the band, so that they owned their own songs, which few bands do even today.

'With hindsight, I've got a lot of respect for Hamish,' said Peter Head, who was also managed by him. 'We all used to rubbish him at the time, can him about being rich — we had no appreciation whatsoever of the value of money — but he was the one who made things possible.'

As big fish in a small pond though, Fraternity were getting nowhere fast. Even Vince dared suggest they needed to 'get off their arses and get some hard work done'.

SAM SEE: 'Even though there was a sense that Fraternity shows were special, we were still doing the same gigs week in, week out. In those days, the concept of making it had no reality at all.'

By January, plans had changed again. The band was now going to go to England. This was yet another mistake — the wrong place to go, at the wrong time — but it was where Hamish had connections. In the past year, as he'd tried in vain to get both T Rex and Yes out to tour Australia, he'd at least made some contacts over there. The plan was to finally use the free time at Armstrong's, then play a tour of South Australia for the Arts Council, then leave.

The band spent a mere few days, again, in the studio, cutting the album which, in a fit of Australianness, would be called *Flaming galah*. It proffered only three all-new songs — 'Welfare boogie', 'Hemming's farm' and 'Getting off' — next to rewritten and rerecorded versions of old material. Hamish set up a deal to release it through RCA.

The decision to leave was a bad one not only because the climate in England at that time wouldn't suit a band like Fraternity, but also because Australia itself was just about to bound into the future. Merely weeks before Fraternity left, Billy Thorpe got the first remote mixing desk ever seen in this country. Of course, right then, Fraternity couldn't wait to get out of Australia.

HAMISH: 'We had this supreme self-confidence, and so coupled with a certain naivety, we couldn't see any barriers whatsoever.'

Prompted by the offer made by Hamish to pay for wives — not girlfriends — to go overseas with their husbands in the band, Bon and Irene decided to get married. They'd known each other for a few scant months.

IRENE: 'Everyone seemed to be doing it at the time. Bon had asked me to go away with him; then he told me that Hamish would pay, and so there was a few weddings going on. But we were really wrapped up in each other.'

Bon and Irene's wedding merged into a blur along with Bruce and Anne's, and John Freeman's. Uncle had taken up with Freeman's wife's sister Vicki, and while they wouldn't actually tie the knot, Vicki would go to England anyway. John Bisset and Mick Jurd had both been married all along; only Sam See was unattached.

BRUCE: 'I didn't like the idea of Bon getting married to Irene, I thought it was too premature. They didn't really know each other that well. But she was a nice girl.'

With the wedding scheduled for January 24, Isa came over from Perth. She wasn't terribly impressed by the whole business either.

Bon and Irene, however, were extremely pleased with themselves. Bon loved Irene as she loved him; but as much as that, he loved the idea of her: that is, the most wanted woman in Adelaide, was his.

SAM SEE: 'Bon and Irene, when they got married, I remember it being like, I was going to say, Paul and Linda — it was all a bit glam, you know.'

A civil service was held in town, with Bruce and John Bisset as witnesses. The bride wore a cream crepe forties-style jacket and a long crepe skirt; the groom, a poo-brown suit with flared trousers and wide lapels. A reception was thrown up on the farm afterwards. 'It was like the best party I ever went to I think,' Irene said.

All possible futures seemed golden.

At the very same time, at a site 50 kilometres north of Melbourne, the first Sunbury festival was taking place. Billy Thorpe and the Aztecs headlined. It was this performance that crowned Thorpie's ascent. The resultant double-live album, released later in the year, outsold every other Australian album released in 1972. Everybody who was anybody was at Sunbury that weekend — except Fraternity.

Any ideas of a honeymoon that either Bon or Irene may have harboured were waylaid in excited anticipation of going to England. Besides which, the band was due to hit the road on February 12, on a tour devised by the Arts Council to take a bit of urban rock culture to the bush.

Trucking through South Australia in a big black bus, Fraternity were their own merry pranksters. Bon, Ronnie Roadtest, was in fine form, even if he was away from his new bride — or maybe because of it. Bruce Howe remembers one incident in particular, at Port Lincoln.

BRUCE: 'It was one of those really still, hot South Australian days, and Bon said, I'm going for a swim. So he put his bathers on, and we walked out on the jetty. All these people were there. At the end of the jetty, they had these scales, for hanging the sharks they used to catch — the big white pointers. The water was so still and so clear you could see everything, and you could see it was just a sea of great big huge stingers, jellyfish, you know, with tentacles ten feet long, all just beneath the surface. Bon looks around, sees he's got an audience, and so what does he do? He climbs right up to the top of the shark tower and dives in. He swims underwater out of the reach of these things, and climbs back up. Of course, everybody on the jetty sends up this big round of applause. That's the sort of thing he was capable of. I was amazed.'

Back in Adelaide by early March, the band played two prom concerts as part of the Adelaide Festival of Arts program, another first for rock music in the State. Repeating a role created by Tully in Sydney, Fraternity accompanied singer Jeannie Lewis and the Melbourne Symphony Orchestra in a performance of Australian composer Peter Sculthorpe's 'Love 2,000'. It was a last gasp for the band's 'classical' aspirations.

'Welfare boogie' was released as a single later in the month. It did nothing, save perhaps provide a glimpse of the sort of themes Bon would later explore more fully.

> I've got me a problem, a real social problem
> I can't find employment for more than a week
> You might think I'm sleazy, but you know it ain't easy
> Finding employment's a job for a freak

The album followed in April. But the general attitude to Fraternity seemed to be that they'd frittered their potential. By then though, the band was in England — not so much a band as a juggernaut, an entourage numbering 16 people and a bus, plus Clutch the dog of course! As far as Australia was concerned, Fraternity would be heard from no more. All the unfulfilled promises would be forgotten; the name Fraternity would just fade away.

England in 1972 was teetering giddily on the stack-heels of glam rock. The glittering stars were T Rex, David Bowie, Gary Glitter, and the Sweet. Fraternity were a bunch of bearded wonders playing what was more than once described as 'country-rock'. It was all they could do to polish their RM Williams boots.

Fraternity's 18 months in England would do nothing but grind the band down and finally out. The experience also claimed a heavy personal cost, as interpersonal relationships, including Bon and Irene's marriage, soured. For the first six months they were there, they did next to nothing. They found a place to live — a big four-storey house in Finchley — and sat around waiting for something to happen.

Had they gone to America as they'd originally planned, they might have fared better, as the music scene there allowed for greater variations. But from the moment Fraternity arrived in London, it was obvious it wasn't going to be the picnic they'd expected. The mountains of gear they'd hauled half way round the planet were already antiquated.

Hamish Henry set up shop, with partner, former DJ Tony MacArthur, as the Mainstreet Gramophone Company. MacArthur was managing French crooner Charles Aznavour, and acting for Dutch artrock band Focus. Hamish got Fraternity on the books with a powerful agency, MAM, but he had little to sell the band on. That they were almost the next big band in Australia just wasn't enough.

With more than a dozen people living under the same roof in Finchley, it was inevitable that friction would occur.

IRENE: 'Being young, you have expectations. I was 21, Bon was 25. The thing in England didn't help matters, because it wasn't conducive to normal life — a lot of pressure, not enough money, no one really with any privacy. If you wanted to go out to the back yard to hang out the washing, you had to walk through someone's bedroom. It was pretty hard to live like that, coming from Australia, having to live on nothing in miserable conditions. I think everyone got to really hate England.'

The girls all had to go out and look for work to support the boys. Bruce and Anne — Anne who was at once pregnant and bedridden with a broken leg — holed up in the attic, above it all. Everyone was feeling the strain. England was cold and grey; Fraternity were nobodies there, and they were broke. Sparks started to fly. The only consolation the band found in England was the price of hash. They smoked blocks of red Leb by the brick.

In November, they played their inaugural English gig at the Speakeasy. It was a nonevent. Beyond that, all the band really had on the agenda was a short German tour. At least it got the boys out of the house.

John Freeman wrote home to the *News*, 'We are now moving into top gear in a flat-out bid to gain the necessary
exposure that is vital for a new group such as ours'. That flat-
out bid consisted of infrequent gigging — the most Hamish
could hustle — playing supports with bands that were
second division at best — Atomic Rooster, Sparks, the Pink
Fairies, Mungo Jerry. The most impressive bill Fraternity
shared was with Fairport Convention.

SAM SEE: 'The basic scam was that the wives went out to
work and the band loafed at home. Really, to be honest about it,
not doing much of anything, just sort of goofing off, watching
telly and playing cricket in the back yard. It was really a
bummer. And so maybe it's idle minds, I don't know...

'It really was a very squalid house, full of people who
weren't united by anything except the music. I mean, the
different personalities in that band, I don't think I've ever
played in a band that was so diverse. And so when the music
dropped off, all these personality differences came out. There
was all sorts of crosspollinations, violence both physical and
verbal, mostly verbal.'

Bon didn't know what to do with himself. He became
frustrated when he was denied the release of performance.
Without it, his whole being — he feared — was thrown into
question.

HAMISH HENRY: 'The essence of Bon was when he was on
stage, his thumbs stuck in his jeans and his chest sticking out,
strutting his stuff. That was all he ever wanted to do.'

Bon was reduced to getting a day job, like the girls. He went to
work in a factory where he knotted wigs. He got Sam a job there
too. He and Irene were squabbling constantly. Bon could be
distant, cold almost, certainly brusque, and Irene felt the brunt
of his frustration. They both grew resentful. It was a vicious
circle. Irene gave as good as she got. She and Bon both had sharp
tongues, and when they were downcast, especially after a few
drinks — which was most of the time — neither of them was
prepared to give an inch. If one slipped, said the wrong thing,
the other jumped on it. Or else Bon just clammed-up.

But there were good times, however few and far between.
Irene remembers fondly how Bon was perplexed by the

English propensity for forming queues, and how he would brazenly jump them, for no other reason than just to rock the boat. She also remembers how he went to see Little Richard, one of his oldest heroes, and came home mortified, since it was obvious that the Georgia Peach was gay. Bon, in his innocence, would never have thought... Alex Harvey, however, was a different matter. Already thirtysomething in the early seventies, the godfather of Scots rock'n'roll was then enjoying his peak, and Bon became one of his biggest fans. His humour, his storytelling bent and his energetic showmanship had a profound effect on Bon.

Fraternity scored only the odd gig. They'd had the wind knocked out of their sails.

Sam See remembers one of the last gigs he played with the band. 'We were all in the bus, the juggernaut, rolling down to Bournemouth to support Status Quo. The only thing we knew about them then was "Pictures of matchstick men"; it would've been just before they broke again with *Piledriver*. This was probably the last sign of the Fraternity arrogance which I always loved. As usual, on the way to the gig, we're having a few drinks, we reckon we're gonna cream 'em. So we're sitting there in the bus, waiting for the hall to open, because we were egalitarian, we all used to help lug the gear in. No stardom for us — bullshit! Anyway, so we're sitting outside the Bournemouth Odeon, and these two Bentleys pull up, and these guys resplendent in Kings Road finery get out. We're there, you know, Look at these pooftas, Bon's going, Yaarrrgh! We're at this point extremely confident we're going to make a name for ourselves in Bournemouth. So we went on, we did quite well, didn't get an encore but did okay, and then Status Quo came on, and they'd changed out of their satin and bells into the familiar Status Quo jeans and T-shirts, and they were three times as loud as us and twice as polished. They were hot.

'We lurched back to London with our tails between our legs. It was probably one of those nights where someone had too much to drink and punched somebody else, I can't remember for sure. But something went wrong within the ego of the band, definitely. By the time winter rolled around, I'd had it.'

Sam moved on to Canada to rejoin the Flying Circus, where they were enjoying a modicum of success. 'It was really the end I think, because we could all see that the band had lost its fight.'

During the winter, Billy Thorpe, in all his arrogance, blundered through London. Fraternity were glad to see a familiar face. Thorpie hit town expecting to lay 'em in the aisles. He left after blowing one gig, at the self-same Speakeasy, where he had the plug pulled on him, ostensibly for being too loud. Thorpie's convenient excuse was that the imminent second Sunbury wanted him back, for a record fee of $10,000 plus air fares. He was on the first plane he could get.

Some time early in the new year Fraternity changed their name to Fang, 'to fit in with the current English trend', whatever they thought that was. To Hamish, this marked the real beginning of the end.

In April, Fang played a couple of gigs with Geordie, the Novocastrian band which, ironically contained Brian Johnson, the singer who would eventually replace Bon in AC/DC. Graeme visited England at that time, and remembers those shows. 'They had the bus, and the thing was, if they'd support a band, they'd take the other band's equipment too, and they were booked to go with Geordie. I think we went to Torquay first, and then we packed up that night and went on to Plymouth. Brian used to carry his guitar player on his shoulders too, I think that's where Ron got the idea, because when he joined AC/DC there was no one around doing that sort of thing. Angus was the perfect guy to carry around. He was so small.'

In May, the band played a short tour of the provinces with Kraut-rock doomsayers, Amon Duul. The headliners, the *Gloucestershire Echo* said, were 'an enormous contrast to the raucous Australian band who started the concert [whose] unambitious but multi-decibel bedecked set sounded much like the rhythm and blues material that was churned out by a million would-be Rolling Stones in the early 60's'.

Relations within the band and its extended family were deteriorating to the point that final implosion was imminent. Uncle hocked Vicki's Mixmaster to buy hash. The drinking became increasingly heavy, putting a surly spin on things.

GRAEME SCOTT: 'It was the boredom I think. They were hardly doing any shows, making nothing, and there was a lot of arguments, wifely troubles as well as band troubles, not just Bon and Irene but a lot of them; nothing was going right, and so I think the drink really came into it then.'

Bon was driven to desperation, and again, one day, he seriously tempted fate.

IRENE: 'I was at work, and when I came home, he was crawling around like a gibbering idiot.'

He'd eaten datura, a poisonous plant once believed to have hallucinogenic qualities. Most self-respecting heads wouldn't touch it, but not Bon.

BRUCE: 'That's when the darker side emerged, and you really knew you were dealing with a person who didn't care if he lived or died. There was this fatalistic side to Bon which was always there. He was fatalistic because he took risks. He took risks with drugs, it's true, it's not a myth.'

IRENE: 'Impulsive is the best word. He liked being outrageous. When he was pissed, he could either be the life of the party, or else, you could see it happen, his eyes would glaze over, almost go black, like there was something there really crapping him off, and a nasty side would come out.'

Irene was in a panic trying to find out what he'd done, what he'd taken. 'I was trying to get him to drink a glass of water or something, but he was just so completely off his face, he couldn't even talk. Uncle was frantically telephoning the hospital trying to find an antidote. Eventually, we gave him some lemon juice, and he just threw up.'

By the English summer of '73 the band had ceased paying rent. Vicki, who was consequently diagnosed as schizophrenic, was behaving increasingly erratically. John Bisset insulted Mick Jurd's wife Carol one time too many, and that spelt the end of him. Bon and Irene were at each other's throats. Resentment was also growing towards Hamish, who the band perceived as living in the lap of luxury at their expense.

In August, the band played what would be its last ever gig, a two-bit festival at Windsor. Hamish bailed out. He'd had enough. He'd sunk a small fortune into Fraternity, and he could no longer see any prospect of a return. The dream was over.

HAMISH: 'I think the real reason Fraternity failed in England was because they were just too loud!'

The band lingered in London, shell-shocked, just wondering what to do. Bon got a job in a nearby pub, behind the bar. Unsurprisingly, he was a natural. But his and Irene's days were numbered.

The band started limping back to Adelaide. Uncle was the first to arrive, in November. 'We just didn't make it in England,' he told Vince in the *News*. 'It's good to be back. [The others] will be home soon.'

Bon and Irene arrived after Christmas, and went their separate ways. Irene stayed at her parents' place; Bon moved in with Bruce and Anne and their infant son, into a tiny house down near the Port. But hope springs eternal. Bruce especially was hopeful that Fraternity would rise again; and Bon, that he and Irene would get back together.

But you can't undo the past, the damage done. And the damage ran deep.

Finally back in Adelaide, Fraternity were in suspension, licking their wounds. Bon felt loyalties strongly, but even he wasn't sure that Fraternity, as such, had a future.

He sat tight, or rather even while he fidgeted, he held his tongue. He had enough to worry about as it was, with his separation from Irene.

IRENE: 'It just got to a stage where you're arguing about everything, and there's just all this bitterness. We were just arguing about anything and everything, stupid little things that you wouldn't normally...'

BRUCE: 'The thing that went wrong with their relationship was that Irene just needed more intimacy, not sexual intimacy, communication, you know. I think she just felt like sometimes Bon just used to shut up shop.'

Isa, never one to mince words, said 'They both liked getting their own way too much'.

Bon was reeling. It was maybe just as well then that he had to go out and get a job. No one else was going to support him, and it might keep him out of trouble. So, like Bruce who was supporting his young family by working as a builder's labourer, Bon started a day job for the first time in almost ten years. He loaded trucks at the Wallaroo fertiliser plant. It was a monumental comedown, but it was what he had to do to stay afloat. Bon could be stoic about such things.

He got a bike, a big Triumph, to get around on. He was mucking around with Peter Head's Mount Lofty Rangers, a band, of sorts, which at least allowed him to keep his hand in. He would drop in to see Irene at the place she'd found for herself in Stepney, but all that did was upset them both.

Bon's stoicism didn't extend to matters of the heart. He would have willingly succumbed to the way of the flesh, and damn the consequences. Had Irene let him, he would have happily climbed back into her bed, and ridden off the next morning. That was his whole philosophy — tomorrow would never come. Bon refused to accept the truth — the marriage was over — and his visits only served to hurt himself as much as Irene.

Irene showed the greater strength. Even for all the love she still felt for Bon — and knew that he had for her — she knew it wouldn't work. Cruel to be kind, to both herself and Bon, she had to cut him loose.

Bon couldn't accept it. And so it was one night after he'd had a row with Irene that he arrived, already drunk, at a Rangers rehearsal, and then stormed off from there, even more drunk, to ride his bike at high speed into an oncoming car. He was almost killed.

Bon was in a coma for three days. Irene didn't leave his side. 'I remember being there once, sitting there with my sister, looking at the screen, you know, the heartbeat monitor, and the line stopping, and yelling for a doctor. The doctor came and banged him on the chest. It started again.'

When Bon came to, he asked Irene if he could come home. What could she do? No one else was going to look after him. He was released a few weeks later.

IRENE: 'He was terribly sick, he just looked like a thin, frail old man. He was hunched from the broken collarbone, his throat was cut — he had a horrible scar there — and his jaw was wired up. He was just virtually skin and bone. And he must have had some sort of internal problem too.

'The clearest memory I have of Bon is of him in a blue checked dressing gown, after his accident, with his teeth missing,' said Peter Head's wife Mouse, 'and I guess I remember it because he just looked so shocking. I mean, his face was scarred, and you know, it had pretty much an impact on us all, when it happened.'

Isa came over from Perth, to tend Bon during the daytime when Irene was out at work.

Bon never fully recovered from the accident, wearing scars and pain for the rest of his life, but he quickly got on the mend. He was nothing if not resilient. He had taken beatings before, and he would take them again. He even managed to find something in it all to laugh about. He sent Darcy and Gabby in Melbourne a picture of himself taken not long after the event, leering toothlessly at the camera, bearing the caption, 'I left my teeth behind on the road'. He was laid up, but he was still able to roll himself a steady supply of joints. He drank — liquor — through a straw.

IRENE: 'He made a bit of an effort then, but [the marriage] was already stuffed. But it was probably like the friendship was a lot better after it was all over, when the bullshit, the bitterness, was out of the way.'

It wasn't long before Bon was back on his feet, if unsteadily. He was already anxious about his professional future.

IRENE: 'We went to a concert, I can't remember who it was, it was an outdoor concert, and there were people there from the industry who just walked right past him, and he said something like, These arseholes used to be all over me. He thought he was just a has-been.'

For want of any other option, Bon joined in rehearsals with Bruce, Uncle, John Freeman and guitarist Mauri Berg, formerly of Headband. Mick Jurd, like John Bisset, had remained in England. But Bon wasn't entirely convinced.

When the *News* devoted a story to Fraternity's ostensible reformation, it started to smell suspiciously like the bad old days. The band came across as full of all the same old bullshit: 'We've got a lot of plans, and we're in no hurry'.

The last thing Bon wanted was a repeat performance of the last three wasted years. He knew he had to find a ticket out.

eight
the youngs

Where the water sparkles on the harbour, in the wash of the Bridge and the Opera House, Sydney is one of the postcard prettiest cities in the world. But the day-to-day reality for most Sydneysiders is a massive suburban sprawl. Crawling along the gritty carbon-monoxide haze of Parramatta Road, you are surrounded by an ever-increasing bleak brick-veneer vista which is Sydney's dreaded western suburbs.

The west is commonly decried as a cultural desert. But that's the exclusive opinion of the snobbish barons of taste who believe that art doesn't belong outside institutions, and don't understand that which does. The first artistic language of suburbia is rock'n'roll, and Sydney's western suburbs have a long venerable rock'n'roll tradition.

When William and Margaret Young emigrated to Australia

*AC/DC's first photo session, Sydney, July 7, 1974, outside Her Majesty's Theatre.
Left to right: Rob Bailey, Angus Young, Malcolm Young, Dave Evans, Peter Clack.*

from Scotland with their six children in 1963, it was here in the West that they landed, and settled.

The rock'n'roll scene was already thriving. George was 15 (born November 6, 1948); Malcolm was ten (born January 6, 1953); Angus six (March 31, 1957).

'Me dad couldn't get work up in Scotland,' Angus later told *Sounds*, 'he found it impossible to support a family of our size, so he decided to try his luck downunder.'

Like others straight off the boat, the Youngs were ushered into a hostel — at Villawood — where they would stay until they found suitable accommodation for themselves. 'It was like a prison camp,' Malcolm later told *Spunky*, 'all these old tin shacks.'

The Young family, as George once put it, was fairly musical in an amateurish sort of way. It was eldest sibling, Margaret, who was largely responsible for turning the boys onto rock'n-'roll; who would, in fact, go on to name AC/DC and put Angus in the school uniform. After the Second World War British seaports like Liverpool and Glasgow were on a direct shipping route to the United States, and so, as rock'n'roll lore has it, Merseybeat itself was inspired by the American records — R&B, blues and hillbilly records — which were accessible there, landing as they did off the boats. Margaret was listening to Chuck Berry, Little Richard and Fats Domino even before they were stars.

Alex, the oldest Young boy, went into music professionally as a saxophonist in Emile Ford's Checkmates. He left home before the family emigrated, to join the Big Six, whose claim to fame was that they backed Tony Sheridan after the Beatles walked out on him. The Beatles connection was strengthened as Alex went on to join Grapefruit, a lesser light on the Beatles' own Apple label.

George was a promising schoolboy soccer player — an interest common among Scotsmen, and certainly shared by brother Malcolm — but he was keener still on music.

Although the Youngs spent barely three weeks at Villawood before they moved out into a place of their own just down the road in Burwood, George managed to get himself together with the best part of a band. His cohorts numbered an Englishman and two Dutchmen, respectively: front-man Stevie Wright, who was lured away from surfsters Chris Langdon and the Langdells; guitarist Harry Vanda, formerly of Holland's premier instrumental combo the Starfighters; and bassist Dick Diamond.

Burwood, with its wide boulevards and solid, free-standing red-brick Federation homes, might almost have seemed posh to working-class Scots. And indeed, today it is becoming gentrified. But in the sixties, it was a rough and ready neighbourhood of 'new Australians', which would play host, down at the station on Saturday nights, to violent meetings of rival gangs. If the rough streets of Glasgow weren't indoctrination enough for the Young boys, this was certainly a fine finishing school.

Burwood also boasted a thriving garage band scene. 'Every new English kid that arrived brought all the latest things with him,' remembers native Peter Noble, who played with Britons in a band called Clapham Junction.

George's nascent band found a drummer, Englishman Snowy Fleet, then resident at the East Hills Migrant Hostel. Fleet was a Liverpudlian and at 24 was much older and more experienced than his new cohorts. He had come out to Australia with his wife and child after throwing in a choice gig with the Mojos, who would go on to join Beatles manager Brian Epstein's stable and produce the classic 1964 hit 'Everything's alright'. Snowy would name the band the Easybeats and initially manage it as well.

The Easybeats are generally acknowledged as the first truly original Australian rock'n'roll band, but the irony is they were in scant part actually Australian. But still the band was immediately, passionately embraced in Australia as our own.

The Easybeats' first gig proper was in late 1964 at an inner-Sydney joint called Beatle Village. From there, they leapt and bounded to the top of the charts.

The Easybeats looked good and sounded good. They dressed sharp, which lent them greater sex appeal than their near Australian rivals, who mostly looked like public servants, and they could both play and write rock'n'roll songs. Plus, Little Stevie was a livewire showman.

Signing a management deal with erstwhile north shore real estate agent Mike Vaughan, the band was introduced to Ted Albert, a friend of the high-flying Vaughan's, who was in music publishing, a budding producer with an ear for the future in beat music. Albert was the middle of three sons of Sir Alexis Albert, whose father Jacques Albert was the founder of a family empire, J Albert & Son, which today still stands as the oldest independent music publishing house in Australia, and is estimated, with interests also in radio and film, to have a total worth of $45 million.

Jacques Albert migrated to Australia from Switzerland in 1884 and set up shop as a music publisher. Immediate success with a single product called *The boomerang songbook* laid the foundations for the family fortune. Turnover was maintained as Alberts picked up Australian rights to an impressive array of song catalogues.

Ted Albert was 26 when Beatlemania hit in 1963, and he got caught up in it. He wanted a Beatles of his own. Initially, he had headhunted the already successful Billy Thorpe and the Aztecs to work with his newly-formed Alberts Productions, but when Mike Vaughan invited him down to have a look at this new group he was representing, Ted, in his own words, almost broke his neck getting a contract drawn up. The Easybeats, after all, did what no other Australian band did, and that was write their own material; to a publisher, obviously, this is important.

Ted immediately took the band into the old 2UW Radio Theatre (the station owned by the family), and cut demos. In March, 1965, a debut single, 'For my woman', was released through Parlophone, and whilst it was nary a hit, it was encouragement enough to Ted to get any sort of reaction to original material. The dam broke with the Easys' second single, which followed two months later, 'She's so fine'. It shot to number one, and in the process dragged the forgotten first single into the top five as well. Easyfever was upon Australia as the group vied only with Normie Rowe for the title of our premier pop attraction.

The Easybeats would go on to produce an incredible run of hits and even cut three albums before they left Australia in July, 1966 for the then Mecca of the pop world, London.

With the rise of the Easybeats, Alberts Productions also established itself as a force in the fledgling Australian music industry. George Young would later praise the urbane Ted Albert as a man who, self-taught in the art of recording rock'n'roll, 'knew as much about feel and balls in a track as anyone I've ever met... and had a very good ear for picking the right songs'.

Ted applied his instincts to running Alberts Productions, and was rewarded with a string of hits for Billy Thorpe and the Aztecs as well as the Easybeats. Dirtier, uglier R&B-merchants like the Throb and the Missing Links fared less well commercially, but left a lasting impact.

When Ted followed the Easybeats overseas, Alberts wound down operations in Australia, at least for the meantime. On the international scene, the Easybeats scored immediately, and massively, with the mod anthem 'Friday on my mind' — and spent the next three years falling apart in the search for a follow-up.

Manager Mike Vaughan was out of his depth overseas. It reached a point, in 1967, where the band was signed 'exclusively' to several record companies around the world, which left them hamstrung. All this experience built the bitter wisdom George would later apply to AC/DC.

Artistically too, George would later rue, the Easybeats strayed off the track, or were led astray. The band progressed through two very distinct cycles, in Australia and then overseas, both of which began and ended with rock'n'roll, but in between went very wayward. Initially, in Australia, flushed with their first success, the band indulged itself and tried to be clever. Whilst the resultant songs like 'Wedding ring' and 'Sad and lonely and blue' were still hits, albeit minor, George at least claims to have derived much greater satisfaction out of the return to rock'n'roll with songs like 'Women' and 'Sorry'.

'Sorry' would reach number one in Australia by November, 1966, as the Easys were ensconced in the studio in London with Who/Kinks producer Shel Talmy, cutting 'Friday on my mind'. 'Friday on my mind' followed 'Sorry' into the number one position in Australia a mere month later, and eventually, after a few false starts, made top ten in Britain and top 20 in America, not to mention hitting very big all across Europe, especially in Germany.

But 'Friday on my mind' would prove, as big hits sometimes can for bands, to be both a blessing and a curse. Certainly, even despite the layers of businessmen who siphoned off much of the Easybeats' earnings, it was a meal ticket for Harry and George at least, who had written the song. George was also made aware of the value of the often overlooked European market.

Despite all the evidence which suggests it seldom works, record companies inevitably want a clone follow-up disc to consolidate the success of a first hit. This sort of pressure, to the artist, is like a red rag to a bull. George and Harry, who by now had taken complete creative control of the Easybeats, would do anything but repeat themselves, or even come close. And so the band's singles that followed 'Friday on my mind' were all over the shop, a grab-bag of psychedelic dabblings which only erratically touched on the vitality of their earlier work. It wasn't until late 1968 with 'Good times', a raging slab of rock'n'roll (successfully revived in Australia in 1988 by INXS and Jimmy Barnes), that George and Harry perhaps realised they'd cut off their nose to spite their face.

The lesson in all of this for George, which he would pass on in no uncertain terms to his eager little brothers, was that you must stay true to your roots.

'Good times' came too late. By then, the public didn't know who or what the Easybeats were, and the band themselves no longer shared the sense of unity they had when they all lived out of each other's pockets. George and Harry had become estranged from the rest of the band, spending all their time together in the studio and refusing to tour at any length. Eventually they moved into their own four-track studio–flat in London.

The band, such as it was, was on its last legs — skint, and with drugs beginning to eat away at it. Stevie Wright began the downward spiral that would lead to the heroin addiction which would blight his life for many years to come.

The last album that bore the Easybeats' name, *Friends*, was barely that. A ragtag collection of demos recorded by Harry and George, with only Stevie otherwise appearing on a few of the tracks, it did, however, yield the Easybeats' last minor hit, the good-rocking 'St Louis'.

On the strength of that, the band managed to get it together sufficiently to tour Australia in the spring of 1969. It would be their last hurrah. At tour's end, Harry and George headed straight back to their London studio lair. Word was that the band had finally broken up.

Harry and George picked up in London where they left off. The next three years would be one long lost weekend as they worked at establishing themselves as an all-round production team, spotting talent, and writing and recording. They sold a few songs and produced a record or two, but nothing world-beating. Little wonder then that Ted Albert — who played an ongoing game of chess with George over the phone — was able to lure them back to Australia in 1973.

Spurred by success with a young pop singer–songwriter, Englishman Ted Mulry, Alberts was reborn in the new decade as a record label in its own right. Mulry's first single 'Julia' was a minor hit. His second 'Falling in love again', penned by none other than Harry and George, and released for Christmas 1970, was a smash.

The signing that consolidated Alberts' comeback was John Paul Young. Englishman Simon Napier-Bell, former manager of the Yardbirds, among other more dubious distinctions (he later managed Wham!) was then working at Alberts on some sort of exchange program. He was looking for a singer to match with another one of Harry and George's demos which was lying around, a song called 'Pasadena'. Cut with John Paul Young, it hit just outside the top ten in April, 1972.

Ted, then, promised Harry and George the world, or at least that he would build them a studio, and that they could run it as they chose. Harry and George, in return, promised to get down to some serious work.

AC/DC always was, and still is Malcolm Young's band. Malcolm formed the band in the first place, and even as Angus has gradually assumed the front man's role, Malcolm was always the driving force, the primary writer, and the one to whom the last word in the band belonged. Angus has come to share much of the songwriting load with Malcolm, but equally, the pair's silent partner in the band has always been big brother George. Having already been around the block with the Easybeats, suffered shortcomings and rip-offs, George was embittered, and so in many ways AC/DC was his revenge. AC/DC would achieve what the Easybeats couldn't — control of their own destiny, and sustained success.

It was George, so much more than merely coproducer of the band, who honed the band's sound and songs into a coherent, commercially viable entity. But George's brilliance was that he never tried to polish a turd. Where less incisive record producers would have tried to iron out AC/DC's rough edges, tart up the sound, all George ever tried to do was harness that power, give it dynamic shape and direction.

As George's crowning achievement, AC/DC also marked the institution of a dynasty in Australian rock'n'roll whose influence is pervasive still. Its presence is not just in the success of AC/DC, but also in the seminal influence AC/DC exert all over the world, and in the rest of the work George and Harry have done as part of the Alberts Productions axis. In the midseventies, Alberts produced an unprecedented string of hits for artists like Stevie Wright, John Paul Young, and the Ted Mulry Gang. Perhaps more particularly than that, George and Harry's production work with bands like Rose Tattoo and the Angels virtually defined the unique Australian rock genre which grew out of the thriving pub circuit.

George Young lived at home in Burwood — when he wasn't out on the road — right up until he went overseas in 1966. Growing up in his slipstream, it was almost inevitable that Malcolm and Angus would follow him into rock'n'roll. Angus would later recall: 'One day George was a 16-year-old kid sitting on his bed playing guitar, the next day he was worshipped by the whole country. I was going to school at the time — or rather, trying not to go to school — and I was very impressed. He was getting all the girls'.

Although, as Angus has testified, there was always a guitar around the house, Malcolm told Glenn A Baker, 'We didn't get much encouragement. Dad was still asking George when he was going to get a proper job. The Easybeats weren't making much money in England by the end and I don't think the family liked the drug thing that was happening in rock by that time.' But music was an irresistible force, and the two brothers picked up as much by osmosis as they did off old records by Muddy Waters, Ike and Tina Turner, Little Richard, Chuck Berry, the Who, the Stones or the Yardbirds.

Both Malcolm and Angus attended nearby Ashfield Boys High, a school notorious for its toughness. Malcolm told *Spunky*, 'Because we were little guys, everyone kept pushing us around, and we had to fight or get beat up'.

The boys' father insisted they get a trade whatever happened, and so when Malcolm left school at 15, he started work as an apprentice fitter. At the time, the inner west was buzzing with music. The powerful Nova agency had its offices in Ashfield, and so the spectre of new local bands like Sherbet, Blackfeather and the Flying Circus loomed large. Malcolm jammed around in mates' bedrooms and garages.

In 1971, when he was working as a sewing machine maintenance man for Berlei, who make the bras, Malcolm met a band presumptuously called the Velvet Underground, who had just landed in nearby Regents Park from Newcastle. They were looking for a guitarist, and Malcolm got the gig.

The Velvet Underground had formed in Newcastle in 1967. With a repertoire based around material by the Doors and Jefferson Airplane, they became top dogs on the coastal dance circuit. When front man Steve Phillopson threw in the towel, the band relocated to Sydney. Finding the guitarist they sought in Malcolm — they knew he was the brother of George Young, but certainly Malcolm didn't play up the fact — they experimented with vocalists until they settled on one Andy Imlah, who was poached off a nondescript outfit from around the way called Elm Tree.

The band was picked up for representation by Dal Myles (now a newsreader on Sydney television), who constituted Nova's sole rival. Thus the Velvet Underground became popular on Sydney's suburban dance circuit, where they would often share the bill with another one of Myles' clients, erstwhile Alberts solo artist Ted Mulry, who was then using the aforesaid Elm Tree as a backing band. Elm Tree had started life, like the Valentines, with two lead vocalists — a young sheet-metal worker by the name of John Paul Young sharing the spotlight with Andy Imlah — but the band was left in the lurch after Imlah went off to join the Velvet Underground.

Malcolm already knew Ted Mulry through George, who'd met him at the 1970 Tokyo Song Festival where 'Falling in love again' was unveiled.

TED MULRY: 'When I came back from Japan, it was around Christmas, and George was home for Christmas, and he said, What are you doing for Christmas? I said, I dunno, whatever; he said, Well, New Year's Eve, we're having a do at the folks' place, come around. So I said, Alright. And you can imagine! You go along with your guitar, and they're all musicians, and you have a few drinks ... The funny thing was, I was the only non-Scot there, there wasn't even any other Englishmen, and you couldn't understand a word they were saying! But what a ball! We had a big singsong, and you'd get everything out, somebody had a squeeze-box, and there was a mouth organ, the bass would come out, guitars. It was great.'

With the Velvet Underground gigging busily, Malcolm threw in his job and became, like the rest of the band, a professional musician. He would never work a day job again.

The young Angus was allowed to go out and see his brother play — and he would sit wide-eyed at the front of stage — as long as he was brought straight home. But the Velvet Underground were pretty well-behaved anyway. They would go back to Burwood after gigs for Ovaltine.

'We used to go round to pick Malcolm up,' recalls Velvet Underground drummer Herm Kovac. 'The first time, this little punk skinhead answered the door, it was Angus. I hid behind Les [the guitarist]; in those days you'd hear about the skinheads down at Burwood Station, Strathfield Station. Shaved head he had, big boots. He said, Eh, come in 'ere. So we follow him into his room, he straps on his SG, jumps on the bed, and goes off on this exhibition, running over the dressing table, showing off, couldn't play any chords, just lead, and when he finishes he says, Whaddya reckon? You had to say, Pretty good, Angus. Every time you'd go there you'd have to go through this same ritual.'

The Velvet Underground were writing a few songs of their own, but their set was still mainly covers — the Stones, 'Can you hear me knockin?' and 'Brown sugar', and T Rex.

HERM KOVACS: 'With Malcolm, he never had guitar heroes, you know when you're a teenager, you have pin-ups on the wall. Malcolm and Angus never had any pictures on their bedroom wall. The one guitarist who was Malcolm's hero, who he did have a picture of on the wall, was the guy you'd least expect — Marc Bolan. Malcolm made us do about six T Rex songs. I said, I hate 'em, they all sound the same. But Malcolm loved Marc Bolan. Mind you, the picture he had of him was tiny!'

Ted Mulry had first cut a version of George and Harry's 'Pasadena', but Simon Napier-Bell was convinced there was a hit in it yet, and so he asked the Velvet Underground to do it. They demurred. They were a rock band, they protested, and 'Pasadena' was pop schlock, even if it was one of Malcolm's brother's songs. The Velvet Underground in turn suggested that maybe 'Mungy' Young, Elm Tree's other singer, would be well suited to the song. John Paul Young was thus launched on his own career.

With the dissolution of Elm Tree now complete, Ted Mulry, who was still producing hits as a solo artist, needed a new backing band, and so he became something of a double-act with the Velvet Underground. The Velvet Underground would open the show, and then play behind Ted for his bracket. But Malcolm was getting itchy fingers. He wanted to go off and get something of his own together. Late in 1972, then, the Velvet Underground folded as such. The rest of the band, plus Ted, transmuted into the Ted Mulry Gang.

HERM KOVACS: 'When Malcolm left Velvet Underground, the reason he left was that Deep Purple had come out then, and he wanted to play all Deep Purple-type stuff. The rest of us weren't really into that. So he went and tried it, couldn't get any gigs, and then the early AC/DC played Beatles songs and all that, just to get work.

George and Harry finally arrived back in Australia for good around the same time that Malcolm was starting to get something of his own together. But if they were going to go back to work for Ted Albert, they did so with a guardedness that would become part of their trademark.

Chris Gilbey joined Alberts around the same time, at the start of 1973, and it was a while before he met George or Harry. Gilbey was a Londoner who had played in small-time bands in the sixties before moving to the other side of the desk, arriving in Australia via South Africa.

CHRIS GILBEY: 'Ted had been giving them a retainer even when they were in England. They came back and I didn't meet them for quite some time. Ted would have these meetings with them. I was doing — I don't know what I was doing! — George and Harry were mysteriously making this record at EMI.'

The record George and Harry were mysteriously making was the legendary Marcus Hook Roll Band album, now a highly-prized collector's item, *Tales of old granddaddy*. This project provided Malcolm and Angus with their blooding in the recording studio, and it was an experience that had a profound effect on Malcolm in particular.

The Marcus Hook Roll Band had its genesis during George and Harry's dying days in England, when a friend called Wally Allen, who was working as an engineer for EMI at Abbey Road, got them into the studio to cut a few tracks just for fun. George and Harry returned to Australia soon after, and it wasn't until EMI's American affiliate Capitol Records contacted them that they even remembered doing the sessions. Capitol was hot for a track called 'Natural man', and wanted more. 'It was a free trip for Wally who wanted to see Bondi Beach,' George told Glenn A Baker, 'so he scored a ticket and came.

'We went into EMI, Sydney, for a month and Wally supplied all the booze. We had Harry, myself and my kid brothers Malcolm and Angus. We all got rotten, except for Angus, who was too young.

'That was the first thing that Malcolm and Angus did before AC/DC. We didn't take it very seriously, so we thought we'd include them to give them an idea of what recording was all about.'

And indeed, Malcolm's eyes were opened by the experience. *Tales of old granddaddy* not only distanced George and Harry from the Easybeats, drawing them closer to forming Flash and the Pan — the mysterious duo persona with which they would have hits like 'Walking in the rain' and 'Hey, St Peter' — it also betrayed seeds of the AC/DC style to come. One cut, 'Quick reaction', was pure riff-driven AC/DC.

Malcolm wasn't impressed by the way the recording process was so piecemeal, so separated, with everything overdubbed and multitracked. That wasn't the way real rock'n'roll operated. Real rock'n'roll was played by a band, together, as a band. All this technology was obscuring the real point of the exercise.

Disillusioned, Malcolm went home and threw his Deep Purple albums in the bin. They were phonies. Not like Chuck Berry, or the Rolling Stones, who were the real thing, who could do it, for real, without hiding behind the veil of studio trickery.

The band Malcolm was getting together was going to be a rock'n'roll band. It was going to be glam, to be sure, because glam was then de rigueur, but it was still going to be rock'n'roll. The idea would prove visionary.

1973, after all, was not a great time for rock'n'roll.

It was a mark of the immaturity of the business in Australia that the spirit of glory year 1971 was allowed to dissipate. Even Thorpie, the movement's spearhead, couldn't maintain his momentum after his ill-fated trip to England in 1972.

By 1973, the scene was split down the middle. 'Commercial' music had taken over the charts. Any new 'progressive' bands had to rely on the live circuit to survive. Radio, with the arrival of American-style programming, adopted rigidly conservative formats.

The two biggest Australian albums in 1973 both belonged to Brian Cadd, whose Americanisms segued smoothly onto radio playlists. Sherbet, who had won the last ever Battle of the Sounds, the year after Fraternity, were rapidly establishing themselves as teen heart-throbs.

A second wave of bands stormed Melbourne's 'underground' ballrooms, discos and pubs in a scene which was admittedly expanding, but beyond gigs in Adelaide and to a lesser extent Sydney, there was nowhere to go beyond that.

Technology was improving, but the talent lagged behind. When Michael Gudinski formed Mushroom Records in 1973, it initially struggled because it lacked genuinely first-rate bands.

The best band of the day was Lobby Loyde's Coloured Balls, but it was typical that they were marginalised and ultimately defeated. Loyde took the groundwork he'd laid with the Aztecs, and sharpened it to a logical conclusion. The most profound legacy Thorpie left Australian rock'n'roll was probably his blithely confrontationalist attitude, and though the Coloured Balls inherited that tradition, volume for its own sake wasn't their weapon — blazing dynamism, aggression and finesse were. Echoes of this sound can be heard in Australian rock'n'roll to this day, but in 1973, complete with their sharpie image, the Coloured Balls were resisted by the hippies that ran Melbourne music as much as the audiences.

In Sydney in 1973, the new band rising was teeny-bopper rockers Hush. Sherbet dominated the national scene. It was enough to make Malcolm Young puke.

AC/DC, named by Margaret Young after a warning sign she noticed on her sewing machine, coalesced around the end of 1973, with a line-up comprising Malcolm, Angus, singer Dave Evans, bassist Larry Van Knedt (a Dutchman, like Harry) and drummer Colin Burgess (who had only recently left the Masters Apprentices).

Angus, at 15, had only just left school, which he hated. He had started work as a compositor (for porn magazine *Ribald*, or so he claims), and wasn't automatically included in the band. Throughout his last year at school, Angus never had a guitar out of his hands. He would run home and straight out again to go and jam with his mates. He wouldn't even change out of his school uniform; it was this image of him, wielding his axe, that inspired Margaret, again, to suggest he take it up onto stage. Angus was putting together a band of his own called Tantrum when Malcolm asked him to fill the gap in AC/DC where keyboards wouldn't fit.

Dave Evans, a Novocastrian Malcolm had met through the Velvet Underground, was in his position more for the way he looked than the way he sang. In fact, he was not a good singer at all, but Malcolm wanted glitter — he himself dressed like a sort of space cowboy — and Evans had it in spades. As a performer, he was a shameless exhibitionist.

Legend has it that AC/DC played its debut at Chequers, in Sydney, on New Year's Eve, 1973. No record exists of this show other than Angus's colourised recollection: 'We had been together about two weeks. We had to get up and blast away. From the word go it went great. Everyone thought we were a pack of loonies — you know, who's been feeding them kids bananas?'

The band's repertoire at that time consisted of Rolling Stones, Beatles and Chuck Berry songs, plus a few old blues numbers and a couple of tentative originals.

By April, the rhythm section had been replaced by Rob Bailey (bass) and Peter Clack (drums). Bailey and Clack had grown as a unit out of Flake, a band that first hit during the radio ban with a version of Trinity's version of the Band's version of Dylan's 'Wheels on fire'. They passed an audition held at George's new place in well-heeled suburban Epping, and it was this settled line-up that would soon go into the studio to cut a debut single. Angus was wearing a Zorro suit, and as well as holding down a residency at the Hampton Court Hotel in Kings Cross, the band was gigging around on the suburban dance circuit.

Harry and George, meantime, were ensconced at EMI with their old cohort Stevie Wright, who had been dredged out of the dual indignity of heroin addiction and the cast of *Jesus Christ Superstar*. Malcolm contributed guitar at these sessions too.

In June, what was probably the first ever press notice of AC/DC appeared in *Go-Set*. The news article stressed the band's youth, which it was putting to its advantage. 'Most of the groups in Australia are getting on rather than getting it on,' Malcolm sneered, 'out of touch with the kids that go to suburban dances.'

The piece also reveals as a lie that AC/DC were innocent of the sexual connotations of their name. Malcolm points out that it refers to electricity, 'but if people want to think we're five camp guys, then that's okay by us'.

Even Molly Meldrum, Australian music's foremost apologist, once described early 1974 as its 'lowest ebb'. But this was only the calm before the storm, a storm precipitated by the comeback of George, Harry and Stevie, with the monumental 'Evie', the first single off the album, *Hard road*, they'd finished recording.

CHRIS GILBEY: 'Everybody had a sense of — it was posthippie — we've decided we don't want to drop out, we're going to drop in and make it really work. Of course, the wonderful thing was that the Albert family had this tremendous cash base, so they could afford to play at being the record business in a way no other indy could.'

In its full three-part form, 'Evie' ran at over 14 minutes long, but even so, on its release in June, it crashed through the radio barrier and went on to become one of the biggest Australian hits of the year.

If ever the Easybeats had a homecoming, it was the now legendary free show at the Sydney Opera House in June, which had Stevie fronting a band that numbered not only Harry and George, but also Malcolm. A crowd of 10,000 had to content itself with the sound from a PA system set up on the Opera House steps as there was no room left in the theatre itself. It was typical of the obstinately forward-thinking George that not a single Easybeats oldie was played that night.

AC/DC played that night too. *Go-Set* noted, 'AC/DC opened the show and showed they're a force to be reckoned with. They play rock'n'roll intelligently, adding their own ideas to sure crowd-pleasers like "Heartbreak Hotel", "No particular place to go" and "Shake, rattle & roll".'

Praising Angus and Malcolm's dual guitar attack, whilst comparing Dave Evans to David Cassidy, the review concluded the band 'looked great and sounded great. Their material is part original and will undoubtedly prove popular as the band gets about a little more.'

If family ties had given AC/DC a kick-start, George had to let them find their own way from there. Even if he was always looking over their shoulder.

When the band was approached by Dennis Laughlin with a management offer, George gave the nod. Laughlin, of course, was the former Sherbet front man and Nova agent who, by 1974, was operating as lone wolf on Sydney's southern beaches. He was running a gig in an old cinema in Cronulla called Last Picture Show, always with an eye for the main chance, and he certainly saw a chance in AC/DC. Laughlin grew up around Burwood too, though maybe more importantly than that, to George, he was a fellow Scot. Laughlin decreed that he would get the band out on the road, beyond Sydney, where a lucrative circuit awaited.

It was quite apparent by this time that Dave Evans had to be replaced. His antics on stage had become an embarrassment. Malcolm and Angus had previously contemplated getting rid of him, but both John Paul Young and future Alberts two-hit-wonder William Shakespeare declined the offer of the job. 'We used to kick him [Evans] off stage,' Angus recalled, 'and me and Malcolm would just jam on boogies and old Chuck Berry songs, and the band would go down better without him.'

The band was desperately looking out for a new front man when Dennis Laughlin scored them the support spot on the August Australian tour by Lou Reed. Reed was then at the height of his junkie-faggot phase, and AC/DC, with their ambiguous moniker and coy debut single, 'Can I sit next to you, girl?', must have seemed perfectly suited to the bill. And hey, weren't they George Young's little brothers? It was in the blood, wasn't it?

As unremarkable as 'Can I sit next to you, girl?' was, it became a minor hit in Perth and Adelaide. So, away from the Reed tour, Laughlin was able to arrange gigs there, as well as in Melbourne, which was then still very much the Australian pop capital.

After playing the last show of the tour with the controversial Reed in Adelaide, AC/DC played a couple of pub gigs of their own, and then went on to Perth for a six-week season at the city's top disco, Beethovens, as support act for famous transvestite Carlotta.

In Adelaide, Bon saw the band. He was unaware of the strings that had been pulled behind his back. He had recovered sufficiently from his accident to be getting around again, and he was doing odd jobs for Vince, painting his office, putting up posters, driving visiting bands. In touch with George, Vince had booked AC/DC into Adelaide.

VINCE: 'George told me, We need a new singer, and I said, Well, what about Bon? George said, But I heard he had an accident. I said, He's alright now, and he wants to leave Fraternity, they're too serious for him. He said, Well, why don't you suggest it to Malcolm and Angus? So I did, and they said, Your old mate? He's too old! I said, He could rock your arse off. I said to Bon, You want to go and check out this AC/DC. He said, Arrgh, they're just a gimmick band. Anyway, we went out to the Pooraka, went backstage, and I remember Angus said, So you reckon you can rock the arse off us? Bon said, You young kids? You bet! And they said, Well, let's see, and they arranged a rehearsal at Bruce's place.'

ROB BAILEY: 'Bon and Uncle turned up, and they were like regulars after that. Bon must have seen the opportunity, thought, This is for me, and set about to woo Angus and Malcolm. After gigs, Angus and Malcolm would disappear with Bon. Bon wasn't silly, he knew where to hit.'

The popular myth that Bon had first been employed by AC/DC as their driver — a myth propagated by the band itself as much as anyone — must have had its origins here, as Bon played host to Malcolm and Angus, all getting around in the old Holden Bon had recently bought for $90.

'I knew their manager,' Bon himself said later in the film *Let there be rock*. 'I'd never seen the band before, I'd never even heard of AC/DC, and their manager said, Just stand here, and the band comes on in two minutes, and there's this little guy, in a school uniform, going crazy, and I laughed.'

'I took the opportunity to explain to them how much better

I was than the drongo they had singing for them' Bon said on another occasion. 'So they gave me a chance to prove it, and there I was.'

Angus, Malcolm and Laughlin went down to the cellar where an aggregation consisting of Bon, Bruce Howe, guitarist Mauri Berg, John Freeman and Uncle were halfarsedly rehearsing. These other guys, though, were unaware that what was going on was virtually an audition for Bon.

BRUCE HOWE: 'Angus and Malcolm picked up guitars and started playing and I started playing bass, and I thought, Fuck me dead, these guys are just so together, with their rhythms, each other; they were almost telepathic. It was one of the best impromptu musical buzzes I had had in ages.'

Bon pulled out all the stops. Laughlin offered him the job on the spot. Bon said he'd think about it while the band was in Perth.

Bon was torn. He went down to the docks and, gazing out over the sea, mulled over everything — Irene, Fraternity, AC/DC. The easiest decision to make was that he didn't want to spend the rest of his life as a working stiff. Next, despite the ties, he wanted out of Fraternity. And he wanted in with AC/DC. The hard part was Irene. Bon had never given up hope that his marriage might yet be resurrected, and he didn't want to forsake that possibility. But in the end, he knew he had to. As Irene put it: 'I was ready to settle down. Bon still wanted to be famous.'

BRUCE: 'He wanted to do it, but he wanted to do it unencumbered by emotional baggage. Bon knew, because he'd done it before, you've got to be in a position where there's no wives, no children, you've just got to be able to get up and take the opportunities as they come.'

After a few weeks in Perth, Dave Evans took to calling in sick. He was drinking a lot. Dennis Laughlin, who himself would occasionally fill in for Evans, rang Bon to reiterate the offer. Bon rang back later to say he'd do it. The band would be passing through Adelaide on their way back to Sydney anyway, so they could get together then. Evans was sent packing. He went on only to enjoy fifteen seconds of fame in 1976, fronting Rabbit on their immortal 'Too much rock'n'roll'. Bon got up with AC/DC for the first time at the Pooraka.

'The only rehearsal we had was just sitting around an hour before the gig, pulling out every rock'n'roll song we knew,' Angus said. 'When we finally got there Bon downed about two bottles of bourbon with dope, coke, speed, and says, Right, I'm ready, and he was too. He was fighting fit. There was this immediate transformation and he was running around with his wife's knickers on, yelling at the audience. It was a magic moment. He said it made him feel young again.'

VINCE: 'The next day, Bon came around to my office, and said, Whaddya reckon? I said, Well, you know, I like them, I think they're great and I think they're going to be big. I said, Why? He said, Because I'm going to join them. I said, When are you leaving? He said, Today.'

DENNIS LAUGHLIN: 'I went round and picked Bon up at his place with Irene. And that was it, that was the end of the marriage too.'

VINCE: 'He just packed his bags. He came around with them in the car, he came around to say goodbye, and he wound down the window and said, Seeya later. And that was that.'

AC/DC begins to coalesce; Melbourne, January/February, 1975. Left to right: Malcolm Young, Phil Rudd, temporary bassist identified only as 'Paul', Angus Young, Bon. Bon: 'Fraternity worked on a different level to me. They were all on the same level and it was way above my head. They didn't have a chance in England. This group has just got it.'

nine
ac/dc
melbourne,
1975

dennis Laughlin was paying AC/DC its wages in drugs and spare change. He wasn't going to last.

But then, the extraordinary thing about this early stage of AC/DC's development is how so much happened so quickly. Bon joined the band at the end of September. Within six weeks, they were without management, but in the studio recording an album. Within six months, with powerful new management and a new line-up, they would have both a debut single and a debut album in the top ten.

Dennis Laughlin and AC/DC parted company within a few weeks of Bon joining. Bon had reasonably expected to be based in Sydney, where the Youngs lived, but a management offer from powerful Melbourne player Michael Browning meant that the band would move south. This was not before they cut the album with George and Harry in Sydney in November. By December, the band had set up base in Melbourne.

When Bon initially arrived in Sydney at the end of September he took up residence on the couch at Dennis Laughlin's flat in Cronulla. Bon knew Laughlin from Fraternity's Jonathans days, and he liked him.

Bon was mucking around with Malcolm and Angus, comparing musical notes. He was convinced AC/DC could be a world-beater. He was astonished by the musical acuity and empathy both Malcolm and Angus had at such young ages, and he was swept up in their single-mindedness. It was as though he'd been reborn. Any lingering pain from his accident injuries was overridden in the general rush of it all. Bon, in turn, gave something back to Malcolm and Angus.

GRAEME: 'I think Ron put a bit of life into it too. I think it was what Malcolm and Angus were looking for.'

'Bon was the biggest single influence on the band,' Malcolm has admitted. 'When Bon came in it pulled us all together. He had that real stick-it-to-'em attitude. We all had it in us, but it took Bon to bring it out.'

'When I sang I always felt there was a certain amount of urgency to what I was doing,' said Bon. 'There was no vocal training in my background, just a lot of good whisky, and a long string of blues bands, or should I say "booze" bands. I went through a period where I copied a lot of guys, and found when I was singing that I was starting to sound like them. But when I met up with Angus and the rest of the band, they told me to sound like myself, and I really had a free hand doing what I always wanted to do.'

The band played its debut proper, with Bon singing, at the Brighton-le-Sands Masonic Hall. They had to get their shit together quickly because they were due to go out on the road in the second week of October. Laughlin had booked gigs in Melbourne, and then over in Adelaide, then back in Melbourne again. They would then return to Sydney to start recording.

LAUGHLIN: 'The biggest problem I had with AC/DC in those early days, being a touring unit, and not having much money, was keeping everything together, keeping everyone happy. There's a few dope smokers in the band, right? Instead of giving everyone fifty bucks a week, it's like, alright, whatever you need, we'll get. Thirty bucks a week plus a bag of dope, a bottle of Scotch. Well, Angus was a pain in the arse, because he says, Fuck ya, I don't drink booze, or fuckin' take drugs. I'd give him a bag of fish'n'chips, a Kit Kat, a packet of Benson & Hedges and a bottle of Coke.'

In Melbourne, the band played the suburban dance circuit, some of the new pubs, and the old discos. On October 16, for the first time, they played Michael Browning's Hard Rock Cafe on its gay night.

From Melbourne, the band headed over to Adelaide, where Vince had booked them into the Largs Pier for three nights. Bon was extremely pleased with himself, being back in town with what he believed was the hottest band in the land. However, with the exception of Uncle, who got up one night to have a blow, Bon's old friends were dismissive, reckoning Bon was selling out. It was the sort of condescension AC/DC faced continually, and would hold against Australia in later years. Bon's attitude was, Fuck 'em. He trusted only his own gut feelings, and they were good.

Adelaide would prove the last showdown for Dennis Laughlin.

MICHAEL BROWNING: 'What happened was that they came down. They had a manager who was a sleazeball. I was just the guy running the club, and I really liked them. They came to collect their money at the end of the night, and told me they were going to Adelaide the following day. So I said, Well, seeya when you get back. Next thing, I got a phone call from Adelaide to say the guy had absconded with all their money or something, and that they were stranded.'

LAUGHLIN: 'I got the shits with them one night in Adelaide. Angus was complaining, Oh, Bon's got a bag of dope, a bottle of Scotch, and I ain't got nothin'. So I said, Fuck ya, I'm not workin' my arse off anymore, here's your books, you've gotta be in Melbourne by one o'clock tomorrow, I'm going home, seeya later.'

BROWNING: 'I sent them money so they could come back to Melbourne, so they could fulfill their commitments to everyone, including me. When they got to Melbourne, they came and saw me and we talked about management. I'd only seen them once then, and I just remember being totally knocked out. They had a new singer then too — Bon Scott — and my immediate reaction, I suppose, was a little sceptical, because my image of Bon Scott was as the singer in a teeny-bopper group, and AC/DC were more of a street rock'n'roll band. But it worked. Malcolm and Angus hated anything that was pretentious, or plastic, poofy, and Bon just exuded character.'

If Bon had liked Dennis Laughlin, he was, however, quite prepared to defer to Malcolm and Angus. If Michael Browning was it, then fine.

Browning himself had been looking for an act to get involved with since May, when after five years, he resigned from managing Billy Thorpe and the Aztecs. 'One tends to become a little complacent after such a long time,' Browning explained to *Go-Set*, but more likely, he was disappointed that Thorpie had failed to give it a serious shot overseas.

George went down to Melbourne to see Browning, and again was impressed with Browning's track record, and his ambitiousness. Browning and George shared a vision: George wanted to get AC/DC out of Australia as soon as possible. Browning wanted a band he could take overseas.

BROWNING: 'My sole personal ambition to be the manager of an Australian band that broke internationally was a motivating factor in AC/DC's success. I mean, it was one thing for Alberts to say, We want to break this band internationally, but without someone to come along with the drive, and the game plan, well, it really wasn't going to happen.'

Michael Browning was, indeed, one of the first Australians to seriously consider going overseas with a band. The first band he ever managed was Python Lee Jackson, which itself made a pioneering foray to England in 1968, only to turn up in America in the early seventies with an album called *In a broken dream*, which featured Rod Stewart on vocals.

Browning went on, in the late sixties, to join Bill Joseph at AMBO, at which point he also took on management of Doug Parkinson. Doug Parkinson In Focus was probably the biggest band in Australia in 1969, having hits like 'Dear Prudence' and 'Hair'. But if Parkinson was never going to go the distance, Browning picked up Billy Thorpe on the verge of his second coming.

By 1973, Thorpie was still a big draw, but his star was descending. Moreover, Consolidated Rock, the Melbourne booking agency Browning had formed with Michael Gudinski and Bill Joseph after the demise of AMBO, had itself folded. Gudinski had formed Premier Artists in its place — the agency that still has a stranglehold on live music in Melbourne — and then went on to launch Mushroom.

Michael Browning too was in need of a new initiative. But if the scene offered few immediate prospects, with a more solid infrastructure now in place, it was ready and waiting for a resurgence.

Over the Australia Day long weekend of 1974, Browning trooped out to Sunbury yet again with Thorpie. The whole thing was becoming rather routine. Neither the Aztecs' nor Sherbet's nor the reformed Daddy Cool's sets were worth getting excited about. But when a new Melbourne band by the name of Skyhooks took the stage and proceeded to tear it apart, people sat up.

Michael Gudinski jumped first and signed the Skyhooks to both management and recording contracts, and by the end of the year, they'd saved the flailing Mushroom's skin.

Between that and a new ABC pop program, launched at the end of the year and fronted by Molly, called 'Countdown', the resurgence was finally on. Michael Browning saw AC/DC, and he knew not only that they could be part of it, but that they could also transcend it.

BROWNING: 'No doubt about it. Otherwise I wouldn't have undertaken it. I mean, I was married, and eventually I had kids and all the rest of it, we dragged them all around the world, and there was no way I was going to do that if the group didn't have the quality that people now recognise. They were definitely special. And still are.'

AC/DC were not strictly speaking a product of the pub circuit. Neither were Billy Thorpe and the Aztecs, Chain or the Coloured Balls, but AC/DC followed on from them in paving the way for pub rock.

What it was was a process of infusion. Sharing the same influences — Chuck Berry, blues, boogie, the Stones, a trace of metal — AC/DC played to the same audience Thorpie had found, an audience that was young, male and left right out. That liked rock'n'roll hard, fast and tough. Loud.

In 1974, these suburban boys had nothing they could call their own. Their sisters had all the poofy pap 'Countdown' could throw at them, like Skyhooks and Sherbet. Their older siblings were bonging on and getting into — whichever's worse — artrock and California soft rock. To these guys, all that stuff was hippie shit, and these guys hated hippies.

Heavy metal pioneers like Black Sabbath were already past it. The only new light was Status Quo. Or, if you were really hip, Alex Harvey or Lou Reed. No one had even heard of the New York Dolls. The local scene was an absolute desert. The sharpies had had the Coloured Balls, but sharpies were dickheads, and the Coloured Balls were falling apart anyway.

It was into this yawning gulf that AC/DC stomped, too late, too ugly to be glam, too clever to be metal, too soon, too dumb to be punk.

They were at once a culmination and a fresh start for the push of what Anthony O'Grady, the editor of the new Sydney-based rock rag *RAM*, described as 'high energy heavy metal boogie bands'. AC/DC were distinguished, to begin with, by the telepathic guitar interplay between Malcolm and Angus, which determined their unique dynamic texture. Bon added colour to movement with his street-smart edge, his strangled vocals, gift for narrative, and his mischievous sense of humour. George's sage sensibilities helped pull it all together.

It was just what the suburban boys wanted.

BROWNING: 'There were a lot of suburban dances, the sharpies used to go to them; there were certain dances that were just sharpies. The big groups of the time were Billy Thorpe and the Aztecs, and Lobby Loyde and the Coloured Balls. It was a scene, an atmosphere, I've never seen anything quite like it. AC/DC came in on the tail end of that. I'd stopped managing Billy Thorpe and the Aztecs, and there was this club called Berties, which had closed down, which I was also a part of. I'd been to London to the Hard Rock Cafe, and I thought, Oh, let's just deck it out and call it the Hard Rock Cafe. So I did that, and that's where AC/DC came in. They became fairly regular performers at the Hard Rock Cafe.'

George was of the old school that doesn't believe a band can even call itself a band until it's done at least 200 gigs. The heavy roadwork AC/DC did helped shape them as much as anything.

ANGUS: 'When we started, as a band, I don't think there was anyone around really that was doing what we did. I think here [Australia] was really what geared it for us; when you first start here, a lot of the places you play all everybody wanted to hear was rock'n'roll, you know. The faster the better. For us, that was great, 'cos that's what we do best. And we were lucky, because of George and Harry, from their time in the Easybeats; they always said that the best time they ever had was just playing rock'n'roll songs, and you know, they said, That's what you guys are going to do.'

Michael Browning proposed a scheme whereby his company Trans-Pacific Artists, which he ran in partnership with Bill Joseph, would absorb AC/DC's debts, set them up in a house in Melbourne, provide them with a crew and transport, and put them out to work, covering all their expenses, and paying them a wage. It was if nothing else an entree to the Melbourne scene.

BROWNING: 'Basically, they were broke. They needed an injection of capital, and an infrastructure placed around them, in order for them to continue.'

George decided Browning's offer was a fair thing.

Bon, like Malcolm and Angus, had already signed a recording-publishing contract with Alberts. Hamish Henry had been prepared to give Alberts his rights to Bon's publishing, but Bon said, Ask them for some money, you never made anything out of me before. So Hamish sold for $4,000. The recording deal Bon signed, calculating back from royalty statements, was for an equal share, as one of five members of the band, of 3.4 per cent of retail. Standard rate today is around 10 per cent; back then, it was around 5 per cent. Alberts has always been known for driving hard deals; no favouritism was extended just because Malcolm and Angus were family.

Before the band was despatched to Melbourne, they went into the studio with George and Harry and cut what would emerge as their debut album, *High voltage*. The band was barely roadtested after only six weeks, but whether it was ready or not, the market was crying out for it.

It is significant that the first single lifted off the album was a cover of the Big Joe Williams blues standard, 'Baby, please don't go'. Widely covered during the sixties, the song had been in AC/DC's set since just about day one.

Of the album's remaining seven tracks, at least one, 'Soul stripper', was credited only to Malcolm and Angus; and another, 'Love song', sounds more like a leftover from Bon's Fraternity days, even though the credit is shared. The remaining five tracks bear the Young/Scott/Young credit which would become so familiar. But to a great extent, not unexpectedly, the album was half-baked. The story goes that the band already had a number of instrumental backing tracks arranged, so Bon simply dipped into his notebooks full of rude poetry to find lyrics to fit. Drummer Peter Clack was asked to stand down during the sessions; the job was done by session-man Tony Kerrante.

Bon himself later conceded, 'That album was recorded in a rush'. 'It was actually recorded in ten days,' Angus said, 'in between gigs, working through the night after we came off stage and then through the day. I suppose it was fun at the time but there was no thought put into it.'

ROB BAILEY: 'Malcolm and Angus would just jam out things, like "She's got balls" — it was just two sequences — slap 'em together and away you go. If they worked, Bon stuck some words on them. He used to walk around with lyric books, and they were full of some of the funniest stuff you've ever read. You could sit down and read them and just laugh and laugh.'

CHRIS GILBEY: 'Because the band was called AC/DC I said to

them, Look, we've got to call the album "High voltage". So that was the title.

'Bon went away saying, What a great title, *High voltage*, we've got to write a song called "High voltage". Well, they wrote "High voltage", but it wasn't until after the album was finished, so it was too late to include.

'Then I created some artwork — we were just making it up as we went — I came up with this concept, of an electricity substation with a dog pissing against it. It's so tame now, but back then we thought it was pretty revolutionary. EMI didn't want to put it out because of the cover either, they thought it was very much in bad taste. But it came out anyway.'

After finishing the album, the band left Sydney for Melbourne, via Adelaide. The band got to Melbourne at the start of December, and holed-up in the Octagon Hotel in Prahran, until Browning found them the permanent accommodation he'd promised. Bon immediately looked up old mates like Mary Walton, and Darcy and his wife Gabby.

AC/DC would take off in Melbourne like a rocket. Boring old farts like Daddy Cool and the La De Das didn't know what had hit them as this snotty young support band blew them off stage.

BAILEY: 'It was a pretty exciting time, because we knew the impact we were having. The band sounded right there, it had a pack of very good songs, the act was great, the whole thing was just in your face, basically.'

AC/DC worked continually, anywhere and everywhere.

BROWNING: 'It was a mixture of pub type crowds to teeny-bopper girls to gays. There used to be a big gay circuit in Melbourne. Bon used to camp it up, he'd wear his leather stuff, and they fitted into that scene quite well.'

'I remember I first saw them, when they were still kicking around Melbourne,' said Joe Furey, who later became a friend of Bon's. 'There must have been about a hundred people there, and there was this little guy rolling around the floor playing guitar, and the whole thing was exceptionally loud, it was about one o'clock in the morning, and everybody was sort of going, Oh, give us a break, it's late. That was one thing I always admired about them, Angus in particular, was that there was a guy who had his act, and whether there was a hundred people there at one o'clock in the morning or what, he was going to do it. It wasn't like, Hey, there's no one here tonight guys, let's cut the set a bit short. Years later I thought that was probably the difference between them making it and not.'

If Bon felt the physical strain from the accident, he didn't let on.

DARCY: 'He was in pain. Those early gigs with AC/DC really stuffed him up. Once you've broken something, it's never the same again. He had to be jumping around singing his heart out, you had to wonder, How's he going to hack the pace? People wouldn't see him to the side of stage hitting his puffer.'

Juke magazine, which sprang out of Melbourne after *Go-Set* folded, called AC/DC 'new faces refusing to be restricted by an established music scene ... brash and tough, unashamed to be working at a music style that many describe as the lowest common denominator of rock music, gut-level rock, punk rock'.

The story went on to describe Bon, 'an old face', as 'charged by the unleashed drive in the group around him, as determined as the rest to have a good time on stage and off, as determined to shake Australian rock where it matters ...'

Juke was taken aback by 'these red-blooded young studs': 'AC/DC quite obviously are not lax to take advantage of the favours in the offering from some of their more ardent female fans. The adjoining motel room was busy with extra bedding and bodies.'

The party had started.

The band moved into a house in Lansdowne Road, East St Kilda. Malcolm and Angus had never lived away from home before, and so at the ages of 22 and 17 respectively, they were running amok, free to come and go as they pleased, to smoke and drink and swear and carry on. And fuck chicks.

ROB BAILEY: 'That place was a bit of a madhouse. A really big, beautiful old house, it had a flat out the back, with what I'm sure were hookers living there. You'd wake up in the morning and there'd be bodies strewn all over the place, nothing left in the fridge ...'

Bon divided his time between the house and Mary Walton's flat in Carlton. He and Mary had consummated their old friendship, since both their marriages had dissolved. But as much as Bon needed that retreat, he joined in the fun and games down at Lansdowne Road.

He wasn't going to be denied his second youth.

Christmas 1974, AC/DC was out on the road in South Australia.

BAILEY: 'We had this Ansett Clipper bus, we'd put the PA in the back, but every trip we did, it would break down. It was supposed to be the logistical answer to all the problems we had, but it just became a bigger logistical problem.'

Spending Christmas in desolate steel town Whyalla might not have been so bad for Malcolm and Angus, because everything was so new to them, and besides, they had each other. But Bon was hit by it. He thought of Irene, and where he found her he found Graeme, because Graeme had taken up with Irene's sister Faye, and they all lived together in Adelaide. And he thought of his folks in Perth, and his other brother Derek, who had a couple of kids by now.

So he had another drink, and rolled a joint. Bon had made his bed, he knew that, and he knew that these little pangs of longing would pass. The Youngs were his surrogate family now, and the music, to paraphrase Duke Ellington, was his mistress. And he could always count on the music's transcendence. The band was starting to find, and define — if not in so many words — its own identity; and self-discovery is an exciting, exhilarating process.

In that process, however, Malcolm and Angus decided the rhythm section had to go. Peter Clack just wasn't good enough, and Rob Bailey, whilst he played well, insisted on having his wife with him all the time. And that was a pain in the arse. Besides, he was too tall.

On returning to Melbourne in January, Bailey and Clack were separately summoned by Bill Joseph and given their marching orders. New drummer Phil Rudd came in almost immediately. Rudd, nee Rudzevecuis, had been playing behind singer Angry Anderson in latter-day Melbourne boogie band

Buster Brown. Erstwhile Coloured Ball Trevor Young (no relation) told him about AC/DC's vacancy, and he passed the audition.

Finding a new bassist proved more difficult. One guy lasted all of a few days. 'It's a pretty rare type of bloke who'll fit into our band,' Bon told *RAM*. 'He has to be under five feet six. And he has to be able to play bass pretty well too.'

Meantime, the band would play as a four-piece, with Malcolm on bass.

Late in January, George flew down to Melbourne to discuss with Browning plans for the release of the single and the album, and to stand in on bass when the band appeared at Sunbury.

Sunbury was a big part of Browning's marketing strategy. He had seen the reach the festival could have, even though it was rapidly decaying, and he wanted to use it as a launch pad in the same way Skyhooks had the year before. But the whole affair was a disaster, and certainly, it spelt the end of Sunbury itself. What happened was that Deep Purple were flown in as an exclusive international attraction; and, as Michael Browning put it, they just jerked everybody around, especially AC/DC. First Purple said they wouldn't play, so AC/DC had to be located in Melbourne and dragged out to the site to dep for them. Then they changed their mind. Angus remembers being disgusted when AC/DC arrived backstage to find a caravan designated to Deep Purple alone, and only one for all the other Australian bands. Then when Deep Purple finished their set, they refused to let AC/DC follow them. In response, AC/DC simply took the stage as Deep Purple's crew was still pulling down gear. A full-scale brawl ensued, on stage, in front of 20,000 people.

BROWNING: 'What really pissed me off on that occasion, and what really made it clear I had to get AC/DC out of Australia, was the fact that the local crew people actually sided with Deep Purple.

'It just really brought home how subservient Australians were to anyone from overseas. How if you really wanted to gain respect you had to go overseas.'

The *High voltage* album and 'Baby, please don't go' single were released simultaneously in February, with the Hard Rock Cafe throwing a 'Special AC/DC Performance, New Album, Adm $1.00'.

Rob Bailey was shocked to learn his work on the album had gone without credit. But then the packaging of *High voltage* gave precious little away, period (and when it did, incorrectly attributed 'Baby, please don't go' to Big Bill Broonzy). The story that got around was that George played bass on the album, though that story is still disputed by Rob Bailey, who certainly has never seen any money from Alberts.

Critical consensus, such as it was, had it that *High voltage* was, indeed, premature. That's when scribes weren't simply damning AC/DC as altogether rude, crude and uncalled for. But certainly the single, with its driving arrangement reminiscent of Golden Earring's 1973 smash 'Radar love', looked set to do business.

Mark Evans joined the band just after the record's launch. Evans, born in Melbourne in 1956, was working in the public service at the time, living with his mother in a council flat in Prahran and just mucking around on bass. There is no truth in the myth that Evans' introduction to AC/DC came when Bon stepped in to save him from copping a hiding off the bouncers at the Station Hotel. Rather, he was mates with one of AC/DC's roadies, who told him about them.

MARK EVANS: 'I just went down and saw them — Malcolm was playing bass then — and they gave me a copy of the album, I took it home, thought, Okay, that's fine, auditioned — straight in.

'That's all it was. I think it was more the look I had than anything else. I don't know how many times people would find out there was two brothers in the band, and they'd think it was Malcolm and me.

'At that stage, the band was on the bones of its arse. Like, I remember at one stage, Phil even running out of drumsticks, so we had to go and get pieces of dowel from the hardware store and fashion them into drumsticks.'

But it wasn't long before Evans was convinced to quit the public service.

EVANS: 'We had this roadie called Ralph, and he drove me home in the bus after I'd rehearsed with the band once, and he said, Oh yeah, things are looking pretty good, we hope to be in England this time next year. The whole arrangement for the band was to get out of Australia. And I remember thinking, Yeah, sure! But once I'd spent a month with them, I realised they were dead serious. One thing I will give them, they had an absolute solidity of purpose.'

Still, it would be some time before Evans met Bon.

EVANS: 'The audition was held in their house at Lansdowne Road. Bon wasn't there, I didn't actually meet Bon until the first gig. He was never at rehearsals. But I knew his name, I kept on hearing about Bon, and I knew, I'd seen the Valentines when I was a kid, at a concert, and I thought, That guy was called Bon, I wonder if they're the same one. I had this suspicion who he was.'

The scene at Lansdowne Road was one of pure debauchery. AC/DC encouraged every kind of rock'n'roll excess Melbourne had to offer — and Bon, Ronnie Roadtest, would again come very close to going over the edge.

EVANS: 'Bon's personality, and demeanour, would lend him to getting into areas where he would endanger himself. Just from, I'll try that! And just being lonely, I think, just being isolated.'

Bon offset the deeper rapport he shared with Mary Walton with the pleasures of the flesh available down at Lansdowne Road.

EVANS: 'A huge amount of women were hanging around, the only thing that kept [the band] going was the girls that would come around.'

It was this environment that inspired 'She's got the jack', though it's ironic that the song places the blame on a woman when it was the boys in the band, so the self-proclaimed legend goes, who were always running off to the clinic. Bon was well aware of the inflammatory nature of the song. When he wrote to Mary in April after she'd gone to London, he admitted it 'may get us castrated by Women's Lib'; and the recorded version also predicted an outraged crowd reaction.

For all the party atmosphere though, Malcolm and Angus

were deeply suspicious of outsiders — other than chicks, of course. It was part of the clan mentality. The approach was all or nothing, and if you weren't with them, you were against them. *RAM*'s editor Anthony O'Grady put it: 'They were like, you'd say, Hi, to them, and they'd look at you sideways like, Whaddya sayin' hi to me for?' Bon was accepted as one of the family, a blood brother, and Mary remembers they were 'very, very tight initially'. Malcolm and Angus looked up to Bon as older, wiser and braver. Bon, for his part, was protective towards Malcolm and Angus, but he felt less like a father figure than a conspiratorial uncle.

Mary remembers feeling a bit like mum and dad to them. 'They were still just babies, and they're sort of so straight in a way too. Angus didn't drink, at least not until his eighteenth birthday, when he got totally blotto, and I don't think he's ever had another drink since.

'They were so family oriented. They would go and buy a roast, a leg of lamb, and they'd bring it around and ask me to cook it. Because they just missed that home life, I guess.'

Angus once said 'Bon gets the women with flats who cook him dinners'. To which Bon replied, 'I like to put my feet up. Not to mention other parts of my body. They say to me, Are you AC or DC? and I say, Neither, I'm the lightnin' flash in the middle.'

Bon's code in life was like his attitude to money: if you got it, spend it. Don't expect it to last, don't expect it, period. This was his bravado. He sometimes didn't even seem to fear for his own safety.

Mary was in no position to carp, but when Bon took up with a young girl called Judy King, well, her response was to book a ticket to London. Judy King was an innocent set on a path of self-defilement. Maybe Bon liked the idea of bringing home a beautiful bird, and just a chick at that, with a broken wing. But maybe the attraction was more basic, as Darcy put it: 'I just think he did his balls over her, she was so young and fit and tight'.

Bon may or may not have met Judy before she showed up at a gig AC/DC played down the coast at Jan Juc — she was, after all, the youngest daughter in the same King family that

Vince Lovegrove had briefly boarded with in 1970. At that time, she was a promising prepubescent athlete, a sprinter. In 1975, at 17, she was an accident waiting to happen.

Within a couple of days of seeing AC/DC, Judy had hitchhiked up to Melbourne. Bon was there, and so was her older sister, Christine, who was working in a massage parlour and maintaining a heroin habit. At the same time, there were a couple of other girls hanging around the band who would wag school to do afternoon shifts in a parlour in Richmond. Within weeks, Judy too was on the game, sucked into the vortex, complete with a heroin habit of her own. If Judy was a working girl, she saved her best for Bon. That she was stoned all the time could be a bit of a drag, but she was caught in the classic vicious circle — she worked to make money to buy dope to make work bearable.

The affair flared up for the first time when Bon was hauled in by the cops to answer for a stack of allegedly pornographic photographs. Phil, a shutterbug, had taken some shots of Bon and Judy rolling in the hay.

'One morning,' Bon told *RAM*, 'I was in bed — completely out of it — and the chick who was living with me at the time was trying to hitch to work — also completely out of it — well, she got picked up by the police and she's so gone she can't speak. [The police were familiar with the house.] So they drive her back and run through the place ... and what happens but they bust me for pornography!'

Bon was pushing his luck.

'Baby, please don't go' was starting to sell.

AC/DC enjoyed the support of radio and 'Countdown'. Ever since 'Evie' was broken by 2SM, radio's faith in rock'n'roll was somewhat restored (if only briefly: the arrival of FM in the later seventies saw it turn back to 'classic rock').

'Countdown' rose in tandem with the music's renaissance. Coinciding with the arrival of colour television in Australia, 'Countdown' quickly became, as Chris Gilbey put it, 'all-powerful, the driving force behind making a hit single'. At its peak, the show had a fair whack of the country's population watching it. 'It was a tough call,' said Gilbey, 'because it was very much Melbourne, very much Molly.'

Molly and Bon knew each other from way back, of course, though their relationship was always tetchy. Molly was a Zoot, and not a Valentines, groupie. Much later, in 1978, Bon said to *RAM*, 'If you don't show your arse to Molly Meldrum all the time here, you're fucked'. But when Molly first saw AC/DC, at one of the Starlight gay discos, he was knocked out, as many people were, and of course, 'Countdown' too got value out of AC/DC.

But as much as AC/DC were becoming part of the Melbourne scene, they would always be interlopers. That they were for the most part native-born Scots, who would soon enough virtually renounce Australia altogether, was the least of it. Similarly, the fact that they were by rights a Sydney band didn't make them so unusual either, because Sherbet, Hush and the Ted Mulry Gang were also Sydney bands.

Melbourne's status as pop capital was because of 'Countdown', its live circuit, and Michael Gudinski's growing power. But it was one of the ironies of 'Countdown's' early days that beyond Skyhooks so much of its talent was effectively bussed in from Sydney, including also Marcia Hines, Jon English, William Shakespeare and John Paul Young.

AC/DC, either way, were like a cat among the pigeons on 'Countdown' — rough and ready for real. Sherbet were clearly little more than froth and bubble, and while Skyhooks were always likely to be 'outrageous', they were also playing down to their audience. But what really distinguished AC/DC was the sense they gave that they were just passing through, that all this was just a stepping stone to bigger and greater things. The transient likes of Sherbet and Skyhooks, it was obvious even then, would never surpass their 'Countdown' heights. But AC/DC had something more.

Back in Sydney, Alberts was well pleased with itself. Cabal-like even in its hometown, it had penetrated Melbourne, and its mafia as well. At a time during 1975–76 when you would sit down to watch 'Countdown' every Sunday night along with virtually every other household in Australia — as 'Countdown' lurched forward, coughing and spluttering and glittering, and if you didn't love it, you most certainly loved to hate it — Alberts enjoyed an incredible reign.

After 'Evie' put George and Harry back on the map, they followed on at the end of 1974 with William Shakespeare, a sort of cross between Gary Glitter and Pee Wee Herman, who scored two consecutive number ones with 'My little angel' and 'Can't stop myself from loving you'.

AC/DC, however, with their long-term potential, became Alberts' flagship act. Even then though, Alberts had other, fish to fry, which were bigger in the short term. Between AC/DC, John Paul Young and the Ted Mulry Gang, AC/DC was the only act not to score a number one before 1975 was out.

CHRIS GILBEY: 'It was an incredibly exciting period. Alberts was so small, it wasn't like a big record company, we were just making up the rules as we went along. And everything we put out became a hit.'

John Paul Young was virtual yin to AC/DC's yang. George and Harry wrote as well as produced his material, which only confirmed their range. 'Yesterday's hero' hit number one in April, from where 'Squeak', as Molly called John Paul Young, would go on to produce a string of classic disco-pop hits. The Ted Mulry Gang, produced by Ted Albert himself, had been on the road even longer than AC/DC — often with AC/DC — when in November, their second single, 'Jump in my car', went to number one.

This was good, George thought. He liked to work, just as much as he liked to drink; both of which he did with a peculiarly Scottish zeal. The studio at Alberts was finally finished, complete with a 16-track mixing desk shipped over from England. George and Harry spent their every waking hour there.

'Countdown' changed AC/DC's audience. The mixed sort of crowd the band had attracted to its live gigs was driven away by the onset of screaming teeny-boppers. Not all the little girls, after all, could swallow the smarmy Skyhooks or Sherbet, or Abba, the Bay City Rollers or Peter Frampton. There were plenty of tough chicks to whom AC/DC's rough and ready image appealed immensely. 'They were everything the Bay City Rollers didn't stand for,' said RAM. 'Maybe it was the way [Angus Young] jumped and rolled around stage like a demented epileptic while not missing a note of his guitar duties. Maybe it was the way Bon Scott leered and licked his lips while his eyes roamed hungrily up and down little girls' dresses.'

MARK EVANS: 'They could see, I guess, there wasn't bullshit involved, like high heels and make-up.'

Teen fandom is, of course, totally partisan, if only so much as it is also transient. The difference between AC/DC and Sherbet or Skyhooks was that AC/DC had the vision for longevity. Skyhooks may have been the first Australian band to write hit pop songs that had overtly Australian flavoured lyrics, but AC/DC surpassed the literal. They had a deep-seated originality that has stood the test of time. AC/DC's old recordings still sound good; who still listens to Skyhooks, or Sherbet?

AC/DC would outlive teen pin-updom because when the little girls abandoned them — as the little girls are wont to do — the boys came back. This to the band was a transient phase, as Australia itself was — a stepping stone to greater things. They were, indeed, just passing through.

At the end of March, as both the single and album entered the charts, and AC/DC were playing a good eight gigs a week in Melbourne and elsewhere, Bon's relationship with Judy King came to an ugly head.

Smack was never far from the surface of the seventies rock scene. Most people still came on like hippies, but the heady days of communal tripping were over. The me-decade demanded a more self-centred high. Harder drugs came in: at the up end of the spectrum, cocaine and speed; at the down end, heroin. No less an icon of cool as Keith Richards was brazenly a junkie.

Bon's drinking had been on the increase ever since he joined Fraternity in 1970. As AC/DC progressed, Bon consumed more of everything. His drinking could be on and off — he was a binge drinker really — but the grog was a persistent presence. And smoking pot was a habit he never kicked, never saw the need.

But if there's ever been a suspicion Bon was more deeply involved with narcotics than it seemed, the fact is that he never really got into heroin. Certainly though, he dabbled in it, as Judy King went down on it. On at least one occasion, in Melbourne in early 1975, he almost died of an overdose. But that, it seems, was enough to warn him off it, even though heroin would surround him and touch him as a codependent for the rest of his life.

Up until the Vietnam War, heroin had been present in Australia in small proportions, mainly in Sydney's Chinatown. As of the early seventies, the drug spread out of Kings Cross. Supply reached Melbourne, where it flowed through massage parlours and hamburger joints on Fitzroy Street, St Kilda.

Judy King was working in the parlour and spending every penny she earnt on smack. One night, Bon found her and Christine out of it as usual. But rather than just being on the nod, they were in high spirits, mischievous as sisters can be. They began goading Bon, trying to entice him to have a taste. Of course, if there was one thing Bon couldn't resist it was a dare, even if it went against his better judgement. He rolled up his sleeve.

The girls tapped out a measure of brown rocks into a spoon. Adding water and a dash of lemon juice over a match, the heated mixture dissolved. Judy drew it into a syringe through a filter from a cigarette. Bon took off his studded belt to use as a tourniquet. Judy found a vein, which wasn't difficult on Bon's sinewy arm, and shot him up.

Bon felt the sickly sweet warm rush, and then — nothing. He slumped in his seat. He had no tolerance, and he was so small anyway. He was turning a hideous blue-grey colour. But still breathing. Judy was hysterical. Stoned as she was, Christine thought quickly enough to shoot Bon up with some speed in an attempt to negate the heroin. She moved in a panicked sort of slow-motion, fumbling with the syringe, having difficulty finding the vein without any tension left in Bon's body. When she did, he let out a whimper, but that was all. It wasn't enough. An ambulance would have to be called. The girls did so. Waiting scared, Judy paced the room as Christine gave Bon mouth-to-mouth, and massaged his heart.

When you overdose on heroin, it is a near-death experience, but it has no romantic qualities. There's no light, or St Peter waiting at the gates, just a falling into a deep grey void. Your life does not flash before your eyes. You are not privileged with the opportunity to repent for your sins.

Bon sat bolt upright into consciousness when the ambulance officer revived him. He felt like he had been set rigid in cement, alive, looking out, but hit so hard upside the head he didn't know where he was. Certainly, he had no immediate past. Then he remembered, and that was the worst part, when he looked up and saw the scene: Judy in tears and Christine relieved, the ambulance men packing up their gear and shaking their heads. He remembered everything, and he felt so bad.

Later in life, Bon resented forgetting. After his body and mind had taken so much for so long, his memory, short and long-term both, was eroded. Remembering may be bad, but not being able to remember was worse. When he was younger, though the pain was sharper, his body was also stronger, more resilient. The spirit, spunkier.

Bon didn't blame Judy. But if this was a case of his nonjudgemental attitude getting the better of him, he was about to have the illusion literally beaten out of him.

In a report in Melbourne's notorious *Truth* newspaper, under the headline, POP STAR, BRUNETTE AND A BED: THEN HER DAD TURNED UP!, Bon told Dave Dawson: 'The girl's father had warned me once before not to sleep with her. But she is 17 and capable of making up her own mind. I had returned from Sydney the night before and she was there waiting for me. We were making love when our roadie Ralph knocked on my bedroom door and said someone wanted to see me urgently. I told him to come back in two hours because I was busy. Eventually I went to the door and was sprung by the girl's father. I was wearing only shorts. He said, I can see you've got your fighting shorts on. He took out his false teeth and said, Come outside.

'I followed him outside where he had two of his mates aged in their 30s. He said, Where's my daughter? I said, She will have gone by now. You are always bashing her up. Suddenly, he started punching me in the head and body. He knocked me into a rose bush and dragged me through it. Then his two mates came over and dragged him away. They could see that because I was just 5' 5" I didn't have a chance.

'That was the worst beating I have ever had. My manager Mike Browning took me to a dentist who couldn't stop laughing when I explained how my dental plate was smashed and my teeth were knocked out. It wasn't so funny for me because the dental bill will be at least $500.

'The girl's father has never given her any love and he certainly showed me none.

'After he bashed me he said, If she is not home by night I will send another ten blokes around to bash you. I'm certainly not going out of my way to see her again.'

Eerily, Bon had almost predicted this incident in Fraternity's 'Annabelle'.

Annabelle's got problems,
The doctors can't repair...
   When her daddy gets here,
He'll come knockin' on my door,
The next thing I replace
Bear-skin rug on the living room floor.

Bon was in disgrace.

In April, the band played a couple of momentous shows in Melbourne, as 'Baby, please don't go' peaked at number ten nationally, and the album lodged itself in the charts, not to leave for an unprecedented 25 weeks. Overseas, Michael Browning had his sister Coral sniffing around.

Coral, who'd met the band in Melbourne earlier in the year, was based in London, where she was well positioned in the music business, working for the management company that handled Bob Marley, Peter Tosh and Gil Scott-Heron. She was very enthusiastic about her brother's new charges.

AC/DC's staple Hard Rock gigs in Melbourne remained. On Sunday April 13, the band played a 'Heavy metal rock nite' with the Coloured Balls; the next Saturday, with Richard

Clapton. The very next day, they played bottom of a big bill on a Freedom from Hunger show at Myer Music Bowl. The following week, they supported the Skyhooks at Festival Hall.

It was a freezing cold Melbourne Sunday, but in spite of that, 2,500 still showed up at the Music Bowl. They paid $3.50 or $2.50 to see the Moir Sisters, Ayers Rock, AC/DC, Jim Keays, the La De Das and Jeff St John with Wendy Saddington. AC/DC, as one newspaper report read, 'got the best audience response... as they walked off the stage at the end of their set, nearly half the audience decided to leave as well'.

'Sure surprised us,' Angus said in *RAM*. 'Everyone always told us we were shit compared to real bands like Ayers Rock.'

Perhaps by way of a gesture of appreciation, AC/DC were presented after the show with supergroupie Ruby Lips. A good time was had by all, so much so that Bon later eulogised Ruby Lips in *Let there be rock*'s 'Go down'.

But not even success opened AC/DC up. Quite the opposite, in fact. 'Countdown' was an opportunity for bands to get together — when they were all busy working by themselves they seldom saw each other — but AC/DC didn't fraternise with other bands. Malcolm and Angus always regarded themselves as separate, if not superior, to other bands. Bon was always going off and meeting other people, but as band, a unit, even Bon hesitated to break formation.

MARK EVANS: 'We hated everyone as a matter of policy, the same way we hated hippies. No other band existed, except for maybe the Alex Harvey Band. Little Richard. Chuck Berry. Elvis. But no one admitted it. We just didn't even talk to other bands.

'Bon could get on with anyone, but Angus and Malcolm had this incredible tunnel vision where no one else counted. It must have had an effect on Bon too. There were times, I'm certain, when Bon would have gone home and said, Fuck this, I'm not putting up with it anymore.'

Being so antisocial was against Bon's natural inclination, after all. He had acquired the nickname Bon the Likeable, after Simon the Likeable, a character on 'Get Smart' whose secret weapon was that he was impossible to dislike.

MARK EVANS: 'My mother was in love with him. He'd come around for dinner and say, Can I do the dishes?'

AC/DC's aloofness and arrogance was party due to a perfectly well-placed self-belief, which is a quality any artist needs to become great. But it was also partly a mask for more troubling undercurrents — an insularity bordering on paranoia. It was an understandable defensiveness at the resentment, if not contempt, so often directed at AC/DC; but it was also a shield for insecurities. Maybe due to having had a sheltered upbringing, maybe just due to a lack of education, Malcolm and Angus were not blessed with many social skills. They were not articulate and were wary of other people. The family had always provided for them, and they saw little need to step outside it now. Bon just had to skate around such obstacles.

The band played with Skyhooks at Festival Hall. 'Needless to say what happened,' said a cocky Bon in a letter to Mary (AC/DC especially hated Skyhooks). Opening support act Split Enz were booed off stage. 'Only the little fellows of AC/DC really pulled it off,' reported the *Sun*.

Bon wrote further to Mary:

> I've been in the badbooks with everybody lately & I'm really such a nice person. I just don't understand...
>
> Off to Sydney on the weekend for a couple of weeks. Life is so boring in Melbourne, still no word on Europe but it shouldn't be too long. I reckon before Xmas or we'll all go fuckin' mad. We just keep copping the same shit week in and out. We feel like packin' it in and going to Sydney and spend all our time putting down songs in Alberts. The rest of the country's fucked. Don't I sound like a bloody whinger. Grrr!!!

The band had started dropping into Alberts on their Sydney visits. They were eager to start recording again, now that they had a proper line-up and even had a few song ideas. AC/DC never rehearsed, as such, but Malcolm and Angus would sometimes sit around together with acoustic guitars. Bon had his notebooks, and he was scribbling away — if scribbling's the right term because Bon's handwriting was extremely neat.

Bon wrote to Irene:

Times is tough at the moment cause Caruso 'ere 'as lost 'is vocal sound, know wat I mean. Worked so hard this last few weeks, it's just said, Fuck you lot I'm havin' a rest. Had to cancel a week's work but because we're in Sydney we can spend all our time in Alberts recording our next smash...

I miss ya sometimes 'Rene. Strange that comin' from me but it's true. It's probably the weather.

Bon was obviously still feeling a little sorry for himself. There can't have been much money around either, as Bon concludes the letter with a PS to Graeme: 'If you can still manage the other $50 I'd love ya f'rever. It's no fun waiting round to be a millionaire!!!'

During the May school holidays, AC/DC played a special 'Schoolkids Week' of daytime gigs at the Hard Rock. It must have seemed a lot like deja vu for Bon, being back under siege at what used to be Berties.

MARK EVANS: 'Because it used to be so packed downstairs, we used to get changed in Michael's office, which was right by the front door, go out on the street, unscrew the air-conditioning ducts and we'd go in through there; they'd close them up after us.'

On the Queen's Birthday holiday in June, in anticipation of the release of a new single, 'High voltage rock'n'roll', AC/DC played, for the first time, their own headline Melbourne Festival Hall show. Stevie Wright and John Paul Young supported. The concert was filmed, and it was this footage, with judicious doctoring, that would strongly argue the band's case in England.

CHRIS GILBEY: 'We did a video, this was before videos were the norm. I was pushing Ted, We've got to do videos. I wanted a video of AC/DC, and I wanted it to be something really sensational. Anyway, we shot it, it was live, they used four cameras, which was unheard of then, it was quite a big budget. And then we added applause at the beginning and end, which we took off the George Harrison *Concert for Bangladesh* album, to make it seem like it was live.'

The gig itself marked AC/DC's conquering of Melbourne. It had taken just over six months.

Bon wrote to Irene:

> HV (LP) has made a gold album (last week) so it caused a slight celebration. I'm going to give it to mum. So I told her to make a space on her mantelpiece. She told me to write some clean songs for the next one but. Wait till you hear a couple of 'em. The band is nothing like it was when you heard it last. Got a couple of better players, better equipment, and songs, just better all round. So watch out.

With Melbourne in the bag, and the lease up on Lansdowne Road, Sydney was beckoning. Bon wrote to Mary:

> I think we'll be living in Sydney soon and try to get the band as big up there as we are down 'ere. We all prefer Sydney to Melbourne but we wish we could drop in and see you over there instead. This country's driving us sane.

ten
sydney

'The Lifesaver was an ungilded palace of rock'n'rolling, easy-going degeneracy,' Anthony O'Grady wrote in *RAM* of the venue which in the mid to late seventies was 'the most prestigious place in Sydney for top and soon-to-be top Australian bands'.

'And if no one could exactly remember the details the next day — like how exactly how or why they ended up in bed with Mandrax Margaret, Amphetamine Annie or Tom, Dick or Harry from the band, well, no blame on either side for the oblivion of the night before. In fact, the bed-hop after the bop caused the place to be nicknamed the Wifeswapper.'

Sydney was a scene then which was very different to Melbourne. In the early eighties, with its pub circuit flourishing, Sydney superseded Melbourne as the centre of rock'n'roll in

Angus, Malcolm and George in the studio, Alberts, Sydney, March 25, 1976, during sessions for Dirty deeds done dirt cheap. *Angus: 'George'd take our meanest song and try it out on keyboards with arrangements like Mantovani. If it was passed, the structure was proven, we took it away and dirtied it up.'*

Australia; but in 1975, rock'n'roll was only just taking root in Sydney.

Initially, while the Youngs went back to Burwood, the rest of the band and crew stayed at the Squire Inn at Bondi Junction. Everyone was happy, not least of all because they were in the studio, recording the new album. Coral Browning was on the case in England. Bon was happy just to be away from Melbourne, free to lick his wounds. Of course, it didn't help that directly across the road from the Squire Inn stood the Lifesaver — before either of the buildings was demolished to make way for a shopping centre and car park.

The Bondi Lifesaver was a dive that's as much a part of Australian rock lore as the Largs Pier, Sunbury or the TF Much Ballroom. In 1975, it was a hotbed, its glory years only just beginning, before it faded by 1979.

'It was the sort of place where you'd be there three nights a week, even if there wasn't always bands on,' said Helen Carter, an old regular. 'It was a bar–restaurant, with music, which meant that you would get there at six, and didn't leave until two.'

With his room across the road, Bon made a virtual office out of the Lifesaver, where the band also played on occasion. He was able to enjoy his celebrity, because it was the same now in AC/DC as it was for the Valentines in Sydney, as opposed to Melbourne — less hysterical, less aggravating. Obviously though, Bon hadn't learned his lesson about jailbait, because he took up with the 16-year-old Helen Carter. But then, the gorgeous young Helen wasn't a fraction of the trouble Judy King was.

Helen, who grew up in Bondi, had been going to pubs since she was 13 or 14, and she was a smart kid. She went on to form Do-Re-Mi, who scored in 1985 with the feminist anthem 'Man overboard'.

HELEN CARTER: 'I saw AC/DC at the Lifesaver — I must have seen them a couple of times — and I just decided one night, I wanted to meet Bon, I wanted to talk to him about what was going on. I guess I thought that sex would be part of it, but I can't say honestly that I didn't think I wouldn't like to sleep with him. So I just walked up one night, and it was quite late, I had to go, so he said, Well, I'll ring you tomorrow. I thought, Sure...

'Anyway, he rings up, and I was at work, so he came and visited me where I worked, at a jeans shop, and he took me out for lunch, so you know, he was courteous I suppose. He always had that, a gentlemanly manner.

'Anyway, he said, Come up to the gig tonight. So I went up and I saw the gig, and I don't remember exactly what happened, but I know that that night we ended up going back to the hotel and I stayed there. And I stayed there quite a lot; and when they went to the Sebel, I stayed there a lot too.

'When they were staying in this Bondi Junction place, they were all in one room. Bon had the double bed because he was the oldest. Everyone else had single beds. But we would sleep together, with everybody else in the room. That kind of irked me a bit, because it was something I felt slightly embarrassed about, but he understood that, and certainly never forced me to do anything I didn't want to.

'He was incredibly gentle. He realised I'd never seen any of this stuff before — not that it was so outrageous, there was a lot of drinking, but there wasn't any drugs.

'The boys in the band — the singer in a lot of bands is frequently apart, you're not actually involved in the equipment or anything like that. Bon very much kept to himself. It was almost as if there was an invisible wall. The boys in the band pretty much did their own thing. But he loved them.

'He was a really hilarious person too; he was really very funny. Cheeky. He would do all sorts of things just to amuse himself and me. He had a very stable view. And meticulous. The way he dressed, and groomed. Just very plain, sleeveless shirt, a pair of jeans, but always perfectly laundered. Belt, studs, that was it, that was the uniform. And he always washed his hair. Dried it properly. He was very proud of his hair. He wasn't just the archetypal grub rock'n'roller.'

Bon and Helen hung out. They went dancing, Helen lurching on her clogs, at Ruffles disco, which was on the roof of the Squire. And they went to the Lifesaver, across the road. Sometimes AC/DC played there; other times, bands like Dragon, Buffalo, Cold Chisel or TMG played there.

HELEN: 'I mean, the stuff that used to go on in that backstage room at the Lifesaver! Like, the room was minute, and they always had the most unbelievable groupies, the loyalty was unbelievable. Not so much a lot of girls, but regular. One in particular, I just couldn't believe what she would do. People would have sex with this girl, in the dressing room. This was a normal thing. Not just blow-jobs either, penetration, actual fucking.

'You know, you'd just be standing there trying to hold a normal conversation, and Bon would just sort of turn his back and say, Don't look. The girl would just lift her dress and they'd start doing it. You'd think it couldn't have been any fun for anybody.

'I guess for Bon, that was part of the reason why he tried to set an example. Although, God, you couldn't have got a worse role model for drinking. I saw him drunk a lot, but he never lost control. He was actually a big sooky drunk, like some people get, just subdued, you know. Not at all violent. He would rather have had a nice soft relationship. He wasn't a wild man lovemaker or anything; to a certain degree that wasn't the only thing on his mind either, despite his songs, which are all just sex or rock'n'roll.

'He loved women, he used to love the attention of women, he loved to have lots of them around. I can say this now and it's probably crap because I look at that sort of behaviour and think, Well... but you see, the difference was, he didn't treat anybody like shit. Even then, when I was 16 and pretty naive myself, if there was any of that we-just-fuck-'em-and-dump-'em attitude, I would have thought, Oh, that's not very nice. But there was none of that.

'Bon would say, Look, if I seem a bit strange sometimes, don't get upset, talk to me about it later. It was obvious even then he was aware there was some kind of public persona that he had to uphold as soon as he stepped outside his hotel room. But in private, he used to say things like... You know, he always used to wear those sleeveless vests, and he'd stand in front of the mirror in the hotel room flexing his muscles. I'd be just sort of sitting there looking at him. He'd say, Do you think it looks good? You know, he was as vain as any other man I've ever known. And I'd say, Sure. He said, You know, I buy them two sizes too small so it makes my muscles look bigger. He was really crucially and sometimes a bit embarrassedly aware of what was expected of him, or what he thought was part of the performance, even though he was very sincere about it. What I'm saying is, he was a professional.'

AC/DC started to make an impression in Sydney, attracting much the same sort of disenchanted kids they had done in Melbourne. Hurstville Rock, a no-alcohol dance held every Saturday night in the local Civic Hall, became a stronghold gig. One witness recalls, 'When AC/DC played it was always huge. You could stand in the middle of the dance floor, and it would be bouncing up and down.

'There used to be this thing between the Westie rockers, who'd come because they liked AC/DC, and everybody else, because we thought AC/DC belonged to us. The audience was mainly surfies, you know. Thongs, jeans, Hawaiian shirts. All these underage people would sneak in, there was no grog allowed but there was always plenty going round. And joints — that was where I got stoned for the first time. People would just pass joints around! You'd get drunk, stoned and you'd chat up girls. AC/DC were great.'

Tireless roadwork was drilling the band into a lean, mean rock'n'roll machine. Malcolm said to *RAM*, before he virtually stopped talking to the press altogether, 'We used to worry about playing what was on the album — we used to play spot on — note for note off the album. But the people weren't getting off on it. Then George said, Don't play the songs, play to the people.'

Bon was also taking his role as songwriter more seriously.

HELEN: 'The thing about Bon was that he really did think a lot about what he was doing. He took it very seriously. He was a very meticulous person. So as a writer, he wouldn't just blurt stuff out. It would be very thought-out.

'Bon would leave his lyric notebooks lying around, and I was always fascinated by the way he would always write in capital letters. He'd have everything really neatly written out.

'And I think he found writing not an easy thing. Angus and

Malcolm used to write a lot of music; they'd just sit down and jam and come up with stuff. So there was a constant flow of material being put to Bon, to write, and I think in some ways that was quite a pressure for him.'

The band spent every spare moment during July at Alberts, mostly through the nights. To Malcolm and Angus it was just like being back home. George was there, running the show with Harry, his redoubtable partner. Also there, as a general trouble-shooter, was Sammy Horsburgh, former Easybeats tour manager who married Margaret Young.

MARK EVANS: 'It had a real family atmosphere. The Youngs, they're real Scottish working class, really good strong family, you know, staunch. Very hard though. Every time I'd go round there — and we used to play a lot of cards, after gigs, we used to play poker — there's seven brothers, and every time one or two or three or four of them would be punching the shit out of each other. Every time, without fail, someone would be having a blue!'

The old Boomerang House, where Alberts used to be located, on King Street in central Sydney, was owned by the Alberts family. It had housed radio-station 2UW, which the family also owned. Alberts Music was also there, though the studio wasn't built until 1975. That was Studio One; other studios were added over the next few years.

With a bare brick wall adjoining it, Studio One looked more like a squat than anything at the cutting edge of technology. Which it wasn't either.

EVANS: 'It was very small — we used to record in the side room, had two Marshall stacks and bass-rig, pointing towards the wall and miked up, and in what used to be the kitchen, drums in there — everything put down at once, generally the fire was in the first couple of takes.'

What Alberts had that money cannot buy, and what every recording studio in business aspires to, was a vibe, an ambience. In recording studios, the vibe is something that goes down on tape, that's why it's so important. Alberts' vibe was thanks to the mere presence of George and Harry, astute manipulators of studio psychopolitics who consistently drew the best out of performers. Their other great strength, as Chris

Gilbey put it, was that 'they were tremendously good song men'. In other words, they had ears for a hit.

TED MULRY: 'You didn't go into Alberts saying, Let's record this song. You were going in there to come up with another hit. And that was everybody's attitude, the buzz going round. You went in to come out with a hit.'

'George produces our material not just because he's our brother,' Angus said. 'He thinks we're good. If we were shithouse he wouldn't do it. But it's nice and easy-going in Alberts' own studio. When you get in there you feel relaxed and at ease.'

Bon told *Juke*, 'He's like a brother, no, a father to the group. He helps us with our writing. He doesn't tell us what to do, he just shows us how to get more out of the things we start.'

AC/DC were much better prepared this time around — tighter, more confident, and even having a few rough ideas to go in with.

Five more new songs were cut during July. 'High voltage' and 'The jack' were already in the can. Next to a rerecorded 'Can I sit next to you, girl', and a version of Chuck Berry's 'School days', 'Long way to the top', 'Rock'n'roll singer', 'Live wire', 'TNT' and 'Rocker' complete the album's track-listing. Nothing of it seems ill-considered.

EVANS: 'Malcolm and Angus would come up with riffs and all that, and then we'd go into the studio. Malcolm and George would sit down at the piano and work it out. Malcolm and Angus would have the barest bones of a song, the riff and different bits, and George would hammer it into a tune.

'Bon would be in and out when the band was recording backing tracks. Once the backing track was done, he would literally be locked in the kitchen there at Alberts, and come out with a finished song.'

Angus once said, '[George'd] take our meanest song and try it out on keyboards with arrangements like 10cc or even Mantovani. If it was passed, the structure was proven, then we took it away and dirtied it up.'

AC/DC would record backing tracks live in the studio — sound spilling everywhere as the band simply played so loud — and then vocals and guitar solos were overdubbed. George and Harry were careful to give the group its head, but at the same time, know when to stop.

MICHAEL BROWNING: 'Yeah, and then just embellish it a bit. George and Harry's most important criterion was rhythm, the whole thing had to just feel right. If you listen to those records today, they feel good.'

CHRIS GILBEY: 'The great thing George and Harry taught me, as a producer, was that if you've got a good rhythm track, you've got the beginnings of a record. If you don't, you've got nothing.'

TED MULRY: 'When AC/DC were recording, you'd walk into a session, and Angus would be on top of the quad boxes, in the studio. He couldn't just sit there, he'd be running around jumping up and down like it was a live performance.'

BROWNING: 'Malcolm used to come up with a lot of titles. He'd sort of come up with a title like TNT, and then he'd play some chords to fit that title, and a lot of the songs were just developed that way. Bon would go away and write a song about TNT, or this or that.'

In his notebooks, Bon had lyric ideas to put to music. Locked in the kitchen, he ran lines through his head one last time, mouthing them out, getting it right. As a singer, Bon was a screecher (there are those who believe his voice was never the same after the accident that did so much damage to his neck and jaw), but like Sinatra or Dylan, Bon's greatness was in his phrasing. And it was the interplay between his phrasing and his words, in their economy, that proved just how seriously he took songwriting.

HELEN: 'Looking through his lyric books, you would see different versions of things. The sort of lyrics they were, you think, Oh, any old dickhead could write that. But it's not true. Even the simplest of lyrics, his timing and metre, he spent a lot of time on.'

TNT was the album that really introduced AC/DC as a band. It still contained a few naff tracks, but its forcefulness was undeniable. If it was as impatient as it was bold, it was impressive for that too. 1975 needed rock'n'roll like this. And certainly, the album's one-two opening punch is as powerful as any ever recorded, with Bon virtually encapsulating his entire life in 'Long way to the top' and 'Rock'n'roll singer'.

Completing side one, 'The jack' overplayed its card-table metaphor, while 'Live wire' was as good a piece of braggadocio as AC/DC produced. 'TNT', the album's title-track which opens side two, was on a par with 'High voltage' — fair but disposable. Next to 'Can I sit next to you, girl' and 'School days', 'Rocker' was hilariously frenetic.

With the new album in the can, sales of *High voltage* were still powering due to the boost provided by the release of the new single of the same name. The band appeared on 'Countdown', Bon doing his Tarzan routine wearing nothing but a lap-lap.

GILBEY: 'At that time, we'd done what we thought were phenomenal units, about 70,000 on it, and that was unheard of, and then the single 'High voltage' took the album up to 120-125,000, and we thought, My God!

'We didn't think AC/DC would become a world-wide phenomenon the way they have. We were all just occupied, tight-focus, on making the act survive. It was just, get a record away. Keep having hits. Try and keep moving. And then it was, Hey, let's get outside the country and see if we can sell it overseas. That was the next step.'

Chris Gilbey was possibly thinking this way when everyone else was thinking about England because he himself had already taken a knock-back on AC/DC overseas. When he went to Midem in January, 1975, representing Alberts generally, he encountered more people interested in William Shakespeare! George, in turn, didn't mind if Gilbey was concentrating on Australia, because Michael Browning was chipping away in England. Browning had sent Coral a copy of the video AC/DC had shot at their Melbourne Festival Hall Queen's Birthday concert, and she was hawking it around London.

To promote a free show at Sydney's Victoria Park in early September, which on the back of the 'High voltage' single would serve as a Sydney launch for AC/DC, Chris Gilbey devised the 'Your mother won't like them' advertising campaign for radio station 2SM. It worked a treat. The single peaked at number six nationally.

GILBEY: 'It was like, instant attitude. Nowadays, everything is premeditated. Back then, we didn't have to philosophise, and come up with a psychological profile of the consumer, to figure out why it was we wanted to sell a bad-boy image in order to have those kids that were alienated from their parents love this group. We just thought, Hey, this is exciting, this is cool. Either you had it or you didn't have it. Rose Tattoo, either you have it or you don't.'

It was another cold Sunday afternoon when AC/DC played at Victoria Park with Stevie Wright and Ross ('I am Pegasus') Ryan. The show was unremarkable — as usual, the band blew everyone away — save for the fact that it saw Angus climb astride Bon's shoulders for the first time.

Bon had obviously climbed back in the saddle because, as Angus said, 'That notorious leader of thieves and vagabonds, Bon Scott, to celebrate the success of the show in Sydney, went out and got a new tattoo and pierced his nipples for earrings. The other boys celebrated in other ways.'

The band was right on target.

In September, AC/DC went back down to Melbourne to renew their expired agreement with Michael Browning — a five-year management contract was signed — and to group for an extensive national tour to promote the release, before Christmas, of the new album. Of course, the album wouldn't eventually be released till February, but this is rock'n'roll, after all.

Bites were being registered overseas. Bon wrote to Mary, 'A&M is wrapped in the band as is John Peel the DJ. Reckons we're the band England needs and we agree.' He also wrote to Irene, 'I'm not doing too bad on the booze thing these days and am getting drunk quite regularly. But I'm a peaceful drunk now. Have I still got any friends in Adelaide?'

Starting in Perth, the tour would take the band all over Australia before winding up in Sydney on Christmas Eve. Before heading to Perth, the band played a few shows in Melbourne.

Booked to play a week of free lunchtime gigs in the Miss Myer department of the big Myers store in the city, the band had barely started their first set on the first day when they were overrun by hysterical girls. Reports of numbers vary between 600 and 5,000. The shop and its fixtures were turned upside down; strangely, a shoplifting frenzy was not reported. The rest of the week was promptly cancelled.

MARK EVANS: 'It was just bedlam. It was probably the only time I thought one of us was going to get hurt. It was really scary.'

The band had to run for their lives. Bon, however, even as he fled, still managed to sneak a peek over the saloon doors of the changing rooms.

A Premier Artists worksheet for the band for the second week of September saw them playing six gigs, plus recording an episode of 'Countdown', between the Wednesday and Saturday, for total earnings of $3,610, which included a $160 performance fee from 'Countdown'. Certainly, it made their old $60 per week pay packet seem inadequate.

At an average of $600 per gig, AC/DC played the South Side Six on Wednesday and the Matthew Flinders Hotel on Thursday, both Bayside suburbs beer-barns, where the band played one set between 10 a.m. and 11.30. At the Matthew Flinders, a scuffle in front of the stage involving Angus cost drummer Phil Rudd a broken thumb, necessitating an immediate stand-in. On the Friday, with old drummer Colin Burgess on Rudd's stool, the band played a free show at the Eastlands Shopping Centre in Ringwood, between 6.00 and 7.00, and then later they appeared at the International Hotel. At 6.00 on Saturday night, the band recorded an appearance on 'Countdown', then played the Tarmac Hotel between 10.00 and 11.30 and then the Hard Rock Cafe between 1.30 and 3.00. On Sunday, the band flew to Perth.

Bon visited his mum and dad in Perth. Chick and Isa were very impressed by the boys. It was the first time they'd all met each other, and they were such nice boys, thought Isa.

The band worked their way back to Melbourne playing through South Australia, visiting even the dreaded Iron Triangle again.

Right on the back of recording *TNT*, the band was in blistering form, but it didn't always get the reaction it might have liked.

'We had been on a tour with AC/DC which led to our first recording ... our big break,' Angels singer Doc Neeson recalled. '... and because we were a covers band and they were an original band, we were getting encores and they were getting booed. People knew our songs and thought that they were a dirty heavy metal band.' AC/DC, nonetheless, went home and told George about this hot new band called the Keystone Angels and, as the Angels, they would serve Alberts well.

MARK EVANS: 'The band itself wasn't hyped, it was good, a good band; but the mechanics of the thing, it was hyped-up, there's no question about that. I don't know any successful band that isn't. But if it had have been left to the reaction from live gigs alone, we would have been struggling.'

The fact that Angus was pushed as the focal point didn't bother Bon. Armed with an axe and a fag and dressed in his school uniform, Angus provided an image so readily identifiable, it became a symbol for the band. In fact, Bon was almost relieved that some of the heat was off him on stage. Jealousies simply weren't possible anyway. The power structure within the band was set, and if you didn't like it, you just had to lump it. Nobody, outside Malcolm and Angus, was indispensable, it seems, including Bon. But if Bon was granted special dispensations, he came close at times to going too far. Like when he OD'd. But even then, the Youngs couldn't come at sacking him. Blood was thicker than water, after all.

Bon was elusive, and though he could have been annoying on a day-to-day level, his saving grace was that he always came through in the end. He was always running late, and he might often be worse for wear, but he never once failed to show, and he always gave everything he had.

Back at the Freeway Gardens Motel in Melbourne, where the band now based itself, Bon was still likely to wander off by himself. But more often than not, he was hanging out with Pat Pickett. Pickett had been living in provincial Geelong, employed at the local meatworks, when he heard about AC/DC, and so he immediately made a beeline for Melbourne. He joined the band's crew in a nebulous sort of role, similar to that which he enjoyed with Fraternity, as Bon's consort, his partner in crime.

Bon's frame of mind was pure reckless abandon.

MARK EVANS: 'We were always looking after him, looking out for him, and we were only kids ourselves. You'd say, Hey, where's Bon? I remember carrying Bon home and putting him into bed. But he had this thing about him where you wanted to take care of him.

'You could see his charm kicking in. You could also see Bon Scott the singer of AC/DC kicking in when the press was around, you know.'

The Freeway Gardens, a shabby motel at the mouth of the Tullamarine Freeway in North Melbourne — devoid of any sort of garden — was a haven for many a rock'n'roll band. TMG stayed there, among others.

HERM KOVAC: 'Bon used to carry around this little shaving kit. That was his whole baggage. It contained a toothbrush, toothpaste, one pair of jocks and one pair of socks. That was it. He'd wear his jeans till he might wash them at the hotel, and so he'd just get around in his jocks till they were dry. But otherwise, he'd have a pair of jocks and socks on the go, and he'd wash them each night in the sink, hanging them up in the bathroom, and get the fresh pair out of the little bag. He'd rotate them. He travelled very lightly.'

MARK EVANS: 'He would do anything. I remember one time he made this bet. It was the middle of winter in Melbourne and he said he'd dive into the swimming pool. Someone took him on for five dollars. A stupid bet. He said, Make it ten. So we went up to the third floor, the balcony, and he just dove straight in. Got out, Where's my ten bucks? He'd do these things that were just over the top.'

Mark didn't know Bon had a history of high diving.

The debauchery of Lansdowne Road continued unabated at the Freeway Gardens. The band, after all, was even bigger now. And so, it seems, were some of the fans.

It was at the Freeway Gardens that Bon met Rosie, subject of the all-time great paean to large ladies, 'Whole lotta Rosie'. The band held in very high esteem anything that was what they called 'depraved', 'evil' or 'filthy'. Put Pat Pickett and Bon together and the conversation would take a seriously funny downward turn. Scatology was a favoured topic, but that was just the beginning. The band ran an ongoing competition — the prize being booze which they would all hoe into — to see who could pull off the most disgusting, depraved, filthy act.

Bon's bedding of Rosie was a big winner in these stakes, but as the lyrics to the song suggest, he derived a lot more pleasure from the experience — 'Whole lotta Rosie' is actually very affectionate — than the band might have imagined.

Rosie was a Tasmanian mountain woman who had started showing up at gigs. An open challenge was thus issued.

PAT PICKETT: 'We were sharing a room at the Freeway Gardens, and I woke up one morning and looked over at Bon's bed and I thought, Jeez, he's done it! There was this huge pile of blubber lying there, but I could see underneath it, this tiny little arm with tattoos on it was sticking out!'

EVANS: 'That's the one thing I will say which was mythical about the band which was pretty true, and that was the amount of females we used to get hold of. It was ridiculous. I used to be fairly lucky, but I was nothing on Bon. He had four days in a row where he got what we called a trifecta, three different girls each day for four days in a row. The man was a genius, I don't know how he did it. He had a huge ...'

Penis is the word that might complete that sentence. At least several reports suggest that Bon was extremely well hung. He liked to show it off too, dressing all to one side in jeans that were inevitably almost sprayed on.

EVANS: 'This other myth, the image the band had as this heavy drinking, you know, brawling bunch, it couldn't be further from the truth. We never got thrown out of one hotel.

'Bon didn't get into any more trouble than your usual bloke on the road. The whole thing was this huge image. There were a couple of instances, a couple. I remember once at the Matthew Flinders, Angus, because he used to spin around on the dance floor, a couple of guys started kicking into him. I remember Pat, Phil and myself jumping off the stage, and getting into that. Phil actually broke his thumb, and so we had to get another drummer for a while, when we were in Perth, we had to get Colin Burgess back.

'But Bon, you could hit him over the head with a baseball

bat, and he'd just say, Hey, what are you doing? But if you hit someone he was with with a baseball bat, you couldn't hide anywhere. Ladies particularly. Guys, he might say, You asked for it. If one of the guys in the band got into trouble, Bon would tell them the next day, You were an idiot last night. But if it was someone you were with who obviously couldn't take care of themselves, my God!'

Pat Pickett remembers a time when Bon was at a pub with Irene, who moved to Melbourne, and a guy was hassling them, perhaps just because Bon was Bon. The guy was a well-known hard man. Bon ignored him, until he went too far. As they were leaving the pub, the guy pulled Irene's ponytail. Bon had a breaking point, and he had just reached it. He took the guy outside and gave him what witnesses remember as a fist-beating to within an inch of his life.

EVANS: 'He was really a pretty mild mannered sort of guy. I mean, I never saw him lose his temper. He had this equilibrium, and he was very, very polite, a real gentleman. Once I saw him get the shits, and it was the strangest thing...

'The band appeared on the *TV Week* 1975 King Of Pop awards show... We played live, and Bon had a terrible time, everything went wrong for him; the mike lead got caught in his shoes, everything. When we got off stage, we went downstairs, and we had to break the lock on the door to get into the bar. There were just all these stacks of *TV Week* there, with Daryl Braithwaite on the cover, the King of Pop. Bon was just standing there staring at them, and he said, Have a fuckin' look at this! And then he started just laughing, maniacally, he said, I don't believe this, and he started ripping up all the magazines. And then, from that point on, that night, he was the most uncouth, awful, rude person I've ever seen. To the point where he took this turkey off the table and was drinking champagne out of it. He just had this turkey under his arm, drinking out of it, offering it to everyone. Something snapped, that one time.'

The band lit out of Melbourne to play rural Victoria, and then ran through Sydney, before returning to Melbourne at the start of November to play a special Melbourne Cup Day show at Festival Hall. Hush supported.

Michael Browning, meantime, was in London. Atlantic Records had gone crazy for AC/DC. A deal would be struck. The album would be released, and the band would go over, sometime in the new year.

All November was spent on the road. The bus was in service when distances weren't too great, speed not of the essence. After Cup Day, the band spent a week in Adelaide, then toured through the deep north of Queensland. Back in Sydney, they played at the opulent State Theatre on November 30. The first two weeks of December were spent in and out of Sydney, swinging through the ACT, before making a quick dash to Brisbane to play a Festival Hall show on the 14th.

It was a hectic time, and Bon was obviously feeling the strain. He wrote to Irene:

What a cunt of a night. Just got back from Canberra a day early and no one is expecting us up until tomorrow. Got no booze, no dope and no body except my own to play with. Shit. And to top it off I left my black book in the bus, which broke down in Canberra...

I reckon we'd have to be the hottest band in the country at the moment. Not bad for a 29-year-old 3rd-time-round has-been.

I don't care if I never get a divorce cause I'm not planning on marrying again unless she's a millionaire and I think my chances of finding one are scarce. But when I pull out my photy album I like saying, And this is my wife. They all fancy you and tell me what taste in spunk I've got...

I'm going through a fucking funny period at the moment. Hope you don't mind a heart balm letter. Don't wanna settle with anybody because I'm always on the road and won't be here long and on the other hand there's twenty to thirty chicks a day I can have the choice of fucking but I can't stand that either. Mixed up. I like to be touring all the time just to keep my mind off personal happenings. Become a drunkard again and I can't go through a day without a smoke of hippie stuff. I just wanna get a lot of money soon so I can at least change a few little things about myself (more booze and dope). Not really. I just wanna be famous I guess. Just so when people talk about you it's good things they say. That's all I want. But right now I'm just lonely.

After Brisbane, AC/DC worked their way down the coast to reach Sydney by Christmas Eve, to play a big shebang at the Royal Showgrounds. Bon spent Christmas with the Youngs, then flew to Adelaide to spend some time with Irene and Graeme, and his girlfriend Faye. 'My wife and her boyfriend, that is,' he wrote to Maria, from whom he had received an unexpected Christmas card. 'Graeme wants to marry my sister-in-law. I'm saying nothing.' Bon also dealt with some legal matters in Adelaide pertaining to his bike accident. He was still paying off bills.

The band played in Adelaide on New Year's Day. Again, as Molly reported in his column in *Truth*, 'The street punk kids of Australian rock and roll, AC/DC, were the cause of a minor riot'. The band had the power cut on them and Bon, inevitably, incited a storming of the stage in protest. 'Power or no power, they were not going to be deterred,' Molly went on. 'Because, would you believe, Bon Scott appeared in the middle of the crowd, on someone's shoulders, playing bagpipes!'

Bon wrote further to Maria:

I'm out on the road again but this time between Melbourne and Adelaide on the coast route. It'll be the third town tonight and there's twenty-one more to go. We've had a week off between Xmas/NY but now it's back to work. Got a couple of weeks off after this tour to record and tie up all the loose ends before leaving for England.

All this touring has worn me out. But it's selling a lot of records and I'm seeing a lot of the country and people that you don't realise exist, so it can't be too bad.

I'm finally making money Maria. About $500 a week and it's all in the bank... I just hope I'm not still stupid cause now I can make a good start at doing something good. Don't know what though. I haven't finished rocking yet and that's all I want to do right now.

With the Atlantic deal now finalised, the rumour was that AC/DC would support labelmates, American band ZZ Top, on a British tour to coincide with the release of their first album; then maybe even do something with the Stones, also on Atlantic. Either way, the band's departure was now certain. It was just a matter of exactly when.

Bon had dreamed as a boy of leading a pipe band, marching beside it swinging the baton, feeling the sounds flow through him, feeling responsible and proud, the agent of so much joy as the drone and flutter reverberated in the air all around him. Now the dream was coming true.

A performance through the middle of Melbourne, on the back of a flat-top truck, was arranged by 'Countdown' so they could shoot a video of 'Long way to the top', AC/DC's new single. Three professional pipers accompanied the band.

This was different to what Bon had originally envisaged, but it was better. Bon was singing his own song. It was rock'n'roll — and it was the pipes.

Traffic stopped as the boys drove slowly through the city and fans ran alongside to catch a glimpse of their idols. Stomping along the length of the moving truck's tray-top (just like Elvis), Bon looked up to see the buildings of Melbourne passing above him under a blue sky and looked down at the adoring faces, and sensed everyhow the power of the music. It infused all his senses, his own body was as if wired, responding involuntarily. Bon was swimming with the power. This was what he lived for.

'Long way to the top' has become an anthem. Certainly, it was AC/DC's best single to date. Bon was best when he was working to his own brief, rather than writing to order — he expressed himself more honestly, more evocatively.

In 'Long way to the top', it's as if Bon acknowledges he's living on borrowed time, and luckily at that. But even then, or perhaps for that very reason, the song remains celebratory.

At the end of January, 'Long way to the top' peaked at number five. Three singles, three hits, and each outperforming the last — it's a record any act would envy.

When the album was released, sent out to media wrapped

in a pair of ladies knickers, it sold 11,000 in the first week, and shot to the number two spot, kept out only by Bob Dylan's *Desire*, which had just knocked *Abba* off.

It was decided then that the band should go back into Alberts to cut another album, not knowing how long it might be before they got another opportunity to record. 'In those days,' said Michael Browning, 'you didn't take two years between records. It was nothing to record two or three in a year.'

The band's rapidly rising star was acknowledged when they arrived in Sydney in February and checked into the Sebel Town House, the five-star hotel still chosen by visiting rock royalty.

HELEN CARTER: 'I was with Bon the day he got a $500 royalty cheque. They were staying at the Sebel, so obviously by then they were making a bit of money, but this was the first royalty cheque he'd got which was substantial, and he was just like, Look at this! His face lit up, he was just really happy at being paid for something he loved doing.

'He was of the old school, where rock'n'roll was everything. To him, it was still rebellion. I mean, it wasn't like he was a guy who was saying, Oh, I've been doing gigs for years now, how come I haven't got any money? That didn't come into it. He was an innocent, I suppose.

'By that stage, everywhere you went there'd be women hanging around, in the hotel foyer, outside the venue, or the dressing room. So Bon would say, Here's the key to the hotel room, I'll be up in half an hour; because he had to deal with not just women but fans. And he really felt he had an obligation to hang around and talk to them.'

The band cut *Dirty deeds done dirt cheap* during February. So quickly after *TNT*, they had virtually nothing up their sleeves.

MARK EVANS: 'Angus came up with the title. I remember when I heard it, I thought it sounded familiar, and ten years later I worked it out — it's some cartoon character, off 'Beanie and Cecil', the villain, Captain Pugwash, he used to say that.'

HELEN: 'Bon would play demos of music he had to write to. He'd just sit around the hotel room and have it going in the background, formulating ideas. He always had a cassette player, and at the time, his favourite song was "Love to love you, baby", by Donna Summer. Which shows another side to him, musically.'

Bon still sought a lot outside the band.

HELEN: 'Angus is pretty straightforward. Bon was almost an intellectual in comparison. I mean, the only way he could gauge anything, or write about anything, was to talk about other stuff, and we did a lot of talking. It wasn't like we went back to his room, had sex for 12 hours and that was that. To be quite honest, I don't think, say, talking to the road crew or whatever, would have been terribly stimulating to him.'

But of course, Bon could mix it with anyone. And if women weren't present, at least not ladies — as distinct from those with whom your secret was safe — then Bon could be a very bad boy. Bon's mythic persona was further fuelled by the subsequent publication of a feature story in the Australian edition of *Rolling Stone*, which opened on Bon vomiting after a show, the victim, apparently, of a 'bad bottle of Scotch', whatever that means. In reality, his drinking was fair to middling. Anthony O'Grady witnessed the same episode, as the band played a few final gigs in Sydney whilst recording the album, and he reported in *RAM*: '[Bon] sometimes gets the same look that battle-scarred alley fighters have — a look of indifferent bloodlust. Kick 'em in the teeth and they'll just spit blood and get up again.' At the same time, O'Grady remembers that at the end of that night, back at Burwood, Bon and he were ushered outside to wait in the car when George wanted to 'talk business' with his brothers, and Bon happily acquiesced, proceeding to simply pass out in the back seat.

HELEN: 'I know that when you get a bit successful, because the pressure and everything else increases, you do drink too much. Especially if you've just done a fantastic show or something, you come off stage and you want to … But it didn't rule his life. It was part of his life, but it wasn't the major feature. The major feature was purely and simply getting up on stage and doing it, he just loved that.

'He used to gargle with Coonawarra red and honey, every morning. This is giving away trade secrets. But that was the secret to his great voice.'

Dirty deeds was rushed; but then, everything was rushing for AC/DC at that time. With an English release of the *High voltage* compilation album now scheduled for May, and a British tour supporting Paul Kossoff's Back Street Crawler locked in for April, the flight to London was finally booked, for April Fool's Day.

When it was completed, *Dirty deeds* was put in cold storage. It emerged as an equally inconsistent echo of its predecessor. The title track was more sloganeering; 'Big balls' is pure vaudeville double entendre; and 'There's gonna be some rockin'' and 'RIP (Rock in peace)' are pretty much the same song, both mindless chugalug boogies. 'Squealer' was an inferior sequel to 'Rocker'.

The remaining four tracks save the album. 'Problem child' fittingly became a staple of the band's live set, a crunching, threatening flurry. 'Ain't no fun (waiting around to be a millionaire)' is a boogie elevated by a superior lyric and greater extension on the band's part.

But it was the album's closing two tracks, 'Ride on' and 'Jailbreak', that were its killers, a double-punch equal to that which opened *TNT*. 'Ride on', despite borrowing the chords from ZZ Top's 'Jesus just left Chicago', is a statement of Bon's tomorrow-never-comes credo whose poignance has assumed a rueful dimension since his death. It segues abruptly but perfectly into 'Jailbreak', a virtual manifesto for AC/DC — relentlessly thudding release.

In March, as 'TNT' itself was released as a single, the band flew to Melbourne to attend a gold record reception cum formal farewell party. Three plaques each for *High voltage* and *TNT* were presented. The band regrouped in Sydney to play one final show at the Lifesaver before they left (at which show Angus stripped for the first time; flashing his bare behind, a routine that features in AC/DC's shows to this day). The night before flying out, a celebration was thrown at Burwood for Angus's nineteenth birthday.

HELEN: 'It was a very quiet affair, just a couple of pizzas and a Billy Connolly record. Bon was excited, but sceptical about it [going overseas]. You know, being 30, not that that's old, but in terms of starting a career, internationally, in an industry which at that stage, if you were an Australian band, you may as well not have existed.'

As 'TNT' climbed the charts, eventually peaking at number eleven, Michael Browning played down the band's departure. He'd been through it all before. 'I've seen too many Australian groups say, Oh yeah, we're going over to England and we'll be big, and when it doesn't happen straight away, no one in Australia wants to know about them anymore,' he told *RAM*. 'AC/DC are an Australian group and we don't want to spoil anything we've built up here.' Maybe he was just trying to cover his arse.

The band couldn't have cared less. As Angus told *Record Mirror & Disc* shortly after arriving in England, 'Success there [in Australia] means nothing. We left on a peak rather than overstaying our welcome, and set out to plunder and pillage.'

Spencer Jones, whose own band the Beasts of Bourbon would later cover 'Ride on', remembers seeing that last show they played. 'It changed my life. There was this girl there, and she got up on stage and started to do a strip. She was quite a big girl, and she was just dancing around without any clothes on. So Bon picked her up. He just put one hand around her neck, and one on her crotch, and he just raised her above his head and stood there with her aloft like that. It was the most macho, sexist pose imaginable, but Bon could get away with things like that.

'And while all this was going on, Angus was up on someone's shoulders, and he was trying to get to the bar, this long bar they had at the Lifesaver. The place was packed, you couldn't move, but somehow they punched their way through, the people sort of parted like the Dead Sea. Angus hopped off at the bar and he did the duck-walk. Meanwhile, Bon's just standing there with this girl on his shoulders. It was incredible. And then when Bon let her down, the roadies came on to help her, but they didn't just throw her back into the audience, she was ushered backstage.'

HELEN: 'No one else could get away with that stuff. I think that was what Bon actually loved about doing what he was doing, he really could, if he wanted, do anything he wanted. And he loved that. He loved that freedom.'

eleven
england

It was a hot summer in England in 1976, a long, hot summer. The country was on the eve of the Queen's 1977 Royal Jubilee, gearing-up for a sustained, jewel-encrusted celebration of monarchistic irrelevance. It was simultaneously on the verge of a revolution.

To chic, would-be subversives, all the Royal Jubilee did was provide a target for pot shots. Following their December 1976 debut single 'Anarchy in the UK', the Sex Pistols' incendiary rewriting of 'God save the Queen' caused the sensation it was designed to. In doing so, the Pistols sparked the world-wide cultural sea change called punk rock.

With his family, Bon had left Scotland to come and live in Australia in 1952, the same year as Queen Elizabeth's coronation. Now he was returning to Britain in time for her jubilee. He couldn't have cared less. He didn't care much for punk rock either.

Left: On tour in Germany, October, 1976. Mark Evans: 'Jeez, Bon was on the turps early that day.'

185

Punk rock, British-style, liked to think it was a political movement; but it was less a political decision than it was, first and foremost, an aesthetic one. It was an aesthetic decision inspired negatively, by an unspeakable hatred for hippies and for practically all the music that then prevailed.

Punk's anger was well-directed; punk was a necessary and overdue flushing out of the stagnant waters rock'n'roll had become. Rock'n'roll was never in a worse state than it was in the midseventies; it was the exclusive corporate domain, to use the preferred punk appellation, of nothing but boring old farts.

Punk ultimately changed the face of rock'n'roll, and more beyond. But like glam, punk was nothing so much as a return to rock'n'roll classicism: the traditional values of teen rebellion and hit-single songwriting. It was getting back to basics because rock'n'roll — if it could be dignified with the name — had lost touch with its underclass roots. It's just that punk was packaged in apocalyptic urban-guerrilla garb.

In April, 1976, when AC/DC arrived in London, the storm was still just brewing. The scene was still stuck in torpor. One of the first gigs AC/DC played, late in the month, was the Nashville Rooms in Kensington, where the Sex Pistols had played their first-ever legitimate gig on the venue's 'new bands' night, merely weeks before.

'It's hard to believe now, but AC/DC were sort of caught up in that punk thing,' said Richard Griffiths, AC/DC's first agent in England, who booked that Nashville gig. 'This was the very early days of punk. The Sex Pistols were playing, the Damned were playing, and AC/DC were playing. There was another band playing, called Eddie and the Hot Rods, who I was also agent for. So there was two things happening at the same time, and they got slightly intermeshed.'

Punk was largely a media-driven phenomenon. The British music press, which wielded even more power (unbelievable though it may seem) than 'Countdown' did in Australia, latched onto punk and propagated it as the new antifashion. But if AC/DC — because they failed to conform to the punk stereotypes — couldn't count on press support, it wasn't the end of the world. They'd never been critics' darlings anyway.

When they got to Britain, their strategy was simply to do exactly the same thing they'd done in Australia: build it up from the grass roots on the live circuit.

It was precisely because of the climate that gave rise to punk that AC/DC also found an audience, and so quickly, in Britain. There were plenty of kids who were just as fed up with all the boring old farts as the punks were — as AC/DC were — but couldn't get into punk because it was so theoretical and confrontational that it was itself alienating. AC/DC had a lot in common with punk — classic roots, a keenness to stir the possum — but they were so much more accessible because they could and actually did play.

MICHAEL BROWNING: 'Building it up in the pubs wasn't that difficult because there was good word of mouth for it. It was just purely down to the kids that liked that kind of music, and they really got off on it.'

'We went over to establish ourselves as a road band first of all,' Bon later told *RAM*, 'and then work for a hit single. Sherbet, a few years ago, got the hit single but they couldn't get anyone to concerts. Then they couldn't get another hit and they couldn't work at all. We didn't want that.'

Angus concurred. 'I think all the good bands are essentially live bands, the great ones, the ones that last, your Stones, Who, whatever. Your only gauge for AC/DC is if we play someplace and people come back to see us the next time we play there. You can't trust the hype side of it.'

AC/DC's initial British schedule was arranged long before the band left Australia. First up, they would embark on an April and May tour of Britain supporting Atlantic labelmates Back Street Crawler, the band fronted by former Free guitarist Paul Kossoff.

Then, in June, they would tour the country all over again as part of a roadshow put together in conjunction with *Sounds* magazine. Coral Browning, with her good connections, had convinced *Sounds* that such a package — boasting a hard rock disco and films, as well as AC/DC, all for the meagre admission price of 50 p — would well serve both the magazine and the band.

Launched in 1970, *Sounds*, of the big three music papers,

was the new kid on the block, and as such it was out to challenge the traditional supremacy of the *New Musical Express* and *Melody Maker*. The *NME* was the market leader, with its fickle, elitist and intellectual championship of punk. *Sounds* took a more down-to-earth approach. It threw itself behind punk too, but not to the exclusion, or denigration, of its already established leaning towards heavy metal.

AC/DC, then, would have been *Sounds'* dream band. Indeed, when the magazine compiled its New Order Top 20 at the end of 1976 — as opposed to the Boring Old Farts Top 20, which was led by the Stones, Led Zeppelin and Rod Stewart — it was AC/DC who topped the list, ahead of Eddie and the Hot Rods, the Sex Pistols, the Damned, Iggy Pop (and the Stooges), Ted Nugent, Blackmore's Rainbow, Motorhead, Judas Priest and in equal tenth position, the Ramones and the Dictators.

AC/DC's first British single, released as soon as the band arrived in April, was 'Long way to the top'. It would be followed in May by the album *High voltage*.

The deal the band had with Atlantic Records was far from generous — a one-album trial, with an option for Atlantic beyond that — but as the only interested party, Michael Browning was pleased just to sign anything. And the band was chuffed just to be labelmates with the likes of Led Zeppelin.

Atlantic is one of the most celebrated labels in rock'n'roll history. Formed in New York in 1947 by Ahmet Ertegun, the son of a Turkish diplomat, it was one of rock'n'roll's mid-wives, making its name with classic R&B. The label survived by adapting to changing trends. By the early seventies, its roster boasted two of the biggest white rock acts in the world — Led Zeppelin and the Rolling Stones. With England providing it further with successful acts like artrockers Yes, and Emerson, Lake and Palmer, Atlantic stepped up its English presence, opening a London office. The label's first direct British signing was the Heavy Metal Kids in 1974, followed by Back Street Crawler.

Atlantic UK's Managing Director Phil Carson was sold on AC/DC from the moment Coral Browning walked into his office in 1975. He asked label manager Dave Dee what he thought, and he was just as keen. Dee thought AC/DC sounded like a cross between Zeppelin and Slade. Maybe they would pick up for Atlantic where the (former Heavy Metal) Kids, a similarly street-urchin-styled outfit, had failed.

RICHARD GRIFFITHS: 'I was at the Virgin Agency in London in 1975, and Michael Browning came in with one of those things — which actually I've only ever seen in Australia — it was like a suitcase, and you pulled it up and there was a screen, a machine, and it played a video. And it played a video of a live concert, in Melbourne, it would have been on the *High voltage* record, and they were just amazing.'

Griffiths left Virgin to form his own agency called Headline Artists, taking with him his own charge, Paul Kossoff, and, among others, AC/DC. It was only natural, then, that the two acts would tour together.

GRIFFITHS: 'Then, the way I've always told it was that in between AC/DC leaving Australia and arriving in London, Paul died.'

Paul Kossoff had maintained a heroin habit for the latter days of Free. He kicked it in 1974, but related ill health caught up with him by 1976.

Bon said in an open letter to *RAM* back home, 'That cunt Paul Kossoff fucked up our first tour (wait'll Angus gets hold of him)'.

BROWNING: 'We were suddenly stuck in England with no work. We had to adopt the stance of doing what any English group would do, and that was just play around all the little pubs and clubs.'

Coral Browning had taken up an office of her own at Atlantic. Often, a record company appoints a liaison officer to an act, and even though Coral wasn't officially on the Atlantic payroll, she served as that and more. She coordinated the band's publicity, and was its virtual mother hen as well.

Although 'Long way to the top' didn't dent the charts, it made a reasonably favourable impression. It was Hit Pick of the Week on Radio Luxembourg; and at least late night Radio One DJ, John Peel — the oldest hipster in the world, the man who discovered T Rex — would give it a spin. That much was a good start. James Hamilton, in *Record Mirror & Disc*, said, 'These Aussie youngsters boogie Stones/Elton John-style' — huh? — 'with bagpipe noises yet!' In *Melody Maker*, Caroline Coon was equivocal: 'up there with the likes of Kiss and Angel... mind-boggling', but concluded cryptically, 'Getting ripped off? Keep laughing.'

Michael Browning and Phil Carson kept chipping away at America. Atlantic over there was not entirely convinced.

The band stayed briefly at a house in the West End, just around the corner from Coral Browning's place, before moving to more permanent digs in Barnes. Michael Browning had calculated it would cost around 600 quid a week just to keep the band; this was a bill footed by Alberts, if in the form of moneys advanced against royalties. The members of the band received the quite generous wage of 50 quid a week.

But they were champing at the bit just to play. To pass time, Mark and Malcolm would go down the local — the Bridge Hotel — to shoot pool. Bon went out on an extended pub and club crawl to check out the competition. Of course, give Bon an idle moment ... He decided to pay a visit to the pub in Finchley where he used to work during Fraternity's last days in London. He came home with a dislocated jaw.

MARK EVANS: 'He walked in and, he said, he'd only been in the place ten or fifteen seconds — he went on his own — and he got hit in the face with a pint mug! And this is like three or four years since he'd been in the place!'

No decent explanation was ever offered for the incident. When Bon wrote later to Pat Pickett, all he said was, 'It wasn't even my fight. I didn't see what hit me.'

The band had a photo session to do, so Bon donned a pair of wraparound shades to obscure the welts. It was excuse enough though to finally finish work on his teeth. Eight hundred quid spent on Harley Street bought him a new set of dentures.

GRIFFTHS: 'I dug [AC/DC] up a gig at the Red Cow in Hammersmith. This show was probably the greatest show I've ever seen in my life. There was no advertising. They came on, they were doing two sets, and to start with there were probably ten people in the pub. They did one set and they did the whole number, Angus on Bon's shoulders, everything, I'd never seen anything like it. Then the place emptied. About half an hour later, they came out to do the second set, and the place was packed. Everyone had run off and said, You have got to see this band. It was packed, it was incredible; I'll never, ever forget it.'

EVANS: 'It was a real battle in London first off, I really had doubts that it was going to work. The Red Cow was, well, it wasn't a regular gig; it had bands on but there was no vibe out on it. People would say, You're playing where? But the reaction was pretty instantaneous. Browning and Coral were excellent at beating stuff up.'

Among the Australians at the Red Cow that night was Silver Smith, with whom Bon had had an affair briefly in 1971. She had left her husband in Adelaide at about the same time Fraternity returned from England, and set off around the world, ending up in London. 'I'd been away for a couple of years then, so seeing the name AC/DC meant nothing to me. I hated the Red Cow, but I had a friend drop in and say, Why don't you come and see this band, they're great; and it was free to get in, so I went down. The place was packed, everybody was really getting off on it, so I weaseled my way to the front, and I got there, and it was Bon! So I went and said hello afterwards. He didn't go home that night, it was all on again.'

Bon was still officially living with the band in Barnes, but he started spending time at Silver's flat in ritzy Kensington.

From the Red Cow, the band graduated to the Nashville. Coral managed to woo a couple of important journalists down to see the show — Caroline Coon and the *NME*'s Phil NcNeill.

Under the headline I WALLABY YOUR MAN, the *NME* ran Phil McNeill's assessment. 'In the middle of the great British Punk Rock Explosion, a quintet of similarly ruthless Ozzies has just swaggered like a cat among London's surly, self-consciously paranoid pigeons ... and with a sense of what sells rather than what's cool, they could well clean up.' Faint praise indeed. The taste-makers at the *NME* decreed that AC/DC were unfashionable.

Even though punk was in one sense very traditional, in

another sense, it was almost avant-garde — and this was where AC/DC and punk most distinctly digressed. If, as is often suggested, the Rolling Stones' great worth was as an advertisement for the blues/R&B artists they ripped off, then the same could be said of punk and the Velvet Underground, the Stooges and the New York Dolls. Today, these three bands are acknowledged as seminal forces in rock's history; but at a time, in 1976, when they were still regarded with contempt — if they were recognised at all — punk discovered them and absorbed their groundbreaking influences. With its do-it-yourself ethic, punk turned to its advantage rudimentary or minimalist, or even inept, technique. In the face of what gave the appearance of modernism, AC/DC, who wore their proficiency and strictly orthodox blues-based roots so obviously on their sleeves, just seemed old-fashioned. Besides, they had long hair, and tattoos. Punk was rude and crude, but it was never gauche. But again, it was precisely because AC/DC bridged the gap between the old and the new, the traditional and the iconoclastic, that they would be so successful.

By now, Back Street Crawler had found a new guitarist, and a handful of gigs were arranged for May, to pay tribute to Kossoff if nothing else. AC/DC would still support. A showcase was held at the Marquee, the famed London club where bands like the Stones, the Who, the Yardbirds, Led Zeppelin and Yes had all paid their dues.

Sounds magazine's Phil Sutcliffe reviewed the show and was so taken by the resurrected Back Street Crawler — who subsequently imploded — that he feared, 'the mere wildly exciting excellence of AC/DC could be forgotten. It shouldn't be. They are heavy, will be huge.' Sutcliffe would go on to be one of the band's most stalwart critical supporters.

The album was released on May 14. The British version of *High voltage* was actually mostly the Australian *TNT* album, with the subtraction of two tracks — 'School days' and 'Rocker', and in their place, the addition of 'Little lover' and 'She's got balls' from the original *High voltage* album.

Though the *NME* did not deign to review the album, *Sounds'* Geoff Barton awarded it four stars out of a possible five. He described it as 'a tonic in the midst of the all-too-serious, poker-faced groups of today'. *Melody Maker*'s Mike Oldfield, however, said, 'It's the same old boogie ... Still, there's hope. The lyrics have a brashness and lack of sophistication that's always useful in the heavy brand of rock.'

In late May/early June, as 'Jailbreak' was released as a single in Australia — to go to number five — AC/DC played the odd pub and club gig in England. Alberts crowed that the band had passed the million dollar sales mark, with *TNT* still shifting 3–4,000 units weekly. The release of *Dirty deeds* was held off for that reason.

On June 11, the band embarked on the 20-date tour for *Sounds*, which had been prophetically dubbed 'Lock up your daughters'. The band got around in a Transit van, which most of the time was driven by Phil, a full-scale car buff and petrol-head who wasn't really comfortable unless he was behind the wheel. Long-time Australian roadies Ralph and Herc travelled in another van with the gear.

MICHAEL BROWNING: 'That was incredibly significant in terms of raising the profile of the group. I mean, we were on the front cover of *Sounds* — for a group that was totally unknown, that had just come from Australia, that was a pretty good score.'

The shows took the form of a revue almost. After a DJ regaled the crowd with sides by Led Zeppelin, Kiss, the Pretty Things, Black Oak Arkansas, Alex Harvey, the Who, Free, Status Quo and Alice Cooper, and some Stones film-clips were screened, AC/DC played a 50-minute bracket.

MARK EVANS: 'That was playing some weird places, it was really breaking the ice. We were booked into some weird little clubs. One place was called the Club 76, I'm sure because it could only hold 76 people! Another place we played in Wales, called Mumbles, in Swansea — five people turned up.'

Life on the road is hardly glamorous at the best of times. Europe probably treats bands better than anywhere else in the world; there, even rock'n'roll stars are regarded as artists. In America, they lay it on thick, perhaps too thick. But touring Britain is without doubt the worst of times.

Former Mott the Hoople front man Ian Hunter wrote a

classic account of life on the road in *Diary of a rock'n'roll star*, in which he said:

> English hotels are really something. They can ruin your day.
> ... We use four-star hotels which are the equivalent of glorified bogs. Oh, the foyer is groovy, but by the time you get to the sixth floor it's beginning to look like Bradford railway station. The slobs that run these dumps really think we're long haired hippies. You know, pockets full of shit and cases full of nicked ashtrays and towels. So they either patronise you or call you into the office and quietly tell you any trouble and we'll call for the fuzz. In the dining room they take the piss first and the order second. We don't tip on principle. Most places haven't got room phones, TVs or anything — you're supposed to get high on Radio 3 and the Bible. Misery and boredom. I sometimes wish we went to the old boarding houses, six to a room...

Going to Scotland, though, was treated as a homecoming by the band and audience alike. Said Bon, 'You can imagine what that was like... hoots, with an "H", mon!'

The *Androssan Herald* commented, 'One fault with Scott's voice is whereas it might be undistinguished most of the time, it does, at others, sound rather like Alex Harvey. This may prove unpopular with Glasgow crowds who might feel that he is imitating their idol.'

But Glasgow was obviously flattered. A *Sounds* review of the gig was glowing. 'The audience even at this early stage,' it began, 'have nearly demolished the staid City Hall. Bon, half-heartedly and mischievously, asks us all to sit down, "or else the management will turn off the power". Nobody attempts to find their seat.'

This minor act of civil disobedience was reported back home as a 'riot'. 'As in Australia,' the *RAM* news item went, 'the group are attracting a young, volatile working class audience.'

While Malcolm and Angus spent a couple of days off visiting long-lost relatives in Glasgow, Bon hired a car with

Phil to go sightseeing. Scotland was his birthplace, after all, and so he thought he might try to find some of his roots. The pair lapped Loch Lomond. But the highlight of the trip, as Bon wrote to old mate Pat Pickett, was coming across two bears shaggin' in the woods. Phil, the camera buff, filmed the occasion for posterity.

The tour wrapped up in London at the Lyceum on July 7, two days before Bon's birthday. Save for the fact that lighting engineer Herc had an accident at the soundcheck, falling from the rigging (and having to be sent home as a result), the show was highly successful. Compered by John Peel, it featured a competition for the 'Schoolgirl we'd most like to...'. The winner was one Jayne Haynes from Harrow, Middlesex, who went home with the first prize of an Epiphone Caballero folk guitar, plus a bonus, bassist Mark Evans — much to Bon's chagrin, mock or otherwise. 'She was beautiful...' he rued, 'really sexy. Garters, suspenders. I was really lusting for her myself ... we all were. But Mark won out. He's just too handsome for me to compete.'

Against all his own forecasts, Bon had made it to the Big 3-0. The band threw him a party, which was missing only one vital ingredient — the birthday boy himself. Bon, as was his wont, had gone AWOL.

One of the few birthday cards he got from Australia was from Mary Walton. He replied, 'Thank you for remembering my B. Day. Not many did. I wrote myself off for about three days and even managed to miss my own party.'

Bon said to Anthony O'Grady, who interviewed him over the phone a few days later, 'Y'know what I did last night? I fucked my birthday in ... started at 11.50 and finished at 12.15 ... It's the first birthday I've done that.'

The band sat around the table at the Russell Hotel waiting for the guest of honour, getting drunk. All except Angus, of course. Bon never did show that night, and he wouldn't do so for a couple of days to come. The band could only surmise he was off with Silver. At that stage, he still hadn't actually moved in with her.

MARK EVANS: 'The basic thing about the band — it was very

insular. There was no real camaraderie, and so being on the road, it could get lonely. And Bon, being a very outgoing person, and older, I don't think there was enough within the band to satisfy his social needs.

'Bon very much needed that space away from the band. So he could do what he wanted to do without having to worry about what we were going to say. Because we used to call him an old hippie. I mean, Bon used to wear his leather jacket and all that, but he was always wearing a kaftan and sandals underneath.'

For one thing, Bon was a self-confessed pot-head. This was a hippie crime which Angus barely tolerated. But Bon would still go off, to be with Silver. He also became friendly with Coral Browning, as she too was more of his age.

Bon and Silver had lost time to make up for. They say you can never go back, but in this instance, Bon was picking up where he'd left unfinished business off. The cynical view was that Bon and Silver's relationship was mutually beneficial, in that Silver provided Bon with an entree to the London scene, and he provided her with a ready-made rock'n'roll star. While this may be true, the fact remains that Bon fell passionately in love with Silver.

SILVER: 'He never made any friends of his own, which is sad. Like, he had friends in Australia; but in London, because of the pressure of everything, he never really got a chance to do that. But then, he had a ready-made assortment of my friends...'

When Silver had first arrived in London a year earlier, she lived in a house with, among others, a guy who worked for Rolling Stones' Ron Wood as his percy. A percy is a personal assistant, a common appendage to most big rock stars — a minder and a gofer, they're often nothing more than drug dealers. Silver met Ron Wood and became friendly with him. She met a few other bands on the scene too, like Thin Lizzy and UFO. If it's not exactly fair to say Silver was on the game at the time, certainly she was supported by sugar daddies.

SILVER: 'They weren't older so much as guys with money. There was a few rich men hovering, I wasn't short of rich men, I travelled around on the strength of that. I just happened to be at the right place at the right time.'

Silver lived comfortably in a flat of her own in the West End. She was a bit of an old hippie, an intelligent woman, a reader, who introduced Bon to books, and no shrinking violet. Like Bon, she enjoyed a smoke, though where they differed was whilst she didn't really drink, she had a growing taste for heroin.

MARK EVANS: 'Everyone was very wary of her. Malcolm would have sussed she was involved with drugs. And once again, that was the band mentality, if Malcolm decided... And Angus, he was very possessive of people, he was funny. Like, when we were living in Barnes, I ended up matey with a few of the guys down the pub, the local garbagemen actually, and you know, it took Angus a while to warm to the idea of that.'

Malcolm and Angus would have felt threatened by anyone who wasn't on their own payroll, let alone a strong woman.

SILVER: 'I think part of it is that they feel inadequate. They're suspicious of anyone that might be in the least bit intellectual. Although they were always very good to me, my personal relationship with them was good.'

They were also two-faced.

SILVER: 'I think it was just that they were young boys that got very successful very quickly, and so they were like fish out of water. They didn't have time to enjoy themselves, I mean, that lifestyle, there was just so much happening. In all the years I've been around, I've never known a band that worked like that band worked.'

For Bon, Silver was his refuge.

By the time Bon returned from his few dirty days off celebrating his birthday, the band was due back on deck.

RICHARD GRIFFITHS: 'We then started booking them around London. I got Jack Barry, who booked the Marquee, I made sure he saw them, and they were incredible, and Jack said — it's a famous quote I can't exactly remember — "The most exciting band I've seen play at the Marquee since Led Zeppelin"; and so we then sat down and worked out a strategy with Jack to basically break AC/DC out of the Marquee.

'This was the summer of '76, a very exciting time in London, incredibly hot summer, and we worked out that they'd do this residency at the Marquee, every Monday night, and then they would get a great slot on the Reading Festival. And somehow, during all this, we went to Sweden too.'

MICHAEL BROWNING: 'We were just totally unfashionable, and so it was hard work, persevering, trying not to worry about the criticism.'

The band recorded a 20-minute segment for Mike Mansfield's 'Superpop' TV program, which also featured T Rex, and then headed off to Sweden.

GRIFFITHS: 'They went off to Sweden for some time, because Tomas Johansen, the promoter there, represented Abba, and he couldn't get Abba into Australia, so we did this sort of exchange. He took AC/DC to Sweden, and Abba went to Australia!'

MARK EVANS: 'We played what they call folk parks, which were like these outdoor barbecue areas with swings and all that, like recreation areas. It was weird because there was a lot of young kids there, but they had blackjack tables and beer, and they were selling beer to 14-15-year-olds.

'But it was enough for the hype to start, and we took hold very quickly in those places.'

Bon was under instructions to keep the Australian media informed, and so in another open letter, this time to the Melbourne *Herald*'s Debbie Sharpe, he wrote:

They love rock'n'roll bands because all the Scandinavian bands are real cabaret. People dance to jigs and polkas, and the bands play Swedish beer drinking (oom-pah-pah) folk songs. The beaches and swimming pools have topless bathing (and I'm a great swimmer!).

AC/DC, however, kept its head down, unimpressed by travelling to new places, seeing new things, meeting new people.

The band had a new road crew. Ralph, for whatever reason, had been sent home with the injured Herc. Bon wrote to Mary, 'We've got two new Scottish roadies now. Madness.'

EVANS: 'It was business as usual, business as usual. There was never any excitement about anything at all. It was taken for granted what was happening to us. Like, there was no difference to us in going from Australia and playing the Red Cow in England, to six months later headlining the Hammersmith Odeon, having this meteoric rise. It didn't faze anyone at all, it was what was meant to happen. It was just this tunnel vision that Malcolm and Angus had: *this is what is going to happen.*

'You could be driving through Switzerland, through the Alps, the most magnificent scenery you've ever seen, and Angus would have his nose buried in a comic. There was nothing that could surprise us, it was just work. The attitude was just, We don't give a fuck, what time do we go on?

'If someone interesting came backstage and wanted to party, Bon would be the one who'd go off with them.'

But if there was an element of joylessness to life with AC/DC, the hour or so spent on stage every night made up for it. Most bands say that going on the road is an excruciatingly tedious exercise, only ever relieved or justified by the actual time on stage itself. The other 23 hours in the day are wasted. You spend a lot of time sitting around waiting: you wait to board vehicles, and then you travel; and then when you get where you're going, you sit around and wait till showtime.

EVANS: 'That was the good thing about the band, whatever happened off stage — and there was always a lot of shit going down — as soon as we got on stage, it was just easy. Angus and I could have a screaming match five minutes before we went on, but then we'd go on, and it was, Bang! I'm biased, you know, but I think that line-up of the band — we just had this ultimate confidence, we had no sense of insecurity whatsoever; we would have played with anyone, we just didn't believe we could be beaten.'

Richard Griffiths remembers being on the road with the band in Sweden: 'It was clear to me it was Malcolm's band. Bon was just a great guy. But even then, I sensed, off Michael, that he wasn't sure that Bon was the singer to take the band all the way. I didn't get that from the band, I got it from Michael. It sounds terrible to say it, but I think that if Bon hadn't died...

'I suppose it was true, he always was sort of separate from

the rest. Phil, he was off on his own, he was actually pretty obnoxious. Angus and Malcolm were thick, obviously. And then Mark, you knew Mark wasn't going to last, he was too much of a nice guy. I mean, these were tough guys, they were pretty tough on each other.

'Bon did have an ability to get into trouble. But I've been around some pretty nasty drunks, and I definitely wouldn't put him in that category. I just remember he used to get pretty... drunk!'

EVANS: 'They would dispute this, but I think they viewed Bon to be ultimately disposable. In hindsight, it seems preposterous, but at the time, he was always in the firing line. And there was a lot of pressure, mainly from George, and record companies. I think within that camp, there's been a certain rewriting of history, about how they felt about the guy — no, that's wrong, how they felt about the guy professionally. Because there was no way you could spend more than 30 seconds in a room with Bon and not be completely and utterly charmed. The guy was captivating; he was gentlemanly, but he had the rough side to him, and he was funny.'

MOLLY MELDRUM: 'When I was in England, AC/DC were breaking there, and breaking in Europe, and I remember Michael taking me aside, and telling me he had this great dilemma on his hands. The Americans wanted to release this group, but what they said was, You've got to find another lead singer. Because they couldn't understand Bon Scott. So Michael was going... But I mean, he was never going to get rid of Bon.'

Back in England, the band relocated into new digs, a house opposite the cemetery in West Brompton, which was chosen because it came equipped with a piano. Bon instead moved in with Silver.

With the Marquee residency kicking off on July 26, 'Jailbreak' was released as the band's second single. Caroline Coon, wrongly referring to it as 'Jail bait', described it as 'a muscle-flexing fine blast of rock'n'roll', but as Charles Shaar Murray observed in the *NME*, 'it will not be helped one whit by the fact that "Jailbreak" is also the title of Thin Lizzy's current album and next single'.

The Marquee residency was heralded with full page ads in the music papers, which reiterated Jack Barry's famous quote, and pictured Angus holding up a reproduction of a letter Atlantic had received from the City of Glasgow District Council, which read, '... have been advised that the audience in attendance at the recent concert featuring AC/DC which you produced were for the most of the performance entirely out of control and were actually standing up on the seats. This has caused some damage to the upholstery and has also resulted in a back being broken off one of the seats.'

It goes to show just how dull the run of British bands was, unable to generate even this modest amount of excitement. Punk was really still waiting in the wings. 'Lock up your daughters' had set the wheels in motion. Playing the Marquee residency, every Monday night through August — and playing other gigs in and around London — AC/DC really caught fire.

Recalls Dave Jarrett, an Atlantic Records promotion man who worked with AC/DC, 'Monday night in London is called Swede Night, because they're the only people who go out, Swedes. The first Marquee show, there was about 18 people there. So what we did, the record company just took everybody we could down to the gig, it was an unlimited guest list. I mean, I used to go down to my local pub, say to the guys, Who wants to go out, and they'd say, How much is it going to cost? They had no idea who they were going to see. But it built up very quickly, to the point where you couldn't get in the door.'

MICHAEL BROWNING: 'There was another group called Eddie and the Hot Rods that were happening in London at the time, both of them had a residency at the Marquee, and it was very much like a competition between the two groups to see who could break each other's record. I think AC/DC to this day still hold the record for the most people in the Marquee. It was quite a small room, and I think we had something like 1,400 people there. I don't think I've ever ever experienced anything as hot and sweaty as that.'

It was a stinking summer in 1976. With the fetid aroma of punk in the air, it was no summer of love; but London when it sizzles is a different world to London any other time of the year — people go out, and get crazy... hot August nights, indeed.

'You wouldn't believe the weather,' Bon wrote to Debbie Sharpe. 'It's been a hotter summer than we had in Australia early this year. It's particularly bad 'cause we're 60 miles from the nearest beach and if you happen to fall in the Thames they treat you for a week with tetanus injections.'

AC/DC were one of a hot summer's hottest items. Molly flew in to shoot a segment for 'Countdown'. Phil Sutcliffe reported from deep in the Marquee mosh-pit; 'The heat is beyond belief... Guys take their shirts off and within half a minute they look as though they've stepped out of the shower. The girls say they wish they could do the same... And that's just for the disco!

'... AC/DC stroll on unassumingly, Bon grins an evil grin and says, This one's just to warm you up.'

Angus was making a ritual of the browneye-flashing routine he'd unveiled initially at the Lifesaver back in Sydney in March; and even that spotty visage, replete in — or rather out of — soiled jocks, didn't turn people off.

''E's the best fing I've seen since Pete Townshend,' a punter said to Molly, who was down there in the mosh-pit with everyone else.

MOLLY: 'It was just this tiny room, and there were all these kids dressed in school uniforms there — which was pretty exciting to me, I can tell you right now! But the thing was, AC/DC weren't doing anything different to what they ever had, and they never have. It was the same as the first time I saw them. They've never had to alter their music.'

The Marquee established AC/DC as the only band in London getting anywhere that wasn't a punk band. That they were swarmed by female fans backstage was proof of the fact — and welcome relief for the band after a veritable drought of feminine attention.

MOLLY: 'By that stage, Bon was certainly drinking a lot. Because it was just part of rock'n'roll, it was part of getting to the next gig, doing the gig ... Bon would be there, and he would have his bottle of whisky, and so we were soul mates in that respect, I guess, because I was into whisky then too, and so we'd be going arrgghh, you know... In those days, quite frankly, you didn't have to worry about it catching up with you. Why would you? You weren't hurting anyone, you were having a lot of fun, and you were doing your job.'

SILVER: 'He was drinking a bottle of Scotch a day, even back in those early days of success. I mean, what he was getting in wages wouldn't have covered his Scotch bill.'

High voltage may not have cracked the charts — if only because its sales, which totalled 50,000 by year's end, were spread over several months — but with the vibe the Marquee generated, even the *Sun*, the pride of the Fleet Street gutter press, outraged though it was by bare bottoms and bad language, had to admit that 'AC/DC are a band we will learn to live with'.

RICHARD GRIFFITHS: 'What was happening was that AC/DC were playing at the Marquee, and just up the road in Wardour Street at the 100 Club, the Sex Pistols were playing, so they sort of got caught up in the whole thing. But what they were, they were a rock band who were different to what had been going on.'

'The Sex Pistols, and bands like the Clash and the Damned, are important because they have brought rock down to earth again,' Caroline Coon wrote in *Melody Maker*. 'The musicians, unimpressed by the trappings of stardom, are as close to their audience as rock'n'rollers have ever been.

'Their lyrics, eschewing the cultural irrelevancies of American R&B, are committed, searching comments about the new morality and tough environment they grew up in. Their music is fast, intensely emotional, fierce and devoid of pretence.'

Just like AC/DC. 'The trouble with these bloody punk bands,' Bon told *Juke*'s Christie Eliezer, 'is they try and look tough but musically they've got nothing, not even a hint of originality.'

The punks also liked to claim they were working class, but if they were that at all, they were, like Pete Townshend and Keith Richards, art school dropouts. The real working-class kids, the punters, didn't know what they were supposed to like, they just knew what they liked. And as it was proved so convincingly — particularly outside trendy London in the industrial wastelands of the North; not just Scotland but cities like Manchester, Newcastle and Liverpool, where the trendy London music papers held less sway — they liked AC/DC. AC/DC, in turn, didn't condescend to their audience.

GRIFFITHS: 'When you compare them to what was going on in England at the time; they came over, and they were so great, because they'd been playing all these gigs, and English bands hadn't been playing. So you had the raw excitement of the Sex Pistols or the Clash or the Jam or whatever else was going on, but you just had this real rock'n'roll band, with this extraordinary guitarist, showman, and Bon who was just great. Kids just loved Bon.'

It probably had a lot to do simply with musicianship. AC/DC, with their greater prowess, got across aggression so much more effectively. With even a measure of flash. AC/DC also attracted older fans — like bikers, who always liked their rock'n'roll loud, hard and fast.

Not only that, they had genuine character and they put on a show. Malcolm, Mark and Phil at the back line — a rhythm section as tight as any — looked like any real, ordinary young blokes. Out front, Angus was pure vaudeville — the errant schoolboy imagery stretching all the way back to Billy Bunter — but the thing was, he was a freak, he could really play that guitar. And Bon, Bon was simply larger than life; but at the core, he too was all real.

If the band mostly copped stick from the press, it didn't matter, because the kids knew what was what.

GRIFFITHS: 'It was all word of mouth, the record wasn't doing much; Sounds was supportive, nobody else, and they were just touring all over. But they were building an incredible live following. Funnily enough, everything was building towards a peak, because by then we were about to come in with the second album, and we thought they were going to explode from the Reading Festival. But in fact, they played Reading and they didn't do very well, and I've never really understood why, because they had a great slot — the Saturday or Sunday afternoon — and they played well, but they really didn't go down very well.'

The annual Reading Festival is an institution in British rock, a showcase that can make or break bands. Sharing a bill in 1976 with Brand X, Ted Nugent, Sutherland Brothers, Quiver, Black Oak Arkansas, and Osibisa, AC/DC had the same hopes for Reading that they'd had for Sunbury back home in 1975. But again, before a crowd of nearly 50,000 they would be thwarted.

An entourage accompanied the band to Reading, including Michael and Coral Browning, George and Harry, Richard Griffiths, Phil Carson, even Silver. On the way there, they stopped in at Richard Griffiths' parents' place for lunch and a quick rubber on the croquet court. Griffiths remembers that Bon, of course, utterly charmed his mother.

But as *Melody Maker*'s 'Reading Report' put it: 'If you think the Sex Pistols are a gang of untalented jerks, then prepare yourself...' John Peel admitted he slept through AC/DC's set — 'probably the first person ever to do so' — but somehow still managed to note, 'Anticipation was high for AC/DC, and response was agitated — people seemed to think them either absolutely awful or great fun. The loutish element definitely dug them, as did I.'

MARK EVANS: 'We drove back to London, and George at that stage had come over with Harry, and we had a pretty heavy meeting, because everyone had the shits. George came back, we were going to play cards, and Malcolm and Angus started arguing. I tried to split them up, and it was the first time George ever said anything more to me than, No worries, mate. He'd given Malcolm and Angus a blast, saying, Who the fuck do you think you are? I don't think it was the band's fault, I think it was the crowd, but George blamed us. And he turned to me, and said, And you! He kept calling me Dave, you know, that was the old singer, Dave Evans — and I said, At least you could get my name right. And then they all set on me.'

GRIFFITHS: 'I didn't like George at all. I felt that George was out to fuck with Michael. In fact, I got the sense that the Alberts people were out to fuck Michael off.

'But then Michael fucked me and took the band away from my agency! But you know, it was probably the right move.

Because I was a small little agency, and he needed someone bigger.

'The last tour I booked for them would have been August/ September. The first gigs we did with them in London they were getting ten pounds a night, by then we were getting 500 to 750 a night, which was pretty decent money in those days.'

Announcing they'd joined the prestigious Cowbell Agency, which handled such topline British acts as Jethro Tull, Roxy Music, Rod Stewart and Alex Harvey, AC/DC were 'bought on' to a September European tour supporting Ritchie Blackmore's Rainbow. A buy-on is when a band pays for the privilege of playing on the bill with another, bigger band. It cost AC/DC a not inconsiderable sum to open on 19 dates for Ritchie Blackmore. The legendary status of the former Deep Purple axeman guaranteed AC/DC an audience which would be not only voluminous but also, almost certainly, the right audience.

Every territory has its peculiar likes and dislikes, and Germany, the third largest market for music in the world, next to producing its own avant-garde strain of rock, has always had a real fondness for the hardest of hard rock. To the Germans, AC/DC might have seemed made in heaven.

AC/DC had excited Germany even before they arrived there. The *High voltage* album shifted 16,000 copies in its first week of release. Prior to the band's joining the Blackmore tour, they played three gigs of their own, and a fourth — a major show for *Bravo* — in Duisburg. *Bravo* was the top rock magazine in the country, and every year it held its own hit-pick kind of concert. Sharing the bill were Suzi Quatro, Slik and Shaun Cassidy.

The band arrived, by ferry, in Hamburg at 9.00 on the morning of September 15. They were greeted by George, who had made his own way over, and brother Alex, who was then based there. It was a family reunion. Bon checked into his hotel room where a letter was waiting for him from Atlantic's German International Product Manager Killy Kumberger.

'Welcome to good old Germany,' it read. 'May I tell you that we at WEA are sure you will be one of the major rock'n'roll bands in the future. Your sound seems to be perfect for our market.

'With your fantastic live appearances, you should soon be able to attract a wide audience. The first reactions to the single and the album have been very positive.'

Accompanying the letter was a schedule for the day, which was typical:

9.00 - Arrival harbour Hamburg
12.45 - Pick up at hotel by Hannelore Kring, promotion co-ordinator
1.00 - Interview at cafe Boheme with Martin Meister, journalist for music magazine Joker
2.00 - Interview at cafe Boheme for magazine Pop with Brigitte Weckelmann
3.00 - Interview at cafe Boheme for daily newspaper Morgenpost with Mario Scheuermann
4.00 - Fabrik open for road manager
6.00 - Rehearsal
8.30 - Concert
11.30 - Dinner at Bratwurstglockle with journalists from Sounds, Pop-Foto, Musikexpress etc and WEA people

In Hamburg, the boys in the band indulged in the not-so-illicit pleasures on offer in the world's most notorious red-light district. All except Bon that is, who delighted as he was by window displays of real live naked ladies, had a date lined up with a fraulein he met when Fraternity visited Germany.

Apart from an uncooperative stage prop — a huge model rainbow which, like Spinal Tap's miniature Stonehenge, kept falling over — the tour was marred only by its star's ill-temper.

AC/DC played with Rainbow in Geneva, Marseilles, Paris and Belgium before returning to England by mid-October. If the French have any particular predilections, it's for the wild men of rock, its gutter poets; and so again, AC/DC must have seemed like a dream band.

Back in London, the band had barely a week off before it was due to go out on the road again, headlining, for the first time, their own British tour. The plan was to do that, and then in mid-November go to America en route to Australia.

A return tour of Australia was booked for December. *RAM* suggested that promoters Evans–Gudinksi had considered calling the tour, 'The little c**nts have done it'. In America, at least two gigs at the Starwood in LA were on offer.

Meantime, *High voltage* was released in the US, and both the *Dirty deeds* album and single were released in Australia. Britain would see the release of the 'High voltage' single, and the slightly amended *Dirty deeds* album, by the beginning of November.

Reviewing *Dirty deeds*, *RAM* suggested the band was simply repeating itself, though had to admit 'they've shown positive signs of a NEW DIRECTION' — even if it came down only to 'Ride on' and 'Jailbreak'.

America bore both good and bad news. *High voltage* — surprise — had polarised reaction. With new cover artwork yet again (Angus struck by a bolt of lightning), industry bible *Billboard* listed it in its 'Recommended LPs' column: 'Australia's newest entry is a cross between Led Zeppelin and the Sensational Alex Harvey Band. Lead singer has a very unique sounding voice and the twin guitars are front and centre from the first cut. Expect airplay on progressive stations.'

Counter culture bible *Rolling Stone*, on the other hand, was contemptuous of it. 'Those concerned with the future of hard rock may take solace in knowing that with the release of the first US album by these Australian gross-out champions, the genre has unquestionably hit its all-time low,' said Billy Altman. 'Lead singer Bon Scott spits out his vocals with a truly annoying aggression which, I suppose, is the only way to do it when all you seem to care about is being a star so that you can get laid every night. Stupidity bothers me. Calculated stupidity offends me.'

As it transpired, the band wouldn't make it to America in 1976. Michael Browning was unable to finally arrange visas, as not only Bon but also he himself had Australian criminal records for pot convictions. This certainly wouldn't have impressed Atlantic, not so much in having been busted in the first place, but in not being able to get around it, and not coming to America to put in some promotional presence.

Critical reaction to *Dirty deeds* in Britain echoed Australia.

Comparing *Dirty deeds* and *High voltage*, Geoff Barton said, 'So alike are they that tracks could be interchanged quite easily' — which was actually the fact of the matter. The single 'Jailbreak' was inexplicably omitted, thus cruelling the album's killer closing, as was 'Rock in peace'. Replacing them were 'Rocker', the *TNT* track dropped from the first English album, and 'Love at first feel', a track the band had up its sleeve which would only see release in Australia as a single the following January. *Dirty deeds* was more of the same, but in Britain, the groundswell of fans had only one previous album to go on, and so it was quite welcome.

Still, neither the album nor the 'High voltage' single went anywhere near the charts. AC/DC's rise was a live phenomenon.

DAVE JARRETT: 'AC/DC and Van Halen, who I also worked with, did a very similar thing. Van Halen did two tours of England, very, very quickly, one supporting Black Sabbath, and then headlined themselves. When they came over and supported Black Sabbath, we'd never heard of them. So it was the young turks with the old warhorses. And they were so exciting, I mean, Dave Lee Roth was in the band. The audience was very responsive. It was fantastic, and again, very similar situation to AC/DC.

'What you had to do, you only had to do a good support or two, and you could cover the whole country, and kids would come out and see you the next time, you didn't need hit records.'

On October 27, the band played the first gig of its headline tour at Southampton University. Oxford Polytechnic refused to grant them permission to perform because their repertoire contained 'blatantly vulgar and cheap references to both sexes'.

Heading towards Scotland always brightened the band's spirits. 'Glasgow would be our favourite place in Scotland, in the whole of Britain, because the kids are really mad — like, half of them are Angus and Malcolm's relatives anyway,' Bon told *RAM*. 'The first time we ever played down there, there were about two rows of seats just demolished. And so this time they had extra men inside and the riot squad outside.

But if the cops had stopped the show and arrested Angus the kids would have gone mad. And no one goes mad like Glaswegians, believe me.'

Arriving back in London and playing the Hammersmith Odeon, even the *NME* had to admit AC/DC was here to stay. 'The emcee only just ducks into the wings and out of the firing range when the Odeon stage explodes deafeningly. Bruised about the head, their breath stolen by the sheer impact of noise, the security men are caught off guard and trampled to the floor as the audience immediately besieged the front.

'And then this schoolboy brat up on the rostrum smirks maliciously as his opening power chord painfully rattles through our bones and makes the unnecessary triumphant gesture of wildly tossing his cap to the floor, as if to say: This is our day.

'The day, Gawd 'elp us all, AC/DC conquered London.'

Dave Dee and Phil Carson, and Michael Browning and Coral, and everybody, knew that they'd cracked it. The 4,000-seat theatre was only just over half full, but it wasn't so much the quantity as the quality of the crowd that convinced them. It was clear then, with even a few kids in the audience dressed in school uniforms, that the band's appeal extended beyond the merely musical. Particularly satisfying to the band itself was the fact that this success was achieved without having to alter its act.

Even *The Times* reviewed the show. Said rock critic Clive Bennett, 'My objections are to their music, not their words, which simply express without inhibitions what most of us have discussed innumerable times with equal frankness in private. Music of any sort must surely require more from performers than just the capacity mindlessly to bash their instruments into oblivion. It is in this primal state that AC/DC exist.'

Any sort of acknowledgement by *The Times* was signal enough: AC/DC had arrived. It was, indeed, a meteoric rise. Their standing in Britain could well yet be improved upon, but the new frontier now was America.

MICHAEL BROWNING: 'There's an amazing photograph of Bon from that first time they ever headlined a major venue in

London. Bon said he'd make his own way to the gig, which of course, we were all a bit nervous about, but anyway... We were all there backstage worrying that Bon wasn't going to turn up. In the meantime, because the band's name was on the marquee out the front, I asked this photographer if he could go around and get a picture of it, you know, 'Sold Out — AC/DC'. So he did that, and then Bon turned up and everything went fine.

'Anyway, this photographer brought the proofs in to show me the next week, and who should be walking past on his way to the gig in the picture but Bon! He was just casually walking to the gig. And that just really summed up Bon, you know, the first ever big headline gig, no lights or anything like that, and he's just casually strolling along. He would have just got off the tube, at Hammersmith.

'And to his credit, he would do things like that.'

Welcome home at Melbourne's Tullamarine Airport, November 27, 1976.

twelve
the little
c**nts have
done it

the story ran on the wire around Australia on November 26: 'A small crowd of screaming girls today welcomed home the controversial rock band AC/DC. The screams, the hugs and the odd tears assured the five member group that it had not been forgotten during an eight month absence in England and Europe. And the members said they ensured that the English public and police force would not forget their act too quickly. At almost every performance the local police vice squad turned up. Guitarist Angus Young provoked the attendance of the law by stripping off his clothes on stage. In two cities, Glasgow and Liverpool, he was threatened with arrest.'

The media was intent on getting something out of AC/DC. Another story went out that teenage female fans were getting tattoos in emulation of the band, which led to an uproar, as the papers put it, among health officials, who feared the risks of backyard tattooing. But if this was a storm in a teacup, it was only the beginning.

AC/DC themselves were happy to be home, although on a professional level, they weren't so sure. They were in line to cop more shit than they ever had before. The matter of AC/DC even got so far as parliament, where one particularly crusty old member expressed fear at the threat the band posed to the nation's morals generally.

The controversy only confirmed AC/DC's suspicion that Australia was a backwater, and even though the band would make a tradition of coming home every year for Christmas, they would never again play Australia — officially — with Bon.

AC/DC would ride out the so-named 'Giant dose of rock 'n'roll' tour — at least, what was left of it after bannings and protests — and then, in January, go back into Alberts to cut a new album.

Bon and Silver had not travelled out together. Bon flew in with the band; Silver went overland from London, her destination being Adelaide where she spent Christmas with friends. She then joined Bon in Sydney in January, as the band worked on the album.

Michael Browning went via New York, where he was really going to have to pull some rabbits out of a hat if Atlantic was to continue its relationship with AC/DC. Support was building for the band in Britain and Europe, but they weren't selling truckloads of records. And in America, they'd sold next to none. Then they'd failed to get into the country to make personal appearances, and the album they'd presented as a follow-up to the first, *Dirty deeds* — at least as far as Atlantic was concerned — stunk.

MICHAEL BROWNING: 'The band really didn't want to do that tour. I can remember arguing about it, but we needed money, because that was the time when the Atlantic contract was up to question, so it was one of those things we had to do just to keep the machine running. I think the band thought Australia was all just a bit rinky-dink, after doing things on a reasonably professional level in England.'

Alberts was determined to distance the band from punk rock. They issued a press release in which the closing question 'Were they a punk rock band?' was answered decisively by Bon. 'No,' he said, 'we are a straight ROCK'N'ROLL band.' But it was the spectre of punk that was constantly evoked as the band was broadly decried as obscene and disgusting.

With all the hype — plus the fact that *Dirty deeds* was still sitting in the top 10 — AC/DC might quite reasonably have expected the tour to sell out. But it was the other major disappointment of the summer that attendances were down. This was probably largely due to the fact that at that stage AC/DC were caught between audiences. The teeny boppers had lost a lot of interest in the band in its absence. However, the image of AC/DC as a teeny phenomenon still persisted, and so the emerging headbangers were still very wary of them. What made all this especially galling for the band was the fact that they were in such fine form, playing like demons.

Some muck-raking wowser had actually bothered to listen to an AC/DC record, and found that the songs' subject matter was frequently less than squeaky clean. At the same time, as *Truth* gleefully reported under the banner POP HIT MAKES WIDOW'S PHONE RUN HOT, 'A wealthy widow was shocked and upset when she began to receive obscene telephone calls'. Kids had taken to trying the number 36-24-36, which Bon suggests calling in 'Dirty deeds done dirt cheap'. Chris Gilbey issued a profuse public apology.

But it was the sight of Angus's spotty behind at every turn that really upset the media. Bon gasped in mock shock. 'You see his backside in the papers more than you see his face — which is preferential as far as I'm concerned,' he told *RAM*.

The tour kicked off in grand fashion at the Myer Music Bowl. The full complement of tickets, at $5.50 and $4.50, was sold out. The show was the triumphant return everybody had hoped for. Things only went downhill from there.

Molly reported in *TV Week* that AC/DC was the 'cause of yet another hysterical riot', bringing 'a 5,000 fan crowd to fever pitch' (other reports had a further couple of thousand outside the cyclone-wire fencing).

'With scenes like this,' Molly went on, 'there is no doubt that AC/DC have become a huge threat to the top positions held by Sherbet and Skyhooks.'

The scene in Australia hadn't changed much. The most successful new talent was a cabaret nostalgia act called Ol' '55, whose debut album *Take it greasy* won out over even Sherbet's *Howzat* as the year's biggest local seller. Split Enz were still too weird for 'Countdown', although sophisticated *Rolling Stone* readers voted them 'Best Band'. Hush had already faded away. Punk was still just grumblings in the underground, not taken seriously at all.

Debbie Sharpe said of the Bowl show in the *Herald*: 'Lead singer Bon Scott played with the audience, singing to them, acting to them... and oh, that glint in his eye'. Bon was, in fact, doing everything short of what Jim Morrison got arrested for in Florida in 1970 — exposing himself — in an attempt to incite the crowd.

Sharpe went on later that night to see the Bay City Rollers, on tour in Australia for the second time in 12 months, and whilst she conceded that the scenes at Festival Hall were not as hysterical, 'for both bands Sunday night was successful'.

AC/DC and company repaired to the Tiger Lounge, a pub in Richmond, where the band took over the stage. An unsuspecting punter who happened to be there remembers the occasion. 'I'd never seen AC/DC, I mean, I wasn't a fan. But they came down to the Tiger Lounge, and they just got up and had a blow. They played some blues songs and some rock'n'roll songs — Elvis; the room was really small and it was really packed, and it was great. I realised how good they were, even as pissed as I was. But the amazing thing was Bon. He was just this scrawny, ugly little guy standing up there, but he had every woman in the place eating out of the palm of his hand. He had this incredible amount of sexual energy, magnetism, and the whole room was electrified by it. No one, men included, wasn't aware of it.'

AC/DC turned a few heads that night. The Tiger Lounge was something of a musicians' watering hole, and when the cognoscenti, who had only ever condescended to AC/DC as a teeny-bopper band, saw them that night, just jamming, away from the usual pressure to put on a show, ripping up old blues tunes, they were impressed. Underneath the set moves, it was clear that they had the chops as well.

Malcolm and Angus didn't care whether they were respected or not. They just wanted to make the money and run. Or at least, that was what they claimed. Certainly though, they knew themselves how good they were. And though Bon too had developed a thick skin — England had inured him to criticism — he was rapt that at last his peers saw the worth of what AC/DC was doing.

The band hit the road on Tuesday, December 7. They hadn't but made it to the Victorian/New South Wales border town of Albury, for only the second gig of the tour on the Wednesday, when the shit started rolling in. Sale of the tour program was stopped after the first gig as some other wowser had found a stray four-letter word in it. Bon was quoted as saying, by way of explaining the theme of 'Ain't no fun waiting around to be a millionaire', 'It means it takes a long time to make enough money to be able to fuck Britt Ekland'. Albury's town clerk claimed to have subsequently received complaints from parents. 'If AC/DC want to come here again, they'll have to change their act,' he said. 'I'm a professional artist myself, and their act isn't entertainment. I'm broadminded, but when you get children going along...'

All over the country, AC/DC would face such self-appointed moral guardians and petty bureaucrats who were determined to place every obstacle in their path.

Gigs in Canberra and Wollongong over the next two nights were tempered by warnings from police: they would pull the plug if Angus pulled down his pants. He withheld his browneye.

Support acts for most of the tour were Stars and Punkz. Stars were the Adelaide band Michael Gudinski signed to Mushroom instead of Cold Chisel, because they seemed more manageable. They were that, but they were also less enduring, the appeal of their cowboy boogie sound wearing thin after 'The mighty rock', their biggest hit. Punkz later became known as Cheek, Punkz being something of a misnomer from the first. Managed by Glenn A Baker and also signed to Mushroom, Punkz was a Sydneyside sixties-style act with which Baker perhaps hoped to repeat the success he'd enjoyed with his other retro protégés, Ol' '55 — but he failed to do so.

'As a young player, in my first serious band, the thing that made a real impression on me was AC/DC's utmost professionalism,' says Mal Eastick, then lead guitarist in Stars. 'And I've never seen anything quite like it since. They just knew exactly where they were going.'

After playing the Saturday, December 11, in Newcastle, on the Sunday the tour played the somewhat more urbane centre of Sydney, at the Hordern Pavilion. AC/DC put on a full-scale show — and no one was known to have gone off into the night speaking in tongues and raping babies. The 4,500-capacity Hordern was barely half full, however.

With the boppers dropping off, 'AC/DC, like Skyhooks,' as *RAM*'s review of the show read, 'must start the whole slow progress of winning over and earning the trust of a more musical audience.' But their prospects looked good, since 'the bulk of the audience resembled the Status Quo crowd who raged and boogied to their heroes just a week before'.

The band's appeal was irresistible either way. 'Loud seems too tame a description for the volume they inflict on an audience,' *RAM* continued, 'it's more a "living sound" that actually penetrates the flesh and bones until movement and rhythm come involuntarily and the audience is swept into the same current... behind the insistency lies an excellent rock/blues outfit with an amazing singer out front in Bon Scott...'

Heading out of Sydney, the band played Orange and Dubbo before the Mayor of Tamworth, Australia's country music capital, stepped in and refused the band permission to play in his fair burgh. Channel Nine's 'A current affair' had a crew following the band around like the Keystone Cops, waiting for the something sensational to happen, which it didn't even then. The gig was blown out, the band just had to hole up in its motel, and then move on, according to schedule, to the next town. No savage retribution, no trail of rape and pillage.

MAL EASTICK: 'We actually had to pinch ourselves to believe it, you know, This is really true, they're not going to let us play. And then the next thing, Willesee arrives in a helicopter, and Willesee was a very big deal on television at that time, and so it was, Hey, this is getting serious! Up to that point, I don't think they were at all perturbed by the controversy, I think they were probably quite amused. But when it was actually loudly expressed that AC/DC were not welcome to play in Australia, in certain parts, they just couldn't believe the pettiness, the small-townness of it. I think they were then inclined to adopt the attitude, Well, fuck Australia, we'll go back to Europe, seeya later.'

The juggernaut pressed on, from Tamworth to Too-woomba. AC/DC made use of any spare time they had to prepare themselves for recording.

EASTICK: 'We travelled together in a small bus. They were always working on songs, all the time. It wasn't like, Hey, I'll wait until I've got some privacy, or until I've had a couple of drinks, gotten loose, none of that. I can remember Angus playing guitar on the bus, and Bon used to stomp up and down the aisle, he would stand behind the driver and he always had a pad and would work on titles first.'

After Toowoomba, which a police spokesman said was 'quiet and without incident' — if quiet is the right word — the band played Brisbane Festival Hall on Saturday, December 18. Strangely, Joh Bjelke-Petersen's blue-shirted storm-troopers failed to exert their presence.

The papers in Sydney still wouldn't let go of the story. 'Members of Australian punk rock group AC/DC must decide if they are strippers or musicians, the General Manager of radio station 2SM said today,' read one report. '"Until they do, the station will not associate with them in any way," Mr Garvis Rutherford said. Mr Rutherford said 2SM would not advertise the group's concerts or play their recordings.' 2SM may have been one of AC/DC's original champions, but the station also happened to be owned by the Catholic Church.

The band headed north out of Brisbane to tropical Bunda-berg and Rockhampton, before doing a U-turn and heading back down the coast again. At Surfers Paradise on the Gold Coast, the band checked into the Pink Poodle for a well-earned day off. Bon made a beeline for the surf, where the diversions were many besides just swimming. He watched the guy with a spray gun full of oil covering barely bikini-clad beach bunnies.

But as occupied as Bon was, he still desperately missed Silver.

SILVER: 'Where I was staying at the beach in Adelaide, this girl didn't have a telephone, so I was just bombarded with tele-grams. Bon was a prolific letter writer, when he was on the road, he wrote almost every day. All those letters I lost. It was sad, because some of the song lyrics were born in those letters too.'

EASTICK: 'Bon was probably one of my strongest early impressions of a rock star living that rock star life, a hard life, you know, where he wasn't really sleeping much, nursing a lot of hangovers — there must have been something inside him that was lonely, or unhappy, to have acted the way he did. But at the same time, he was a totally dedicated profes-sional. With that strong obsession, like, We're gonna be better than everybody else.'

On Thursday, December 22, the band played in Murwil-lumbah, just an hour or so's drive south of the Gold Coast, in the lush Northern Rivers of New South Wales, next door to the Aquarian Age commune town of Nimbin. AC/DC made as much sense to the hippies as they did to banana farmers. At least Bon scored a bag of killer home-grown.

The following night, the band played on the Gold Coast itself, at the Miami High School Great Hall, with the Saints. As if from out of nowhere — or the wilds of western Brisbane suburb Oxley — the Saints had set faraway England on its ear with the single they'd recorded and released themselves, the blazing '(I'm) Stranded', a pioneering punk classic. Chris Gilbey had got wind of this and located the band to offer them a gig. They arrived at the gig in a couple of beaten-up old station wagons, a few of the Oxley boys lugging their gear just so they could hang around.

Even at the height of school holidays, the hall held only a smattering of suntanned teenagers. Michael Browning was manifestly unimpressed by the Saints, although Chris Gilbey would go on to manage the band briefly. AC/DC themselves were equally unimpressed, the Oxley boys narrowly averting a confrontation with their crew as all they were doing was getting in the way.

At eight the next morning, the band climbed in the bus to do the thirteen hour drive back to Sydney. 'THEN,' as the worksheets put it, 'EVERYBODY FUCKS OFF! BUT MAKE SURE THAT YOU MAKE ARRANGEMENTS TO BE BACK IN MELBOURNE BY THURSDAY 6TH JANUARY.'

It was almost as if Michael Browning had only just sat down to Christmas dinner with his family in Melbourne when the phone rang. Phil Carson was calling from London. A problem. Atlantic in New York reckoned they didn't want to take up the option on AC/DC.

MICHAEL BROWNING: 'There's no doubt that Atlantic Records in America were really lukewarm on the group at first, in point of fact, would have preferred to have dropped the group. They had a guy called Jim Delahant, who was head of A&R at the time, who quite clearly wished to have them dropped. Jerry Greenberg, the president of the company, was kind of half into it. It was only for the fact that Phil Carson in London talked them into dropping the advance commitment that they held onto the group. Which was the difference between having to pay twenty thousand dollars instead of thirty; nothing by today's standards, but then, it was the only way we could keep the deal.'

Carson was confident that AC/DC could do the business in Britain to start with, and then, in turn, America. He shared the belief with Browning and the band that this next album was going to take AC/DC up the next step.

The band, as usual, was unaware of these goings on. Bon checked into Hyatt Kingsgate in Sydney's Kings Cross, and spent Christmas with the Youngs at Burwood. But with the news coming through that the city fathers of the Victorian coal-mining town of Warrnambool had barred the band from appearing there on January 12, something was going to have to give.

ROCK BAND THREATENS TO LEAVE COUNTRY read the headline on New Year's Eve. 'AC/DC — Australia's raunchiest rock group — have threatened to quit the country and settle in England because of alleged "hounding" from local authorities,' the story opened.

'It's no good if we drive half way across the country to stage a concert to find that someone has cancelled it because they consider us obscene,' Angus was quoted as saying. 'It will only take a couple more hassles from the authorities and we will leave Australia.'

The point was academic. Leaving Australia, so to speak, was what the band was doing anyway; they were never in one place long enough to call anywhere home. But from this point on, AC/DC almost disowned Australia, even if it was where they all returned every year at Christmas. They would go so far as to play down being an Australian band, proclaiming instead their Scottish roots.

On New Year's Eve, Bon went out to see the premiere performance by Rose Tattoo. They were guys he knew: singer Angry Anderson had fronted Buster Brown, the band whence Rhil Rudd came; slide guitarist Peter Wells was previously in Buffalo, and bassist Ian Rilen in Band Of Light; the line-up was completed by rhythm guitarist Mick Cocks, and drummer, 'Digger' Royal. Overnight, the Tatts became notorious, a self-styled gang of rock'n'roll outlaws intent on mayhem and destruction. Bon loved them, and in fact, it was his tip that led to their signing with Alberts.

MICK COCKS: 'In the early days, when we first started, we could only work two places, the Lifesaver and Chequers, everybody hated us. But Bon was a big fan. And that's basically how we met. If Bon was in town, he'd pop up somewhere, and we'd go and have a drink.

'In those days, Angus and Bon used to get up for a blow. 'Cos Bon would be out drinking with his girlfriend, just having a good time, and we just got on really well. I suppose we were one of the few bands he could get up and have a sing with and feel comfortable. We'd just do standards — Little

Richard, 'Johnny B Goode', 'Goin' down', old blues songs. We were a rock'n'roll band, in a period when everything was a bit glam, or whatever.'

AC/DC got out on the road again on January 5. They played out the rest of their tour, six gigs, without undue incident. Bonds were paid in Portland and Bendigo, $500 and $2,000 respectively, and they were not forfeited. With the last gig on January 14 in Ballarat, the band was simply relieved it was all over. Now they could get in the studio. They hightailed it immediately to Sydney, where they checked into the Hyatt Kingsgate. Silver joined Bon there.

The band was back in the familiar — indeed, familial — confines of Alberts' Studio One. Bon added Silver's name, in silver spray-paint, to the graffiti wall at one end of the studio, such was his devotion to her. Such was everyone else's suspicion of her, it was promptly erased.

MARK EVANS: 'The band sounded different in the studio. We were all playing well, we were all happy to be back in Sydney, we were enjoying that, and so recording that album, the confidence was right up. We were recharged because we knew we had to go back over to England again and really do it. And I think that album was one of the better ones of the whole lot, it was a real turning point for the band.'

RAM asked Bon whether there would be any change in AC/DC after three straight rock'n'roll albums. 'But that's all there is,' he replied, 'there's no more than that. You play what you were brought up on, what you believe in. I can listen to other bands that play really intricate stuff and I can appreciate it, and I even like some of it, but I'd never attempt to play it. Like Alex Harvey took the rock'n'roll thing and told stories but that's going too far for me. I wouldn't try to tell anything more intricate than "Jailbreak" 'cos that's still basically rock'n'roll.'

George and Harry were just as fired up as the band. If George accepted that *Dirty deeds* had been knocked back in America because his production of it was poor — rather than blaming Michael Browning — then he was going to make amends with *Let there be rock*, as the next album would be called.

Alberts had continued on its winning streak in Australia

during 1976. The Ted Mulry Gang trailed only Sherbet and Skyhooks as the biggest band in the land. John Paul Young was the leading male solo artist. George and Harry themselves won a *TV Week* King of Pop Special Award for Best Australian Songwriters. Late in the year, when they released their own first single under the Flash and the Pan aegis, 'Hey, St Peter!' it went to number three.

By now ensconced at Kangaroo House, George and Harry were raring to go with AC/DC. Sessions progressed smoothly, in typical AC/DC fashion — George, Malcolm and Angus honing riffs and ideas, with the addition of Bon's lyrics, into structured songs, and then putting it all down in rapid-fire sequence. One of the most oft-repeated stories concerning AC/DC's studio method emanates from these sessions. At one time, as Angus was overdubbing a guitar solo (and guitars and vocals were about all that was overdubbed), his amplifier started smoking, fusing out. George gestured wildly from behind the desk. Keep going! Keep going! 'There was no way,' he later explained, 'we were going to stop a shit-hot performance for a technical reason like amps blowing up!'

Let there be rock was the first fully rounded AC/DC album. The band had finally found itself.

George and Harry gave the band plenty of room, and the band rose to the occasion and brought it all home. George and Harry got AC/DC sounding better than they ever had on vinyl, capturing with clearer definition and crisper dynamics, all the savage attack of the band's live sound. Bon's writing too was more assured, more coherent. The band stretched themselves to wring the most out of every bar of every song — and still they never overdid it.

Let there be rock saw AC/DC abandon the last vestiges of the pop band they had once been. 'That album sort of put us on the road,' Angus agreed, 'and I think it also set the style of the band.'

Its feature track, 'Whole lotta Rosie', was, of course, a play by Bon on Led Zeppelin, and his tribute to the self-same Rosie, an ode to making fat ladies sing as fine as Jimmy Castor's like-minded funk classic 'Troglodyte'. If Bon had returned to Melbourne in 1975 for that song's inspiration, others betrayed the same source: 'Go down' was inspired by supergroupie Ruby Lips, and 'Overdose', which appropriately borders on the turgid, harks back to Judy King.

On previous albums, simple stomps like 'Dog eat dog', 'Bad boy boogie' and 'Hell ain't a bad place to be' might have been filler tracks, but on *Let there be rock,* they more than justify their presence. Only the requisite slow blues, 'Crabsody in blue', a creaky play on George Gershwin, falls short lyrically, like 'The jack'. The title track, however, is a masterpiece which in its extended instrumental passage enters a realm of pure white noise equalled at the time only, ironically, by the Saints, with their first album's anarchic opus, 'Nights in Venice'.

AC/DC had almost finished the album — and a new, previously recorded single, 'Love at first feel' had been released — when they went out to play a special show for the Festival of Sydney on January 30. Five thousand people turned up at the old Haymarket warehouse to see them headline over Taste and Chariot, and blow away any echoes of the 'rock' stars of the festival — the Little River Band — who had earlier played the same venue.

MARK EVANS: 'When we finished the album, we had to go back to England. We did a couple of gigs in Sydney, then we went back to Melbourne to do some gigs; we did a gig in Melbourne on Thursday night, then we did Friday and Saturday in Adelaide, then we did Sunday night in Perth, then we did the following Wednesday night in Edinburgh.'

'Can't wait to get back [overseas],' Mark said at the time in *RAM.* 'They treat you properly, food and booze provided, none of this hassling with hall managers shit.'

The band had had enough of Australia. Australia had failed to show the required amount of respect, so Australia could go fuck itself, AC/DC just wanted to be where the action was. In America. 'Love at first feel' performed even less well than 'Dirty deeds', and would, in fact, stand as the last AC/DC single to breach the Australian charts until 'Highway to hell' over two years later.

After playing to mixed reception in Melbourne and Adelaide, AC/DC played its last Australian date in Perth, which at least enabled Bon to see his folks. His mother didn't quite know what to make of this mysterious, dark lady by the strange name of Silver. But Bon seemed to cherish her — that was the right word — so like always, she just had to go along with him. Silver was extended every hospitality, and she could see just how devoted to Bon his parents were.

Like the other four members of AC/DC, Bon had received a missive from Ted Albert just prior to leaving Sydney which he was still clutching proudly. It contained a royalty cheque for the second half of 1976, and a letter, which read:

> As you will see from the enclosed statement, the total record earnings for the whole group for the period total $24,733.06. After deducting the manager's one-fifth, the total of $19,786.45 remains and your one-fifth of this is $3,957.29. A cheque for this amount is enclosed.
>
> My personal thanks to you for all the many hours of hard work that you have spent in the studio during the last few weeks. Also on behalf of the whole company our thanks for your efforts overseas and our best wishes for the coming year.

Four thousand dollars in six months was a paltry sum when expressed as barely three cents for every seven dollar album sold — but to Bon, it was a fine old going-away present.

Isa saw Bon and Silver off at the airport. Chick couldn't be there as he had to work. The band was glad just to get on the plane, putting Australia and all its petty aggravations behind them. They would not return to play again until after Bon was dead.

Now, not only Britain and Europe but also America beckoned. And they had a new album so hot in their pocket it was burning a hole.

Bon's feet barely touched the London ground before he was back in the bus on the way to Edinburgh, where the band commenced a 26-date British tour on February 18. 'Dirty deeds' had been released as a single in January.

AC/DC was playing like a band possessed. The obvious quality of *Let there be rock* had given them another injection of confidence, although none of its material had yet been introduced to the set. The ecstatic response back in Britain was encouraged by kids who had bought the *Dirty deeds* album over Christmas and were now getting a chance to catch up with the band.

But if the majority of critics still demurred to AC/DC, Bon hit the nail on the head when he told the *NME*, 'The music press is totally out of touch with what the kids actually want to listen to.

'These kids might be working in a shitty factory all week, or they might be on the dole — come the weekend, they just want to go out and have a good time, get drunk and go wild. We give them the opportunity to do that.'

Celebrating the drooling, banal raw glory of sixties prototype punks the Troggs — creators of 'Wild thing' and 'I can't control myself' — critic, the late Lester Bangs wrote of a 'no-jive, take-care-of-business band churning out rock'n'roll that thundered right back to the very first grungy chords and straight ahead to the fuzztone subways of the future. And because it was so true to its evolutionary antecedents, it was usually about sex, and not just Sally-go-to-the-movieshow-and-hold-my-hand stuff, but the most challengingly blatant flat-out proposition and prurient fantasy...

'The reason why this band ultimately cut their competitors and successors at raw high-energy electro-fertility stomps was their consistent sense of structure and economy — I don't think any of their songs ran over four minutes, the solos were short but always slashingly pertinent, and the vocals were not to be believed... leering, sneering punk snarl... raspy and cocky and loose and lewd...'

AC/DC exercised the same appeal. Stripped of all artifice, of everything unessential, leaving only the rhythm and the blues, AC/DC got to the point with an elemental force, allowing Bon, with a glint in his eye and tongue in his cheek, to tell his tall tales.

'You get on that stage,' said Bon, 'and the more crass, gross and rowdy you sound, the more they love it. So I just go up there and scream away, sometimes to a point where I can't talk the next day.'

'We're on the crowd's side,' he said, 'because we give 'em

what they want, and everybody gets into our show — because it's a band/audience show. We're not like performing seals, we're all in it together.'

AC/DC's audience appreciated the fact.

Back in London by the end of March, the band had a moment's peace prior to taking off for Europe to tour with Black Sabbath at the end of April. Malcolm and Angus moved into a flat together in Ladbroke Grove; Mark and Phil moved into one just around the corner. Bon was snugly shacked-up with Silver, who was still living by somewhat dubious means and dabbling with increasing enthusiasm in heroin.

Heroin in London in the late seventies was in plentiful supply, and of a consistently high quality and low price. It was enough to tempt anyone. Bon resisted it, maybe because he knew how dangerous it was, maybe because it just wasn't his style of drug — preferring anything more social — or maybe because he knew that as far as the Youngs were concerned, it was just not on. Silver, however, had no such reservations. And Bon was happy if she was happy.

SILVER: 'As far as my life goes, I don't think anyone has loved me as unconditionally as Bon. He had no complaints — they were all on my side. It gave me the guilts for quite a long time. Because Bon was really good to me. He accepted me exactly as I was. He was really attentive too, you know, two or three letters a day bombarding you when he was on the road, and he was always bringing flowers and little presents. I mean, it was full on, right up until we split up.

'No one gave Bon drugs. He could have used any time he wanted, but the thing was, we just wouldn't let him. Partly because he wouldn't metabolise them well, and also, if he was in that devil may care frame of mind, he wouldn't stop to think that the person he was using with may have had a tolerance, and he had none at all, and so he would have ended up blue on the floor.

'Bon wanted to get married and have kids and all that sort of stuff. At the time, I just couldn't get my head around that, it seemed like the world we were living in was so mad, it didn't make any sense.

Pin-up idols, 1969.

ABOVE: The Valentines in their last incarnation, Autumn 1970, not long before breaking up. Left to right: Ted Ward, Bon (wearing his 'Super Screw' T-shirt), Paddy Beach, Wyn Milson, Vince Lovegrove.

BELOW: Fraternity, by now rechristened Fang, on the road in their own magic bus; England, April 1973. Hamish Henry (centre) wearing shades and a moustache.

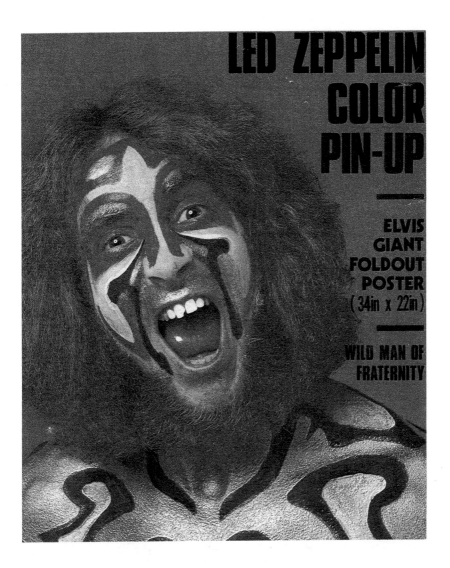

Bon, 'Wild Man of Fraternity', gracing the cover of short-lived Australian rock rag *Sound Blast*; November 1970.

ABOVE LEFT: On stage, Melbourne Festival Hall, New Year's Day, 1975.
ABOVE RIGHT: The same day: after a quick change into the kilt, Bon introduces
'Young Talent Time' graduate Debbie Byrne. Bon: 'She wanted me to be her
"boogie man" and it just happened that I had a bit of costumery (like me balls).
Said I ruined her image.'
BELOW: On 'Countdown', 1975. Bon's appearance in a schoolgirl's uniform
prompted howls of outrage.

ABOVE: With Irene at Fraternity's Finchley house in London, 1972, before the rot set in. The house degenerated into a squat.
BELOW: Bon at Bondi on the bike he rented over the summer of 1977/78.

ABOVE LEFT: With Silver at her flat in London, circa 1977.
ABOVE RIGHT: With Mary and Peter Renshaw in Melbourne, after a few drinks; Christmas 1979.
BELOW LEFT: With Anna Baba
BELOW RIGHT: At Angus and Ellen Young's wedding; London, February 1980.

ABOVE: The block of flats in Overhill Road, Dulwich, where Bon died.
BELOW LEFT: Isa at home with 'the boys' after Bon's funeral.
BELOW RIGHT: The oft-stolen plaque marking Bon's grave at Fremantle
Cemetery. After the first such theft in early 1988, Isa told the *West Australian*:
'We know there are plenty of visitors as we sometimes find fresh flowers. And
we often have to remove empty beer and whiskey bottles, but there has never
been any damage until now. How can anyone do a thing like that?'

Mary: 'This photo was sent to Graeme by a fan after Bonnie died, and then Graeme gave it to me. I just think it really captures Bon.'

'Bon was very pipe and slippers. He liked peace and quiet. He had this public image, but he was probably the most domesticated male I've ever known. He liked everything to be clean and tidy. When he was home he liked to just see people, you know, sit around, entertain — at home, not going out. He liked having roast dinners on Sunday and all that. But he could go very quiet and sombre if he was hurt. He was a typical Cancer.'

Silver's recollection of the kind of records they used to listen to together throws a different light on Bon as well. He had a special fondness for female soul singers — Millie Jackson, Gladys Knight, Lorraine Ellison, even Joan Armatrading — and he also liked Roxy Music and Bryan Ferry, and Steely Dan, J Geils.

SILVER: 'He knew the lyrics to an enormous number of songs. Everything from *Oklahoma* through to ... all that Broadway musical sort of stuff. He had a great memory for lyrics... well, his short-term memory was stuffed, he couldn't remember which plane he was supposed to catch! But yeah, his taste in music was very different.'

He still felt an obligation to live up to his image though, as a profile he filled out at the time, but which seems to have gone unpublished, suggests.

Favourite Drink: Whisky
Favourite Bike (Don't Like Cars): Harley Sportster
Favourite Colour: Silver (Preferably Metal), Black
Guitarist: Don't mind the Young brothers
Singer: Don't mind Jess Roden
Record: Don't mind Tres Hombres
AC/DC Record: 'Carry me home' (as yet unreleased)

Before the band left for Europe, they shot a video in London, for the special fifth anniversary episode of 'Countdown', of their new Australian single 'Dog eat dog', the first to come off *Let there be rock*. With 'Carry me home' on the B-side, it went nowhere. When *Let there be rock* itself was released in May, it went in and out of the charts before it even got any higher than number 20. Ironically though, as Mark Evans put it, 'That was the point at which things started to look really strong, that was when America started'.

With the British release of *Let there be rock* in the offing, Atlantic in New York was finally starting to come around. This was largely due to the appointment of two new executives to AC/DC's case, Michael Klenfner and Perry Cooper. Klenfner and Cooper had just joined the company as part of a package from Arista Records, and they could see something in AC/DC.

MARK EVANS: 'The thing was, the reason the band always had a level head, was because there was always something to do, a new objective. We always seemed to be starting at the bottom and working our way up.'

The Black Sabbath tour would prove to be ill-fated, precipitating Mark Evans' sacking. Sabbath, by 1976, were well past their prime, and AC/DC were all but blowing them right off stage. Only the showmanship of Ozzy Osborne kept Sabbath alive. Substance abuse within the band was rampant. It was in this atmosphere, then, that relations between the two bands came to an ugly head, when Sabbath bassist 'Geezer' Butler apparently pulled a flick knife on Malcolm. Fistic retaliation was swift, with the end result that AC/DC were simply shown the door.

EVANS: 'I don't think the band took too kindly to being on the road in Europe for some reason. Every time we went to Europe, things seemed to get strained. When we were in England, Scotland, no problems. And yeah, things did get very tense between Angus and me, basically, I suppose, because we just didn't get on. And so what happens, if you've got your brother in the band, and somebody doesn't like your brother...

'Europe could be a lonely time for Bon too. He never socialised with the band. It would not be unusual for us to be out, and not return with Bon. He would just wander off in some other direction. Do whatever it was he did.

'The last six months I was in the band, his drinking did escalate pretty quickly, to the point where he started showing up at gigs with a bottle of Johnnie Walker.

'In hindsight, after we had a problem with the Americans,

going, What the fuck is this? knocking back *Dirty deeds*, I think with the negativity of that, and then getting thrown off the Black Sabbath tour, I think I was made a bit of a scapegoat. It was, What's going wrong, we'd better make a change. And it was gonna be both me and Bon!

'I didn't know, and I'm sure Phil didn't know either, that *Dirty deeds* was knocked back in the States. We just weren't told. We were in Helsinki, after the Black Sabbath tour, ready to fly to America, right, we're going, but then it was like, Guys, sorry, we're not going, you're going back to England. Things aren't ready yet.'

Next thing, as *RAM* reported on June 3, 'Mark Evans, the quiet, well-behaved member of AC/DC has left the group'.

All Mark said at the time was, 'Both me and the band are better for it'. He was sent packing, given a $2,000 golden handshake in lieu of all future royalties. He returned to Melbourne, where he continued a career in music, initially as bassist with a band called Finch. And though it would take him ten years, he would eventually win settlement over the royalties which had been denied him.

MICHAEL BROWNING: 'I got a phone call from Malcolm and Angus, and they said, Could you come over, we've got something important we want to talk about. At that stage I had a sense the Americans were a little bit negative towards Bon, I had a sense it might have been something to do with that. So I got there and I was actually surprised they wanted to get rid of Mark.'

MARK EVANS: 'When I got the bullet, Michael Browning rang me and said, Listen, the guys are going to call a meeting, what do you know about it? I said, Michael, you've called the wrong guy, I don't know anything about a meeting. He said, Well, it's at Malcolm and Angus's place tonight, I think they're finally going to give Bon the arse. I said, I don't know about any meeting, so I said to Phil, Do you know about a meeting, and he said, Yeah, I do. And I said, Michael, it's me. And Michael's words on the phone were, Oh fuck. He said, I thought it was going to be Bon.'

On the road in America. Left to right: Phil Rudd, unidentified ligger, Bon (with perm, and bottle), new bassist Cliff Williams, Angus, unidentified liggers, Malcolm, Michael Klenfner and Perry Cooper of Atlantic Records, and Michael Browning, AC/DC manager.

thirteen
america

the replacement of bassist Mark Evans by Cliff Williams saw AC/DC change its operation up a gear.

The band was clearing the decks in readiness for its first assault on America, the biggest and most competitive music market in the world. With the stakes now so much higher, nothing could be left to chance, no excess baggage would be trucked. Cliff Williams could be expected to hold his end up, no more, no less. You had to know your place, or else forfeit it. Nobody was indispensable.

There's no reason to believe Bon was beyond this law either, even if the Youngs reserved an inordinate amount of loyalty for him. But Bon knew himself he'd come too far to throw it all away now. An atmosphere of increasing venality was something he would just have to learn to live with. When he joined AC/DC in 1974, it was a new lease on life for him; but in the end, for the last couple of years of his life, the band became a business, and it was more like a job, a daily grind that Bon endured as price of finally 'making it'.

As everything else other than the music itself congealed around him, Bon drank more and more just to get through the day. Cliff Williams, as it turned out, was a saving grace, a new friend for Bon who relieved some of the day-to-day tedium.

It was Michael Browning, again, who found Williams and engineered his joining the band. Malcolm and Angus were keen on a bassist called Colin Pattendon, who had previously been with Manfred Mann's Earth Band. But as Browning said, 'He just didn't fit the image. At that juncture, I felt that whoever came in had to look the part as well.' Browning was alerted to Williams by a friend. When Williams passed the audition, Browning gave his friend a tenner by way of a spotter's fee.

Williams was born in the Essex town of Romford, just outside London, on December 14, 1949. His musical background was not unlike Bon's, having spent the early seventies as a member of an obscure English country-rock band called Home. He was playing with an outfit called Bandit when AC/DC's better prospects presented themselves.

SILVER: 'That was a bit of a relief when Cliff came in, because Cliff was more our age, our interests. The boys — they were kids. I mean, they were kids from the western suburbs, and they were really aware of it, they had a lot of fronts up, and they weren't going to change. Whereas Cliff, you know, he was 28, he'd been around, and he read books, went to the movies, had a girlfriend. Because none of the boys had girlfriends at that stage.'

The band returned to Australia at the start of June to work Williams in, in preparation for touring throughout the rest of the year.

America had finally fallen into place. The band would have to be in top form.

Michael Browning had gone over to New York to meet with Perry Cooper and Michael Klenfner. As the new kids on the block at Atlantic, Cooper and Klenfner needed to earn some

kudos. When President Jerry Greenberg came to them one day early in the piece with that same old film of 'High voltage' they saw their opportunity.

PERRY COOPER: 'He said, Look, we've got this band, we've signed them for the rest of their life, and we put out an album, but we can't get fuckin' arrested with it. He said, Why don't you have a look at it. Klenfner says, I haven't got time, so I go into my office — and I really liked the whole thing.

'So I went back to Klenfner, and I said, You gotta look at these guys, and so we started talking. We thought, What's going to break this band? Obviously, radio isn't. The only thing I could think, If they get over here and tour, if they're as great live as they look, they've got something different. We had to find out, Are they willing to work their asses off, for the next — you know, nonstop, like the Stones. The Stones, in the very beginning, used to just go around in a station wagon. AC/DC ended up doing exactly the same thing.

'We met with Michael Browning, and it was agreed that they would just come over and work their asses off, touring. Michael said, That's what these guys do, don't worry about that.'

Browning signed AC/DC on with a booking agency called American Talent International, and gigs were lined up.

The band arrived in America at the end of June. Club dates were booked along the line from Texas to Florida. The Deep South had given the world redneck boogie bands of the order of ZZ Top and Black Oak Arkansas, and if an opening existed in America for AC/DC, it was here. In 1977 punk rock meant about as much to middle America as it did to middle Australia.

MICHAEL BROWNING: 'One of the important factors in the group's American campaign was that there was a guy called Sidney Drashin, in Jacksonville, Florida, who was a promoter. There was a radio station down there too, and for some reason they must have got hold of an AC/DC record and actually listened to it, and just fell in love with it. Programmed about four or five tracks. And so the guy from the radio station was calling up Atlantic, and so was Sidney, saying, you know, What are you doing with this group? So that one town formed

the basis, it gave the record company living proof that it could work. And so when we went there to tour, we picked up a couple of dates here and a couple of dates there, we'd play for $500 and travel 500 miles, playing dates with a variety of acts, but we did Jacksonville and played the Coliseum to a packed house.'

AC/DC supported REO Speedwagon at the Jacksonville Coliseum in front of as big a crowd as they'd ever faced, nearly 8,000 strong.

BROWNING: 'There was Jacksonville and there was Columbus, Ohio, which is a college town, and that was a similar situation there, the radio station people were fanatical for the group. So you just had to go there and build it from the ground level up. It was all done on a shoestring, in hire cars, staying at Red Roof Inns, Holiday Inns.'

The band headed north from Florida, through Columbus and Chicago on its way to New York. Bon wrote to Mary:

I'm enjoying our tour of America. The band is playing good and going over great… The money's good… The chicks are outta sight (right now they are outta sight) and everything is better than I ever thought it could be. We're touring here till Sept 7 and then it's Europe for eighteen dates, England for twenty, America for another month or so and then Australia for a tour. So I should be able to break your door down early next year. Bon's love life ain't goin' too well at the mo. I haven't seen my lady for four months and it's kinda painful… Love will prevail. My hair's getting long and the perm is almost out. I'm a regular shaggy dog… But I like it.

In New York on August 24, AC/DC played on the bottom of the bill at Palladium, under old wave punk band the Dictators. They then raced downtown to the Bowery, to put in an appearance at CBGB's, the decrepit, hallowed home of New York new wave, where they were met with stony silence opening for a nowhere power-pop outfit called Marbles.

Variety at least gave them the thumbs up over the Dictators.

Supplanting Angus's asshole, which was deemed unfit for

puritanical American consumption, the band's new set-piece — the walking-the-floor routine, Angus astride Bon's shoulders — was improved since Angus had acquired a new toy, a cordless guitar pick-up.

A New York fanzine called *Punk* interviewed Bon and Angus. Bon succeeded in his attempt to outgross the gross-out standards of punkdom. The only telling thing he said was in answer to the question, What's the meaning of life? 'As good a time and as short as possible.'

In a way, AC/DC was a little confused by America. Britain, Europe, even punk rock, they could understand, but America is so big and so diverse, contradiction is inherent.

'I hadn't even heard a lot of the music here at the time — I thought there would be more rock,' Angus told *Guitar World*. 'But when we got here it was a disco type thing. What was real strange was that although the media was pushing this really soft music, you'd get amazing numbers of people turning out to hear the harder stuff. We were playing big stadiums and getting a great reaction.'

The band was duly unimpressed meeting staff at Atlantic, finding the stereotypical image of the gold-sporting, cigar-chomping, cocaine-sniffing record company executive not too far from the truth.

From New York, AC/DC jetted to the West Coast. After gigs in the northwest states with Ted Nugent, they played four well-attended shows at the Old Waldorf club in San Francisco. In LA, at the Whisky A-Go-Go, LA's legendary Sunset Strip equivalent of London's Marquee, they pulled a crowd of fewer than 100; but as *Variety* again enthused, made an indelible impression.

Touring America was at least an improvement on Britain in terms of service, and lifestyle. Like most rock'n'roll bands, AC/DC would forever suffer condescension in Britain, even — especially — at the best hotels. But Americans have never let class tarnish the colour of people's money. In LA, AC/DC stayed at the Hyatt House, just up from the Whisky, where Mott the Hoople had stayed a few years earlier. In *Diary of a rock'n'roll star*, Ian Hunter described the scene, which hadn't changed much in that time:

I've just come back from the coffee shop, doing my observation bit. The guy at the till snorted coke while he was sorting out my change. Two groupies to my left looked quite reasonable while three hideous ones ogled from my right...

It's all fucking boring anyway. They're lousy lays as a rule and you can never get rid of them once you let them in. They don't even listen to the music anymore and you run a big risk in the dose stakes if you decide to dabble. The best thing to do, young and inexperienced musicians (if there is such a thing), is to whip their spotty little arses and lay back and enjoy a professional blow job; then tell them you got crabs and they'll be gone before you know it.

Bon, however, fully intended to make the most of his first ever visit to Hollywood. He wasn't seen without a blonde on one arm and a bottle in his free hand. He and Phil went to Disneyland on a day off. They rustled up a couple of extra special joints for the occasion. They didn't know what they were in for. The joints were laced with angel dust, an erratic seventies psychedelic, which sent them off on a trip more unnerving than any Disneyland big dipper. It was just a question of who was more put off, Bon and Phil or the regular Disneyland patrons, who couldn't tell if these two tattooed men walking around wide-eyed and legless, holding hands, were one of the attractions or just some sort of terrible mistake.

AC/DC boarded the plane back to Britain feeling quite pleased with themselves. The prospects ahead were looking good.

With 18 gigs in Europe (France, Holland, Belgium, Germany) before a 14-date British tour commenced on October 12, the band had already sold out two London shows at the Odeon.

Bon was long enough in London to unpack his bags, do his laundry, and then pack and leave again.

The album had just been released. It couldn't have got off to a better start, gaining good reviews, and for the first time, actually penetrating the charts.

Simpatico critics were in agreement that *Let there be rock* was a more complete AC/DC offering. It would go on to peak in the British charts at number 75, a quite respectable first entry. George and Harry were celebrating back home, because at the same time, Flash & the Pan's 'Hey, St Peter!' was hitting in Europe, going to number six in Belgium, number seven in Holland and also selling well in France.

The tour confirmed the band's stature beyond any doubt. Said stalwart supporter, *Sounds'* Phil Sutcliffe, 'Live [they] are the most insanely compulsive heavy rock band I've ever experienced ... who offer the rare combination of wild excitement and consistency.

'The schoolkid image will have to go one day but at the moment it's still dead right ... Bon is vital. He's the spice and flavour with the heavy hardtrack. An appealing rogue and buccaneer, give him a wooden leg and a parrot on his shoulder and he'd be the image of Long John Silver.'

It was the sheer, irrefutable power and appeal of AC/DC's live gigs that accounted for their growing following and its diversity. AC/DC traversed Britain's tribal barriers, pulling punks, bikers, hippies, headbangers, 9-to-5ers, old rockers and young boppers all along.

The band got back to London on the first day of November. Silver was worried about Bon's drinking. This was ironic, as he might well have worried about her increasing drug dependency, which he presumed not to do. But even as Silver let her own habit run away from her, she couldn't bear to watch Bon boozing it up.

SILVER: 'When Bon was drinking and I was drugging, I didn't know what I was running from, and yet I could see what Bon was running from. It's always easier to be in denial about yourself. I see it a lot differently now. We both really had the same disease, it was just a matter of a different drug of choice. But I was judging him. It was also just really painful; I couldn't bear to be around him when he was drinking. He didn't ever nag me, he didn't have a problem with what I did — but then I was a lot more manageable than what he was. Basically, it was just a lot of people in a lot of pain, trying to rage on regardless.'

Bon and Silver's relationship was starting to show some cracks, but the couple enjoyed a reprieve on a weekend away in Paris. The Stones were in the studio there cutting the *Some girls* album, and Silver's friend, Stones guitarist Ron Wood invited them to drop in.

SILVER: 'Ron had been in town, and he said, Come over. The strange thing was, there was a French punk band [Trust] recording in another part of the same studio, and they were more impressed by the fact that Bon was there than Bon was by the Stones. Though he liked the Stones. It was good actually, because they took us around everywhere, and we didn't have a word of French. That was a buzz for Bon.'

The album was out in America by now, confounding the critics. Even *Creem* magazine, with its metalesque predilections, was succinct in its dismissal of AC/DC: 'These guys suck'. Maybe America was just going to be like Britain all over again. The band was rising there despite the critics' best efforts to quell them. *Let there be rock* cracked the Billboard chart at number 187. It's difficult to enter lower than that, but it was a start.

AC/DC returned to America in November, and spent the next six weeks crisscrossing the country. They would be back in Australia by Christmas, like the year before, to record a new album. Their American home base was New York, where Atlantic had its headquarters, and where Michael Browning had by now also set up an office on Broadway. The band themselves stayed at the Americana, a hotel located near seedy Times Square. They played a few headline club gigs of their own in the South, with support acts like British bands UFO and the Motors, and then as a support act themselves, they played big stadium gigs with Kiss, and pomp-rockers Rush.

'We toured around in a station wagon,' Angus told *Guitar World*. 'We got put on with Kiss. This was when they had all the make-up and everything — the whole hype. They had everything behind them, the media, a huge show and stuff. And here we were — five migrants, little micro people.

'It was tough to even get into the show with that station wagon. Many a time they wouldn't let us into the venue 'cause they didn't see a limo!'

On the road, Bon drank even more than he did at home.

MICK COCKS: 'What happens, you're playing to 5 to 10,000 people a night, an hour and a half on stage, it's fantastic, it's real high; and when you come off, you travel in the bus back to the hotel room, you've got to come down, it can be really difficult to find something to do that makes sense. And if you're doing a long tour, it builds up, you know, and you drink, there's not a real lot of alternatives. I once did a tour without drinking, and phew, you can keep reality.'

Silver joined Bon as the band played through a blizzard in Chicago with Kiss. Stoned though she may have been herself, she hated to see Bon drinking himself into oblivion.

SILVER: 'I couldn't deal with seeing this incredible, together, really wonderful person that half the world was in love with, and then seeing this dribbling mess that you could have no respect for. I found it just too hard in the end. He wasn't like that all the time either, but when he went, he went. He was one of those drunks, he wasn't aggressive, he was just unmanageable. He wouldn't know what city he was in, he'd just lose it.'

Silver was starting to think that maybe she'd had enough.

The band swung back through New York in the first week of December, before returning to Australia, Bon and Silver travelling together. They played a radio broadcast from Atlantic's studios on December 7, and opened for Kiss at Madison Square Garden, then flew out of JFK for Sydney.

The band hoped and planned, also, to tour Australia again.

Bon and Silver checked into a motel at Coogee. They needed some space of their own. At Coogee, they were right on the beach — and it was going to be a sweltering summer.

SILVER: 'A lot of the hoohah had died down by then, that teeny bopper thing was over, so it was much more laid-back. Bon hired a motorcycle to get around. You know what it's like on the road, you get sick of eating out all the time and that, so at least at this place you could have some stuff in the fridge, and a frypan and that, some of your own stuff. Because we were there for three months.'

No tour materialised. With an English bass player now as

well as crew, absurdly protectionist Australian immigration authorities refused to issue AC/DC the appropriate visas.

'We used to think of ourselves as an Australian band,' Angus told *RAM*, 'but we're beginning to doubt that now. The fuckers won't even let us play here.' The band found itself with time on its hands, not due to return to Britain until April, after the album was cut at Alberts in January.

With a slipping local profile, AC/DC could well have used the exposure afforded by a tour. The 11 months the band were away from Australia this time had seen a great many changes on the scene, changes which would have been greatly to AC/DC's advantage; changes which, in fact, might even have been indebted, in a way, to them. Sherbet and Skyhooks had both dropped right off. 'Countdown' still held a huge sway, but its reign was no longer autocratic. Pub rock was taking root, and this was music, by definition, which sold itself through live performance.

Pub rock left no room for punk. Any Australian new wave was consigned very much to the fringes. The old hippies who had only just got their act together — and assumed seats of power in the music industry — were hardly about to hand the reins over to a bunch of young punks. First generation Australian 'new wave' bands like the Saints, Radio Birdman, Nick Cave's Birthday Party and the Go-Betweens were forced to go overseas to find a significant audience.

'We don't have the kind of culture punk needed,' Ross Wilson once explained. 'We're quite comfortable. Groups like the Angels and Rose Tattoo transferred that aggression into a macho rock, using better musicianship than the punks.'

It was in Sydney that pub rock really came to the fore. Why, Rose Tattoo were a band that actually formed in Melbourne but moved to Sydney because its work prospects were better. Melbourne bands like the Sports and Jo Jo Zep and the Falcons trailed the leaders. Adelaide bands Cold Chisel and the Angels gravitated to Sydney. Dragon had arrived from New Zealand. Sydney itself produced Midnight Oil, Mental As Anything and Icehouse.

On almost any given night in Sydney in the late seventies, venues like the Bondi Lifesaver, Chequers, the Stagedoor

Tavern, the Civic Hotel and the Grand Hotel would be pumping. Suburban beer barns like the Manly Vale Hotel, the Comb & Cutter and Selinas were taking off.

But even as Sydney was buzzing with new energies, the most pervasive influence on the scene was still that of Alberts. As a label in its own right, Alberts proffered Rose Tattoo and the Angels, but maybe even more than that, it was Alberts' mere presence, its independent heritage and its innovative drive, that confirmed its patriarchal hold.

CHRIS GILBEY: 'I don't think Alberts set out to become a rock'n'roll label, but it became a rock'n'roll label due to the momentum set in motion by rock'n'roll bands like AC/DC.'

Everybody, but everybody recorded at Kangaroo House, where the vibe George and Harry generated was palpable, and something they all hoped would rub off on them. With the Tatts and the Angels specifically, George and Harry took the work they started with AC/DC to a logical conclusion, orchestrating and stylising a rock'n'roll genre which in sum total was unique.

The pub band that set the standard was Cold Chisel. But even for all their maverick spirit, Cold Chisel owed AC/DC, and Bon especially, an enormous debt. Cold Chisel had grown out of Fraternity's alma mater, the Largs Pier, and singer and fellow Scot Jimmy Barnes, who had replaced Bon briefly in Fraternity, saw himself as Bon's heir apparent.

AC/DC had become a given in Australian rock'n'roll.

The Angels and Rose Tattoo institutionalised pub rock. The ferocity which was their trademark became one of the distinguishing fundamentals of the genre.

'[People] come to our gigs, or gigs generally I guess, to let something go, a sort of catharsis,' Doc Neeson once told *Rolling Stone*. 'We always feel that there's this implied confrontation between band and audience. They're saying, "Lay it on! Do it to us!" and it's like a veiled threat that if you don't, you'll get canned.'

Rose Tattoo's debut single 'Bad boy for love' was released in October, 1977. By December, when Bon arrived back in town, it was near the top of the national charts.

MICK COCKS: 'It was the first record I'd ever made, it went top five; I thought, This is easy!'

Cocks was among the number of reprobates, including Joe Furey, who were living at the time in a big old hotel in Kings Cross called the Eaglefield. 'We just took this place over. Downstairs we had a music studio and an art studio — the girls painted, the boys played music.'

The scene was riddled with drugs. Killer weed was equalled in its abundance by speed, mandies and heroin. In Sydney, like London, in the late seventies, top-grade smack was plentiful and cheap.

MICK COCKS: 'Bon came back to town, and he would stay at this hotel he liked in Coogee with his girlfriend, and I got into him one night and said, Oh, come and stay with us if you like, because things weren't going so well with his girlfriend, and so he'd come and crash at our place.'

Powerage, as AC/DC's new album would be called, was cut like every other AC/DC album — quickly.

JOE FUREY: 'Of course, with the album being recorded, and guitar parts going on later, Bon had done most of his stuff; he was sort of hanging loose around town, so he used to drop over. The Tatts were playing around, the Lifesaver was happening, it was pretty rockin'...'

Powerage followed very much in the footsteps of *Let there be rock* — so much so, in fact, that there was something almost rote about it. It contained some great individual tracks — 'Rock'n'roll damnation', 'Riff raff', which would become a highlight of the band's live set; 'Sin city', and 'Gimme a bullet'. 'Gimme a bullet' was perhaps Bon's most accomplished piece of writing to date, in which his penchant for hardcase metaphors finds more genuine pathos and humour than it had before. Even the album's second-string tracks sustain a more consistently high standard than earlier albums' fillers. However, altogether, *Powerage* just seemed to lack the uncompromising coherence and relentless body and soul that was its predecessor's greatness.

Bon was happy just to finish his work in the studio. He didn't necessarily enjoy recording, with its alternating intensity and tedium. 'Recording can be a bit of a pain,' he once said. 'You have to think. The rest of the time you are just cruising.' You might wait around all day till a track was set up, and then have to get your part down within a couple of takes. It was just fortunate Bon was so capable. No singer so filled Alberts' Studio One with the sheer presence of voice that Bon did.

His obligations in the studio fulfilled, Bon spent long hot days on the beach, sunning himself, swimming and thinking. He was worried. Silver was acting strangely. He knew she was losing patience with him because of his drinking, and at the same time, she'd struck up a friendship with Joe Furey. Bon liked Joe himself, but even if, as Silver always maintained, they were never actually lovers — their relationship more akin to that of soul brother and sister — and whether there were drugs involved or not, Bon still felt threatened. But knowing the independent Silver as he did, he just had to grin and bear it. He decided to try to get off the grog, which he thought might win him back some favour.

He was rapt when Graeme showed up to see him. 'He knew that drink was getting to him. He was going to a hypnotist, to stop from drinking. But a hypnotist, you've got to do it all the time, not just once or twice. And so of course, touring all the time, I think the loneliness got to him. You drink.'

Sitting on the beach all day at Coogee, the only thing Bon wanted to do once the sun went down was go out raging. He fell off the wagon. It was too much to ask, he had too little to do otherwise.

GRAEME: 'He'd go down to the Bondi Lifesaver, and he'd be drunk most nights, and he'd still go home on his bike.'

MICK COCKS: 'Bon was one of the last true rock'n'rollers, a real person, it wasn't a business to him, it was an addiction, something he had a gut feeling for. He lived it. You know, he had that dream — because you're talking about a period of time when it was a dream, a romantic dream. You were outlaws, that was the only way to look at it. You only sort of paid lip service to the social side of things — like paying tax, or registering to vote — when you had to. You didn't have any sense of community, you weren't really interested in what was going on, you didn't have the same problems the average person had. It was like you were in a different world.

'And when you did achieve it, it's still a dream, you know, it's not like it ever becomes a job, going up on stage.'

It's just maybe everything else — the soul-destroying rootlessness of life on the road, the phoniness endemic in showbusiness, the purely exhausting demands of celebrity — that becomes hard work. Bon wasn't tired of it all yet, and he still had a fair way to go to get to the top, but maybe the only way to do it was in a numb, alcoholic haze.

With Bon going on tour in Britain and Europe, Silver had arranged with Joe to go away together, off on the hippie trail through southeast Asia. They had arranged to meet Bon's brother Graeme in Bangkok.

SILVER: 'I made the decision to break up when we left Australia. Bon couldn't accept it, he was still very emotionally dependent on me, so we said, Okay, 12 months, have a 12 month break.'

Before Bon and Silver went their separate ways, AC/DC played a couple of shows at the Lifesaver under wraps. Billed as 'the Seedies', as the band was affectionately known, word got out, as it was doubtless meant to, and more than 4,000 people tried to get into the Lifesaver over the two nights.

Let there be rock might have only sold a miserable 25,000 copies in Australia, but as Bon pointed out in *RAM*, it had sold nearly ten times that internationally, and 'word builds up when people hear you've been going well overseas. People want to see you. A lot of people just haven't seen the band.' AC/DC had by now completely shed the stigma of being a teeny-bopper band. They were acknowledged as a godfatherly force. And when they played those two nights at the Lifesaver, they proved the point.

JOE FUREY: 'It was probably one of the best shows I've ever seen. I mean, you had a band that had moved into virtual stadium mode, a big rock band, playing in the Lifesaver, to a capacity crowd, and the band was on a real high then, playing really well...'

In Australia, like Britain and America, AC/DC had to take the step that only a hit record makes possible. A lot hinged on *Powerage*.

Bon left for London with the rest of the band, clinging to Silver's promise that he would see her there in a couple of months' time, after he'd been to Europe and before he went to America again.

Critical reaction to *Powerage* was generally positive. Any suggestion that the band was merely repeating itself was offset by the fact that this would only make the album an easier sell. And indeed, it got a strong start out of the blocks.

Bon defended the album. 'Look what happened to the Rolling Stones,' he said. 'They started looking for a new direction, going off on tangents, and they produced shit. And then the punk bands came along and scared 'em, and now you will notice, they are going back to producing what they've always done best — rock'n'roll. You progress, sure you do, but you move forward in the same direction. You do not shoot off on some tangent.'

On April 28, the band embarked on its most comprehensively mounted British tour to date. A full range of merchandising — T-shirts, patches, posters — was available — a first for AC/DC and an early example generally of a practice which today is second nature, and extremely lucrative, for rock bands.

DAVE JARRETT: 'They were right in that era when patches on denim jackets started happening, all that, and so the AC/DC logo was just everywhere. It was really easy for kids to identify with.'

AC/DC were making the transition every band has to make in pursuit of American superstardom, and at which many falter — the transition from a club band to a stadium band; that is, a band able to project to the farthest reaches of a venue so big and cold that rock'n'roll should never have been put into it. The trap is that as every gesture is amplified, the act becomes bloated, bombastic, impersonal. AC/DC somehow managed to avoid that. They scaled up but not out, retaining their trademark leanness and vitality even as they drew so much broader strokes.

Bon wrote to Irene:

Hi sugar . . . I'm writing from Birmingham. We're about half way through the Brit tour and most of us are suffering from the flu or bubonic plague or something. It's been great so far gig wise as most have been sell outs and we've been getting good reviews for the concerts and the album. Stand to make a bit of money at long last...

Our album went into the British charts first week at 26 so it looks like being a Top 5 at least. We only have about ten gigs to go on this tour and then it's off to Germany for two TV shows and then we have three weeks off before America. Cliff and I are going to Paris for a root around. I have some friends in a band there who'll put us up for a few days. They're a punk band called Trust. They recorded a couple of our songs in French and just last week got banned from French TV for singing suggestive lyrics. The song they did was 'Love at first feel'. So I've struck again!

'Rock'n'roll damnation' was released as a single in Britain at the end of May as the band left for Europe. It went to number 24, the best performance yet by an AC/DC single.

Bon and Cliff returned to London from Paris in mid-June. Bon was anxious because Silver was finally on her way there too. She and Joe hadn't got far down the hippie trail. They waited around in Malaysia for an old girlfriend of Silver's who never showed, and then went on to Bangkok, where they met up with Graeme and got 'bogged down', as Silver put it. People go to Bangkok for two reasons — sex and drugs. And these weren't people who had any kind of interest in either little boys or girls. The best and cheapest smack in the world was available in Thailand.

SILVER: 'Bon was in London when I arrived there, he was staying at a friend of mine's place, and I was a bit pissed off actually, because I'd planned on staying there myself. I felt intruded upon by that, because we had this agreement, and he was just there all the time. He couldn't kind of let go.'

Angus was despatched to Australia to promote the release of *Powerage*. 'We drew straws to see who'd come, and I lost,' he grumbled. Neither the album nor 'Rock'n'roll damnation' made any real impact on the charts, but at least the album sold steadily enough to go gold by the end of the year.

By the start of July, the band was back on the road in America, where the album was now out, playing support spots anywhere and everywhere with the likes of Rainbow, Alice Cooper, Journey and Aerosmith. They were starting to get a reputation as a bad support act, because they were so good, often upstaging the headliner.

In Chicago, playing in front of 40,000 Summer Jam revellers, they pulled the rug out from under bands higher on the bill, like Foreigner, Aerosmith and Van Halen. Working their way to the West Coast, they did the same thing in Oakland, outside San Francisco, as Pasadena's *Star-News* reported: 'While the big name on the bill was Foreigner... it was little known Australian group AC/DC that brought 70,000 fans to their feet... The quintet's 10.30 a.m. show aroused the crowd with a moving set of power rock'n'roll.'

AC/DC were connecting because they were rock'n'roll and they were real, and American audiences, at least in part — it was again, a symptom of the emergence of the new wave — were starting to tire of bland FM radio fodder.

Powerage was selling quite respectably, especially considering it wasn't getting any airplay to speak of.

Back in New York by the start of August, the band repeated a familiar routine, at the Palladium, blowing Ritchie Blackmore's Rainbow off the stage, before pulling out again for the Deep South.

The road was simply a way of life for AC/DC. On August 12, they headlined over Cheap Trick and Molly Hatchet in Florida stronghold Jacksonville, and sold out 14,000 seats.

'I enjoy touring; I've had some great times,' Angus told *Sounds*. 'I think touring is what you make of it. I do get fidgety if we have a day off, because touring is geared around twiddling your thumbs and getting ready for the show. If the show's missing, the day just doesn't feel right.'

MICHAEL BROWNING: 'There were grumblings sometimes, because it's hard for these young guys to appreciate that you can play to 14,000 people in Jacksonville, Florida, and earn whatever it was, 20 or 30 grand, and then you could drive 100 miles up the road and play to 20 people! There were a lot of gigs, I guess, that they questioned. But it was all part of the building process.'

'It's sometimes a drag being in a different hotel every night,' Bon allowed, 'but it's not as bad as being stuck in front of a lathe every day of your life for 50 years. I am here and I am free and I'm seeing new faces every night and touching new bodies or whatever. It's great, there's nothing like it.'

'Bon is fine,' said Angus. 'We call him the old man, but he's always there. And he will be in the future.' It was almost as if Angus was trying to convince himself of the fact. He admitted, after all, in a contemporaneous interview, 'You can have so many women and so many drunken nights, but it's going to take its toll some day'.

Rock'n'roll bands on the road in America don't have to pursue sex and drugs — sex and drugs pursue them. Cocaine is chopped out under your nose. Bon found it difficult to just say no.

Vince Lovegrove and Bon hadn't seen each other in a dog's age when Vince met up with the band in Atlanta, Georgia. After wearing out Adelaide, Vince had moved to Sydney, and then Melbourne, where in 1978, after a stint producing the 'Don Lane Show', he got up a proposal to make a documentary for Channel Seven on the international emergence of Australian rock'n'roll. AC/DC naturally occupied a prominent place in his script, and so he sought them out. They were playing a show that night at the Atlanta Symphony Hall, with Cheap Trick supporting.

Vince found a lump coming to his throat as he watched from the side of the stage, his old mate 'struttin' across the boards like the eternal Peter fuckin' Pan he was...' After the show, when Bon had changed out of his ragged, denim stage threads into a very flash plaid drape coat he'd just bought, and grabbed the bottle of Scotch that was always present in the band's rider for him, he and Vince repaired to the hotel, the very plush Peach Tree Inn, to catch up.

Vince wrote in *RAM*:

Very impressed, I was. Personal driver, ritzy hotel, the best lookin' groupies I'd ever set eyes on. I mean, it was the real thing. I thought, if anyone deserves it, Bon does. He's been at it for long enough, and at last, he was showing 'em. He said he'd make it and he was making it... in style.

Out of the car, and up into Bon's room. Not yer average hotel room, but one that reeked of a very determined effort to emulate all the comforts of a luxurious home away from home.

So there we were. Bon and me, an Australian photographer, a few groupies, and the odd Seedie wandering in and out in an attempt to find the action. Not that there would be too much action in Bon's room that night. The groupies would eventually be bored, the photographer would almost nod off to sleep, room service would be cut off at 2 a.m., and Bon and I became self-indulgent about the good old days... and to top it off, there was nothing to smoke. We used the completely legal drug of Scotch to ignite the memory cells.

'I'm getting tired of it all,' he finally confessed. We were both wasted. Totally. There were no inhibitions. His burbled confession came as a total, almost sobering shock. I mean, his scenario appeared complete. Success was almost there, and so were its trimmings. And Bon tells me he was getting tired of it; he must be joking.

'No way, Vinnie. I really am getting tired. I love it, you know that. It's only rock'n'roll and I like it. But I want to have a base. It's just the constant pressures of touring that's fucking it. I've been on the road for thirteen years. Planes, hotels, groupies, booze, people, towns. They all scrape something from you. We're doin' it and we'll get there, but I wish we didn't have these crushing day after day grinds to keep up with.'

I'd never seen Bon like it. He managed to laugh it off and have another swig. He set a fast pace, the old Bon, but if you dug deep enough, you found an accumulative exhaustion that threatened to sap his upfront energy.

'Rock'n'roll, you know that's all there is,' he said. 'But I can't hack the rest of the shit that goes with it.'

From the Deep South, the band dashed across the continent to the Northwest, where they played around with Aerosmith, before dropping in on LA for a headline show of their own at the Starwood. In September, they played a few more dates with Aerosmith through the Midwest, before heading back to Britain.

Aerosmith, then hitting their drug-addled midcareer crisis, suffered in the face of AC/DC's hunger. They — Aerosmith — were persistently blown off stage. In LA, AC/DC managed to drive a typically jaded LA audience 'wild and calling for encore after encore'.

The band wasn't exempt from crises of its own though. If Bon was beginning to feel, if not show, the strain, it also was around this time that Phil Rudd buckled under it. Phil had always been highly strung, and in the bleak American Midwest heartlands, he was suffering what might only be described as an acute case of white-line fever.

SILVER: 'When Phil cracked up, Bon was pretty upset about it. I mean, Bon wasn't one to rock the boat, but he was pretty freaked out by the way they just propped Phil up and made him perform.

'I think it was a bit of a strain for Bon too, because he did all the PR. Like, if there was a radio station, Bon had to do all that, pretty much.

'And I mean, that's what happened to Phil, because he was doing a lot of the driving as well. And because he was the quiet type. I mean, I'm getting this second hand, I'm getting this from Bon, what happened to Phil.'

Like Bon, Phil was a dedicated pot-smoker. He was also always partial to a toot. Put that together with life on the road itself, and the result can be pure paranoid dementia. Phil was a mess. On a couple of occasions, he had to be hauled off to hospital for sedation.

SILVER: 'Instead of, like, giving him some time out... there was no actual concern for Phil's long-term wellbeing. And basically, that was pretty much their attitude to Bon too, with his drinking. Nobody really seemed to give a shit that he was killing himself, as long as he got out there and did it. If I wasn't there to make sure he caught the right plane, then someone else would be, and that was it. As long as they could do the job on the night.'

Bon wrote to Irene:

Hi there. Tis about four in the morn (Mon)... the bar's closed... the bottle of Black Jack [Daniels] is empty... we're outta dope... the TV's finished... I don't have anybody to fuck... I've dropped a quaalude [downer]... I could go on all night but I won't... We're two days from the finish of our US summer tour... It's been fourteen weeks and of course we did a month in England before that. We have six days off before touring Europe and England again for a month... Boring innit. I should be back in Sydney around Nov 16th. We're recording for maybe a month and hopefully January will be off... Now I've had days off since I joined this band... But not one whole thirty-one day month.

The band landed back in Britain in October, just as the live album *If you want blood, you've got it* was released, a mere six months after *Powerage*. Alberts had been planning a greatest hits album called *Twelve of the best*, but at the last minute changed its mind. The greatest hits in live form would obviously extend the album's appeal and indeed, *If you want blood* wasn't exactly planned, but it turned out to be the record that paved the way for AC/DC's breakthrough. Live albums, which tended to be double or triple sets in which songs short in their studio versions were stretched out into extended tedium, were for some reason popular in the seventies. *If you want blood* reversed that tradition. Culled, by George and Harry from tapes 'recorded live', as the sleeve notes asserted, 'during Australian, UK and American tours', the album was indeed just like an AC/DC gig itself. Packaged simply, wearing the indelible image of Angus impaled by his own axe, Bon glancing over his shoulder, it boasted a blunt ten tracks and, allowing nothing extraneous, got straight to the point, that being raging AC/DC rock'n'roll. For a band whose forte was live performance, it was the perfect souvenir, and the punters responded accordingly. In Britain, they pushed it to number 13, a new high for the band.

In America, it propelled AC/DC into the top 50 for the first time. In Australia, the album went unreleased until Christmas, by which time it was quite apparent the authorities were still not going to relent and allow the band to tour the country, which would ideally have promoted the release of *If you want blood*. The band was suffering for this stupid stalemate. The album sold slowly.

At the end of October, the band embarked on yet another British tour, playing 16 dates in 18 days. They would return to Australia after that — as had become the tradition — to spend Christmas at home, and cut a new album at Alberts.

The British tour was an unqualified success.

At the Glasgow Apollo, as legend has it, Bon got lost backstage after walking the floor with Angus, and then managed to lock himself outside the theatre. The only way he could convince the stagedoor bouncers that he was, in fact, the evening's attraction, was to ask them, Why else would I be running around in the freezing cold without a shirt on? Asked about the incident a couple of days later, Bon said, 'I can't remember that — it was two days ago'.

DAVE JARRETT: 'They had this incredible work ethic, and the fact was that each time they made a record, it seemed to be so much better. So it became a matter of how many Hammersmith Odeons you were going to do.'

In America too, they were finally taking off. The success of *If you want blood* reflected on *Powerage*, and by year's end, its sales, at over 150,000 units, outstripped those of the previous two albums put together. Even *Rolling Stone*, which had studiously ignored the band since mercilessly panning *High voltage* in 1976, was starting to take notice. A news story ran in its November 16 issue. It read in part, 'Bon Scott mentions some influences that are difficult to glean from listening to his music. He is particularly impressed by the way Frank Zappa has been able to manipulate his image over the years. Fondly remembering the old PHI ZAPPA KRAPPA poster of Frank sitting on the toilet, Bon suggests a successor: "Bon Scott pulling himself".'

In London to play two conclusive Odeon shows, Bon was herded into Atlantic's offices to drink the liquor cabinet dry whilst doing phone interviews with the press in other parts of the world. He spoke to the *Herald* in Melbourne, claiming success hadn't spoiled him. 'All that has changed is my intake of alcohol. I can now afford to drink twice as much.'

Talking to David Fricke in New York for a feature on the band which would be published in *Circus Weekly* in January, he bemoaned the lack of critical acuity applied to AC/DC in Britain even as the band scaled the heights. 'This guy came to see us at Leeds University. We did two encores that night and the crowd went wild. Then I read the review next week and he puts shit on the crowd — "How could 2,000 mindless people like this bunch of idiots". He didn't see what we were doing for the crowd and what they were doing for us.'

Bon went on, 'There's been an audience waiting for an honest rock'n'roll band to come along and lay it on 'em. There's a lot of people coming out of the woodwork to see our kind of rock. And they're not the same people who would go to see James Taylor or a punk band.'

Asked about the band's unrelenting touring, Bon kept up a brave face. 'It keeps you fit — the alcohol, nasty women, sweat on stage, bad food — it's all very good for you!'

But Fricke asked, what if his voice ever gave out?

'Then I'd become a roadie,' Bon replied matter-of-factly.

The two sold-out Odeon shows the band played on November 15 and 16 merely confirmed their status. Atlantic threw a party backstage after the first night's show. Bon proceeded to get so drunk that in the wee hours, according to *Melody Maker*'s Steve Gett, he 'needed the stomach pump before getting to his feet again'.

Success, for Bon, was bittersweet. He had no one to share it with and no home to go back to.

Definitely not the Glimmer Twins, Angus and Bon size up to their prospects.

fourteen
highway to hell

'If Bon Scott is lucky,' Pat Bowring reported in the Melbourne *Sun* on December 9, 1979, 'he'll see his parents in Perth at Christmas.'

'I haven't seen them for three years,' Bon, back in Sydney, told Bowring. 'I hope they recognise me.'

'Some of the guys in the band are buying places here this time,' he continued. 'I'm not. I've bought a bike. That's all I want. I'll sleep on that. Besides, I'm too young to settle down!'

Bon's bravado didn't let up for a moment. With his Kawasaki 900 throbbing between his legs, he found a flat in O'Brien Street in Bondi. Moving in, he said to Pat Pickett, 'You know, Pat, this is the first time I've ever had a flat of my own'. Bon

257

was still aching for Silver, but this new, forward-looking experience was some compensation.

The band was waiting on the nod to go into Alberts to start work on a new album. Bon threw himself into a strict regimen, getting up at 8.30 every morning to go for a swim, eating well, and drinking only saki — in moderation — in anticipation of a likely tour of Japan in February. He was working up ideas for the new album.

All the band's plans, however, were about to come undone. Bon wasn't lucky enough to make it to Perth for Christmas or anything else. In fact, the developments of the next month or so would be the most traumatic AC/DC had ever endured.

The story broke late in January when Pat Bowring reported, 'The Vanda–Young songwriting and production team may not be working on the next AC/DC record'. The storm had been brewing for some time, right back, perhaps, to the very beginning of AC/DC's relationship with Atlantic in America. The records AC/DC were selling in America were due to the band's live profile, not because they were getting any airplay.

MICHAEL BROWNING: 'Atlantic, at that time, quite clearly felt that they weren't getting records delivered that were radio-friendly, sound-wise, for the American market. And it was true.'

First thing in the new year, Atlantic's Michael Klenfner flew in to Sydney from New York. His mind was already made up. AC/DC needed a hit single. George and Harry were off the case. Within a week, a new producer had arrived in Sydney and started working with the band.

BROWNING: 'Klenfner's idea was to get a guy called Eddie Kramer involved. And so Eddie Kramer was flown out to Australia and met the band, and then the band flew over to Florida and did some pre-production with him — they were virtually forced into using this guy.'

Never one to give anything away, especially to the press, George seemed to take it all on the chin. Privately, he was fuming. He had made all this possible only now to be unceremoniously dumped. Malcolm and Angus were equally taken aback.

BROWNING: 'Outwardly, there were no signs, but I think

Malcolm and Angus felt very strange. I think they felt like their brother had been shafted, and that I was part of that process, or that I'd allowed the record company to get away with it.'

Bon too was perturbed, but he also knew his was not to reason why. He'd seen the axe come down before, and thicker than water though blood may be, Malcolm and Angus were also extremely ambitious. Maybe the Yanks were right, anyway. Besides, if the band didn't acquiesce, they could expect little future favour, if any, from Atlantic. They agreed to work with Kramer. Kramer's claim to fame was that he'd engineered Jimi Hendrix, and more recently produced Kiss. He came on more like a cigar-chewing hustler than a music man.

Malcolm and Angus assuaged their guilt at George's sacking by blaming Michael Browning. From this point on, things would never be the same again. What was once a defensive insularity now degenerated into fully-blown paranoia. It was an atmosphere of fear and loathing that would escalate for years to come, and only exacerbated Bon's growing sense of dislocation.

BROWNING: 'I think it was really a question of, all bets are off.'

Bon was running late, as usual, when he was due in one night at 2JJ's Darlinghurst studios to do an interview. Presenter Pam Swain was becoming anxious. She'd been warned about Bon; told, among other things, that she should have a bottle of something in waiting for him. All she could afford was a can of beer. It sat getting warm on the desk.

When he did finally show up, he didn't touch the beer. He and Pam became so absorbed in the interview that they continued talking together in the studio even after the show was over. Pam liked the guy, found him funny, warm, and sincere, even for all his ladykiller charm. When Bon finally climbed aboard his bike to leave, he promised to give her a call, maybe they'd go out together sometime.

The band was rehearsing at Alberts, putting material together. Kramer was sitting in. Bon took Pam to the speedway out at Parramatta. It was a lovely night, Pam remembers, marred only by the speeding ticket they got on the ride home.

Pam invited Bon over to a lunch she was having the next day, not expecting him to come. But come he did. The scene was quite outside Bon's experience — polite society almost, the intellectual types that tend to work at the ABC — but Bon was the life of the party. Pam was smitten.

All this was enough to keep Bon's mind off his deeper woes. The theft of his bike a couple of days later, however, threw him back into a spin. At least it wouldn't be long before the band left for Japan. A farewell party was held at the Strata Inn, a pub in Cremorne. Bon, Malcolm and Angus got up with George, on bass, and Ray Arnott, drums, and played a few numbers. It would be Bon's last ever performance on Australian soil.

On his last night in town, Pam arranged to meet Bon at the Lifesaver after she'd finished work. When she got there, he was nowhere to be seen. She raced back to Double-Jay, thinking he might have got the arrangements mixed up. He wasn't there either. She went back to the Lifesaver, but still he hadn't shown up. She was dismayed more than anything else. Bon was about to go away indefinitely, and they weren't going to see each other again. She drove home across the bridge cursing him. Bon, meantime, had managed to climb through a window into her bedroom, and was in repose when she got there. All that was missing was a rose between his teeth.

Of course, Pam's flatmate was horrified when this ravaged, tattooed figure emerged the next morning and went straight to the fridge for a beer for breakfast.

But the band wouldn't be going to Japan, after all. At the last minute, visas were denied. Bon killed a couple more days at Pam's place while new flights were booked to go direct to Miami. *RAM*'s Stuart Coupe met up with the band in the departure lounge. Bon, he said, who had Pam on his arm, was 'batfaced'. 'True to form and reputation he informs my female companion she "should look after that great body". He looks me up and down and continues, "and if he doesn't let me know and you can have my phone number".'

AC/DC were not enamoured of either Eddie Kramer or Miami. 'This time of year, it's an Elephant's Graveyard for geriatric

Jews and totally boring,' Bon wrote to Maria. Maria and her husband Jim had just had their first child, and Bon extended his hearty congratulations on the 'wean'.

Bon wrote further to Uncle:

Atlantic reckoned we should use a top Yank producer and appointed one Eddie Kramer to the post. It turns out the guy was full of bullshit and couldn't produce a healthy fart. He was a good engineer with a big mouth ('I can hear this note...') and a lot of front. We gave him the arse and got hold of one John Lange who we start work with on Wednesday in London.

MICHAEL BROWNING: 'I got a phone call from Malcolm in Florida, to say, This guy's hopeless, do something, he's trying to talk us into recording that Spencer Davis song, "Gimme some loving", "I'm a man", whatever it was...'

'Three weeks in Miami and we hadn't written a thing with Kramer,' Bon told *RAM*. 'So one day we told him we were going to have the day off and not to bother coming in. This was Saturday, and we snuck into the studio and on that one day we put down six songs, sent the tape to Lange and said, Will you work with us?'

These demos were cut by Malcolm, Angus and Bon, Bon sitting in on drums, which by now had become their practice.

BROWNING: 'I was at that stage based temporarily in New York, I'd met some people who'd invited me to stay with them, one of whom was Mutt Lange's manager, Clive Calder. I got the phone call from Malcolm, and I got off the phone, and Mutt was there, in the apartment, and I said, You've got to do this record. At the time, Mutt had really only done City Boy, the Boomtown Rats, but I happened to think he was incredibly talented. So within a couple of days they agreed to do the record.'

Not before Michael Klenfner lost his job over the matter. It was Klenfner who foisted Eddie Kramer on the band, and he disagreed violently with the idea of now getting in Lange. But if Michael Browning ever had a reputation for being soft, he stood fast this time. Klenfner was left out in the cold. The band flew to London to start work with Lange.

Bon's letter to Uncle continued:

A couple of days later: Landed in London yesterday on one of those beautiful rain-drenched two-degree mornings. Today's not much better. Gee, it's great to be back… We meet our new producer tonight and hit him with fifteen songs that need shaping. My fingers are crossed.

Robert John 'Mutt' Lange was a South African who, after getting his start in music as a singer and songwriter, crossed to the other side of the mixing desk. He was reported to have felt on trial with AC/DC initially. But the band too, unused to outsiders in the studio, felt vulnerable. Either way, a sufficient, if guarded mutual respect developed.

BROWNING: 'It turned out, he was the best person on earth to do it.'

The band virtually moved into the Roadhouse Studios in Chalk Farm, spending the best part of three months there. That, to start with, was a shock to AC/DC, who had never previously spent more than three weeks on any one album.

Highway to hell — as the completed album was called, after the name Angus had given the band's last American tour — was as much of a progression upon *Powerage* as *Let there be rock* was on *Dirty deeds*. But more than that, it was groundbreaking in any terms.

'Mutt was brought up on the rough side of town which helped him in the studio,' Malcolm told *RAM*. 'He's like Harry, a bit more commercial. We learnt a lot. You really need an outsider because we can all go too far and disappear up our own anuses.'

Sessions for the album — 15 hours a day, day-in day-out, for over two months — were gruelling. Songs were worked and reworked. Staying at the Swiss Cottage Inn, Bon bore up under the prolonged pressure, maintaining a brave face, but none felt it more deeply than he.

SILVER: 'He was a bit lost. I mean, I still ran his bank account for him. He was never in one place long enough to keep it together. He got used to me organising everything, keeping the bills paid, all that sort of stuff. Plus the emotional stuff, like, he was no longer in a relationship that he was dependent on, stuff like that.'

Silver was herself by then a fully-fledged junkie.

The album was finished — mixed at the Basing Street Studios, near Ladbroke Grove, in a comparatively short eight days — at the end of June. Lange managed to inject a greater sweep into the band's sound on *Highway to hell*, and it was this, plus the smoother touch of melodic backing vocals, but without loss of any of the band's characteristic dynamic crunch, that gave the album its poise and potency.

The title track, which opens the album, assumes anthemic proportions even before Bon's vocal comes in. Few albums in rock open quite so ominously, and few, as this one proceeds, are ultimately quite as monolithic. Bon's lyrics were more universal — few characters appeared in the songs and the narratives were more compact — but they were no less evocative. His turn of phrase, and better-balanced vocalising, counterpointed perfectly the band's controlled explosive grind. Every track bar 'Love hungry man', which the band quickly disowned, became an AC/DC staple. Mutt Lange had achieved precisely what George and Harry couldn't — a blend of accessible polish and raw power which satisfied both the band and Atlantic.

MICHAEL BROWNING: 'When they were in England recording, I spent a fair bit of time in Australia, so I wasn't really part of that process. I was also having a few immigration problems with America, so I was waiting for that to be resolved too. I next saw the group in New York, after they finished making the record. By that time, I think a few American management companies had started to sniff around.

'At that point we were strapped financially, the whole thing had put such a strain on the whole financial system, and so this guy called Peter Mensch, from Leber & Krebs, had just damaged my position, and so I think they were quite impressed by the prospects in that.'

Alberts was already in the hole to a massive tune (touring America as a support band is a money-losing proposition), and simply couldn't afford to increase the amount they were putting into AC/DC. Michael Browning had been talking to an upstate New York promoter by the name of Cedric Kushner with regards to him buying in on the operation. Malcolm and Angus, understandably, weren't keen on another unfettered outsider staking a claim on them. It didn't help, either, that Kushner was questioning, among other things, the very deal the band had with Alberts. It was clear now it was time to give Browning the chop too.

PERRY COOPER: 'He [Browning] was getting pressured by a lot of people; people were going over his head at times. The band had its own mind — and when they make up their mind, they don't talk to anybody about it. So whatever happened — Michael gave his all for that band. But they're as tough as nails, these guys. There's an old saying, Off the charts, outta your hearts, and when you're off their charts, forget it. But the guys, I've gotta say, they always were very cooperative with us.'

Exactly when Peter Mensch first approached AC/DC on behalf of Leber & Krebs, the powerful New York management company for whom he worked, remains unknown. But certainly, AC/DC was a rising star which had often brushed against Leber & Krebs' tentacles. Aerosmith and Ted Nugent were managed by the company, after all.

Leber & Krebs was formed in 1972, when David Krebs and Steve Leber left the William Morris Agency to form their own operation. They made a mint out of musicals like *Jesus Christ Superstar* and *Beatlemania*; then, in 1974, whilst also acting as US agents for Focus, Argent and Hawkwind, they took on management of Aerosmith and Nugent. In 1977, those two clients alone grossed them nearly ten million dollars.

Leber & Krebs capitalised on the fact, as Steve Leber once explained to financial magazine *Forbes*, that 'an unknown group couldn't walk into Citibank and get a loan if they tried to use their talent as collateral. But we're willing to be the banker for the artist.'

The marriage of Leber & Krebs and AC/DC was made in heaven. Not only could Leber & Krebs inject cash into AC/DC, but the band was impressed by their aggressive, evasive style. In return, AC/DC was just the hot prospect that might revitalise Leber & Krebs' ailing stocks.

Michael Browning still had a year to serve out on his contract, but he accepted a payoff. His excision at least provided the smarting George back in Sydney with cold comfort. Even if George thought the settlement was too large, Browning, of course, thought it was too small.

Bon had no strong feelings either way about Browning, but he was saddened to see the end of Coral, whom he'd always liked. He stayed in contact with her as she moved to LA, calling her regularly.

Browning himself returned to Australia and continues to this day to work at a high level in the music business. On the immediate rebound from AC/DC in 1980, he formed Deluxe Records, the label that first signed, among several other fledgling pub bands, INXS.

MICHAEL BROWNING: 'It was hurtful, no doubt about it. I personally think I did a pretty amazing job. Sure, we made a couple of mistakes here and there, but it was a pioneering situation. And what made it more hurtful was that over the years, everyone, me included, with the Youngs and AC/DC, tends to get written out of history. It's like you never existed. Even Mutt Lange, who did an amazing job of delivering to Atlantic Records exactly what they wanted, it's like, Mutt Who?'

AC/DC hit the road again in America in 1979 at the end of June, with *Highway to hell* due out in a matter of weeks. *If you want blood* was still selling, had by then, in fact, surpassed the quarter-million mark, which neatly maintained a rising curve. The band would play its own first stadium headline tour, through partisan territories like Texas and the Deep South.

Atlantic had high hopes for *Highway to hell*. Perry Cooper said at the time: 'I don't believe you can break an act in the United States 100 per cent by touring. It takes you to a certain level and then drops dead. The only thing I can equate AC/DC with over here are Cheap Trick and Van Halen. They've both toured extensively over the years and neither one of them has broken from touring. They've created albums that are a little bit more acceptable and bang! they've become Platinum artists. AC/DC can do that too.'

Bon called Pam Swain to invite her to join him on the road. He also asked her a favour — could she get him some money from Alberts? A thousand dollars would do. The request struck Pam as strange, but she told Bon she'd do what she could.

Highway to hell was released simultaneously in Britain and America on July 27. It immediately registered the desired response — good reviews in Britain, and airplay in America.

Even the arch *NME* now had to come to the party, though it wasn't without snide qualification. THE GREATEST ALBUM EVER MADE (IN AUSTRALIA), read the headline, the review going on to describe AC/DC as 'a band who practise the science of overstatement to a ludicrous degree and succeed'.

Highway to hell quickly became AC/DC's first British top-10 album, going to number eight, and the first American top 20, peaking at number 17. European returns were also very encouraging. Stalwart support continued in Germany and Scandinavia, while the single went to number 15 in Holland in its first week of release, and France too looked better than ever.

This was the big time. Strangely, Bon was still harping on to Pam about the money. Maybe it was because the band was caught in the transition between Browning and Leber & Krebs that there was no cash around; whatever, Bon seemed desperate.

In Australia, the single was released first, in August, and it climbed to number 24, marking the return of AC/DC to the charts after an absence of nearly three years. When the album followed in October, it completed the strategy of re-establishing the band in Australia. After the last two albums had failed to chart altogether, *Highway to hell* went up to number 13.

The road snaked its way to the Midwest. Billed as an 'Australian–Scottish new wave punk band', AC/DC were special guests on good friends Cheap Trick's gala fourth of July show in hometown Rockford, Illinois.

Pam Swain joined the band in Chicago, and travelled with them to Omaha, Nebraska. She felt like she really shouldn't have been there. Bon seemed distracted, a different person altogether to the one he was in Sydney. It wouldn't have helped his mood that Pam couldn't bring any money either. Alberts had refused to write a cheque. But Bon still tried to accommodate Pam.

With a full entourage numbering 25, the band was by now travelling in greater style, which meant a fitted-out bus. It was a home away from home that could never be. But Bon didn't have a home to go to anyway. He was just another weary traveller on that lost highway.

'Some days you wake up and you never want to see the blokes again,' tour manager Ian Jeffery told Pam. 'But those days never come near the others when you can see what you're working for — five, ten, 15 thousand people shouting their heads off for the group.'

That was what kept Bon going too. 'I'm in love with rock'n'roll, that grows, you know,' he told KSJO San Jose radio show 'Livewire'. 'I'm more in love with a couple of things, but ... I was in love with one, but, ahh, she left me ... I just hope rock'n'roll never leaves me.'

Bon fed off the crowd, finding fresh inspiration for songs he'd sung literally hundreds of times. Fifteen thousand faceless heads, all bobbing in unison, hair swinging, arms outstretched, fists punching the air, just a-spittin' at the moon.

The band was still playing a lot of the same songs they were when they first arrived in Britain over three years ago, still opening the set with 'Live wire', and running through 'Problem child', 'The jack', 'High voltage' and 'Rocker'. 'Riff raff' and 'Sin city' were more recent, off *Powerage*, but even 'Let there be rock', 'Bad boy boogie', 'Hell ain't a bad place to be' and 'Whole lotta Rosie' — the band's standard encore — were over two years old. But as a support act, you can't afford to muck around.

They say that performing is like making love to an audience, and yet then at the end of the night you find yourself alone in a hotel room. But if the experience is less like making love than having sex, Bon was always prepared to personalise his audience. A lot of artists won't do that, preferring to remain inside their cocoon. But Bon was too much a true man of the people. He happily spent time with fans —

and not just groupies — having a drink and a smoke, entertaining them; perhaps it allayed his loneliness.

'Often he would trail off with fans who came back after a show,' Angus later told *Sounds*. 'He judged people as they were and if they invited him somewhere and he was in the right mood to go, he went.'

Pam asked Bon for the record for a story she wrote for *RAM*, whether life on the road was glamorous.

'Bloody oath,' he replied almost indignantly. 'What do you think I do it for? The money, or the music? I do it for the glamour. The women and the whisky... What else is there in life? Let me think...'

'You get used to being on the road,' Malcolm said. 'You can get boozed up like Bon. He can get right out of it. Then you get sick and have to stop drinking. Now I've learnt to pace myself; it works better, because you've got so many hassles all the time.'

Privately, Bon was talking a lot about settling down. He was telling Pam he wanted to buy a house somewhere.

On July 30, a headline ran in the Melbourne *Herald*: TWO SHOT AS FANS RIOT AT AC/DC SHOW. Sharing a bill with Ted Nugent, Aerosmith, Journey and Thin Lizzy, the band had appeared at a huge open-air gig in Cleveland, Ohio, which turned very ugly. One youth was killed and another seriously wounded when a gunman let loose among the crowd of over 60,000. Three hundred police were called in to quell panic. Throughout the day, nine people were treated for stab wounds, and 75 arrested, mainly on drug charges.

Bon later claimed that AC/DC knew nothing, at the time, of this unrest, but it can't have not touched the band. At least, that's what Pam Swain thinks. She had got off the bus in Omaha to go to New York for a stay, and when the band got there, a few weeks later on August 11 — to open for Ted Nugent at Madison Square Garden — she found Bon to be more remote, dark even. Maybe it was just her, she thought, but maybe it was other things too. Maybe it was the kid shot dead in Cleveland. Maybe it was just all the pressure. Maybe it was the booze and drugs — Bon was gobbling down pills by the handful. Maybe he was just having a bad day or few.

Pam would never see Bon again after that.

Molly Meldrum was in New York for the same show. He saw a different Bon. 'He was as fine as ever. He was being warned by the doctors, Stop drinking, and I said to him, Are you going to stop drinking? He said, Of course not. I've never been sick for a day in my life, and I think that's one of the reasons why! Any germs that get into my body, Johnnie Walker goes, Pow!'

PERRY COOPER: 'As far as the drugs and stuff? I mean, he did a little blow — and everybody was doing it — and he had his marijuana, but he never got to the point where he had to have it, or he was paranoid.'

The band had been invited by the Who to appear with them on a one-off London show at Wembley Stadium on August 18. It was an offer even AC/DC couldn't refuse. The Who were one of the few bands Malcolm and Angus had any time for, and so it was an honour to be asked to share the stage as they made their return to live performance after a three-year hiatus, and debuted new drummer, former Small Face Kenny Jones, who had filled the chair left vacant by the death of wild man Keith Moon. As such, the Who wanted to make a grand entrance, and so a bill was assembled that was meant to stand as a sort of state-of-the-rock roll call. It featured the latest American guitar-slinger Nils Lofgren, and new wave old farts, the Stranglers, as well as AC/DC. The gig stamped a seal of approval on AC/DC, and only further broadened their scope.

Checking into the Swiss Cottage Holiday Inn, Bon was pleased just to get back to London, where at least he had a few friends. And old friends were becoming dearer to him as it became increasingly difficult to tell who your real friends were.

JOE FUREY: 'Touring all the time, you can become cut off from people, you're unable to sustain friendships. You just end up living the whole rock'n'roll stereotype on the road. Bon knew how important it was, keeping that family of friends he had together. People like percys, they keep that side of an artist's life intact. You've got to have that infrastructure, and I think when Coral Browning went, you lose that, when you suddenly go with another management company that doesn't know.'

SILVER: 'Once they signed with Leber & Krebs, it was getting to be big business by then, the personal touch was gone. That social thing, where you saw everybody around, was over. The band had their respective lives they were leading. Angus was close to getting married. Malcolm was with Linda. Cliff had a girlfriend, and an ex-wife he saw as well. So it was fragmented socially.'

JOE: 'A lot of the time, when Bon lobbed into London, he was just completely hanging loose. So in a lot of ways, that was the relationship Bon and I had, because he could always get in contact with me when he got to town, and I'd know where so-and-so was, you know.'

Joe himself was then working as a percy for UFO guitarist Paul Chapman.

JOE: 'The feeling in London when Peter Mensch came in and started trying to run AC/DC was that he was just like somebody's nephew or something, you know, an accountant who was related to the boss at Leber & Krebs in New York, where it was like, let's give Peter a job, you know — and he came in, like, This is the way it should be done. He was treating it like you would have run a factory, you know, and it doesn't work like that. Bon would only get a phone call from them when they had something for him to do.

'But he worked within it. Those last couple of months, there was definitely the feeling, I mean, they were the hottest band in the world. They knew they could blow anybody off the stage. And Bon was aware of that too. But he was never one to bitch about things, and that comes back to his professionalism. He was smart enough not to do that. He was going to reap the bounty of what he'd just spent 20 years pushing to do.'

The Who's Wembley show was indeed a 'gathering of the tribes', as hippies, punks, old and revival mods, and headbangers alike all made their way in the summer sun down to the famous Twin Towers. But between the tepid Nils Lofgren and the turgid Stranglers, it was only AC/DC who aroused the crowd's unanimous enthusiasm. Read *Juke*'s review of the show: 'AC/DC are not "good" or "bad". They are perfect AC/DC, a heavy metal archetype overblown to the point where stereotype meets parody. Is Bon Scott serious or what? Is he just playing out a real-life comic strip of an HM lead singer? Do they smirk when they write those giant three-chord riffs? Or do they just know that the world will love something this crass?'

After repeating the performance supporting the Who again at a couple of similar European summer festivals, the band flew back to America more confident than ever. The rest of the year was mapped out for them: after doing another lap of America, they would return to Britain in late October to tour, then tour Europe, and then they'd be free to head down-under, as usual, for Christmas.

Bon wrote to Irene late in August:

Hi kid, how's tricks. At the moment I'm in California to start our Fall tour. We've been running round like blue-arsed flies this past couple of months between America, Europe and the UK doing all kinds of concerts, TV shows and promotion shit for the new album. Have you heard it yet? I don't even know if it's been released in Australia yet. It's on the charts all over the world and selling like hot crumpet. I think we've done it with this one. Should be able to pay the rent for a couple of years. I wanna buy a house in California, a place like Fraternity had. I have some friends here who are in the real estate business and I've had some good offers but it'll take another year and I'm in no hurry. It's just a nice feeling to know you can do it at last...

I might get a chance to see you round Christmas–New Year. I plan to get to Sydney round the 23rd of Dec, buy a bike and ride to Perth. I've got a couple of weeks off and I just want to take it easy and unwind (this touring takes it out of you)... I'm still a very single man and having a ball right now. America's certainly the place for a good time. I've become a bit of an alco (what's new) but I'll cut down when I go on holiday and leave off for a couple of hours... I'm not doing a lot of letter writing at the moment you might have noticed but I'm always thinking of you. Say hi to Graeme if he's still alive.

The band toured America through September, into October, headlining exclusively in big venues over bands like Molly Hatchett, Sammy Hagar and Pat Travers. Bon somehow still managed to find enough energy to get into trouble.

A famous incident was recalled by Angus: 'We were going from California to Austin, Texas, and we stopped off at Phoenix for fuel. We were just taking off again when someone says, Where's Bon? He'd followed this bird off the plane and we reckoned he'd drunk so much he wouldn't even know which country he was headed for ...'

'We'd been drinking in the airport bar for about ten minutes,' Bon picked up the story, 'when I says, Don't you think it's time we caught our plane? She says, What do you mean our plane? I'm staying here. I run back and the fuckin' flight's gone.' Bon went on to describe, true or otherwise, the night he spent in a Mexican bar whipping all the regulars on the pool table, before he was chased off by a fierce-looking black lady of Rosie-esque proportions. He managed to get on another flight to Austin just in time to make the gig.

With 'Girl's got rhythm' out as a single in Britain, the tour the band was due to start there on October 26 was practically sold out before they left America. They didn't even stop over in London on their way to Newcastle, where the first gig was at the Mayfair.

DAVE JARRETT: 'I flew up to Newcastle, and when we got there, there'd been a small fire in the hall, so they had to cancel that night's show. So I thought, Alright! Back to the hotel, party time! The band all went to bed. It was just me and the road crew. I think they were all just so tired.'

Prior to concluding in Leicester on November 9, the tour played an unprecedented four-night stand at the Hammersmith Odeon, which unequivocally confirmed AC/DC's status in Britain as, simply, one of the biggest bands on the circuit.

The band then headed to Europe. They were accompanied by freelance photographer Robert Ellis, who had somehow convinced a 'loud American' (Peter Mensch) that he could serve the band well. He wrote later of Bon: 'Like Keith Moon, he was a real danger to himself and needed constant minding ... but he was nearly always the first down in the lobby of a morning, spruced up and ready to go. I warned him and anyone within earshot of the impending danger, but no one took much notice, least of all him.'

Due to public demand, another, albeit shorter, tour of Britain had been hastily convened for the first week of December. Yet another two shows at the Odeon were locked in. The tour's first gig, at Southampton, had to be cancelled when a leg muscle Bon had pulled in Europe became inflamed.

JOE FUREY: 'That was the sort of period when Bon... well, when he'd come to town before, he was very much the rock'n'roller on the make. But at that point when he came back to London, he almost had a statesman's air about him, a sort of serenity. I said, So you reckon you've made it? and he said, Yeah; not boasting, but satisfied. He knew that he was financially set for the rest of his life regardless.'

Getting back on his feet, Bon climbed aboard a bus bound for the Midlands. He had an unexpected passenger in tow, Mick Cocks of Rose Tattoo, or rather, formerly of Rose Tattoo. Mick had arrived in London in November, after leaving the Tatts under something of a cloud.

MICK COCKS: 'Bon said, Look, I'm going on tour with the band, why don't you come? I said, yeah, alright. He wanted some company, he was pretty lonely. I figured, he was playing in a band, but that doesn't mean he's got friends, right?

'What Bon would do, was go and have a drink with people he didn't really know, and because he was sort of famous, you'd get a lot of hangers-on. He knew who was leeching off him and who wasn't, but he'd reached the stage where he didn't really care. He just wanted the company.

'The first four days on the bus, I just sat there before anyone actually spoke to me from the rest of the band. It was a coach, a 40-seater coach, and so Malcolm would sit up the front with his entourage, and Angus had his possie, the rhythm section theirs, and so I just sat up the back there with Bon. The band gave me the impression they were very set in their ways. Every band has its own way of doing things, but it was like, This is what we have to do. If I had any respect for them it was for that. Then I remember one day, one of the roadies came down and said, Malcolm wants to have a word with you. Just this message. So I went down to Malcolm and said, Yeah, gidday. And he said, Well, what are your intentions? I said, What do you mean? He said, What's the story? I said, Well, Bon asked me to come along with him for the ride. Malcolm knew me well enough, but he was playing the grandfather. So I said, Look, mate, if you think I'm taking advantage of him you've got it all wrong. I was sharing a room with Bon; it wasn't as if they had to spend money on me or anything. And he was just very lonely at the time.

'It gets like that. I'm not putting anybody down, but if you've been in a band for a number of years, it's a bit like having five wives. So what you try and do is, if you can, set up your own little situation that doesn't create friction, then you go with it. It's not unfriendly, it's just the way it is.

'Bon was drinking a bit at the time. But he'd give it a nudge for a while, and then he'd go off it. I think he was looking for some sort of romantic love he knew didn't exist. You know, because he'd stopped chasing girls. He was thinking about other things. In those days he was talking a lot about his ex-wife, saying he had some things there he wanted to sort out. He was doing a lot of thinking, in terms of how he saw things working out.'

The two more Odeon shows were merely a postscript to AC/DC's ascent.

MICK COCKS: 'You got the sense, Shit, they're going to go up another level again. That they were really comfortable with what they were doing, and they just needed a bit of luck to kick on even further.'

JOE: 'I think it was at that point in time that everyone knew it was going to happen. I remember we went to Tramps one night, and we were joking about the bill, which Bon picked up, so things were obviously going well.'

MICK COCKS: 'He said, Look, I'm going to take you to this restaurant tonight, and he was all giggly. I said, What's the matter? He said, We're going to have steak tartare. I said, I love steak. And so these two piles of pink, raw mince show up, and I say, I'm not eating that! And Bon's sitting there, he says, Okay. He says, Taste it. I say, No. Of course, I'm getting hungrier and hungrier, and so in the end I ate it. It was good.

'The food he'd eat, he was quite fussy about it. After a gig, he'd say, Let's find a restaurant that's open; and we'd go and eat. I was shocked. I mean, I used to tell people, I'd say, Oh, I ate this last night, and they'd say, Ah, get away. They'd say, Who took you? I'd say, Bon. They'd say, Piss off. And liqueurs. He had a cultured side that he liked to... I used to call him a toff. He used to laugh at that.

'He never gave me the impression money meant anything to him. The guys in the band, Phil, he'd go out and buy a couple of Ferraris; the bass-player, he was just happy with the security; Malcolm and Angus, I'm not sure, but they always gave me the impression they were pretty level-headed about it. But Bon was like, well, Fuck the money.

'He was very aware of not owing anyone anything. I remember actually giving him some money one night, not because he didn't have any but because he didn't have any cash, and I remember at the time thinking, well, you know, he'd spent hundreds of pounds on me, wining and dining, and he was like, You've done me a big favour. I thought, it just didn't match the ten quid I'd given him. It was a bit silly, really.'

Mick lost sight of Bon then, because Bon went to Australia. AC/DC dropped in on Paris to play a single show with Judas Priest — which was filmed and subsequently released, on video, as *Let there be rock* — and then Bon flew on to Melbourne. He went straight to Mary Walton's place in Prahran, where he was always welcome. Mary's future-second husband Peter Renshaw provided him with a serious drinking partner.

Since *Highway to hell* had put them back on the charts, the band was all the more determined to get an Australian tour together; but now it depended more on Japan falling into place, which would justify the expense of hauling the huge AC/DC roadshow to the eastern hemisphere.

Bon was doing the rounds of all his old haunts, looking up all his old mates. Irene and her boyfriend Nick arrived home one day to find a bottle of Scotch and a few bottles of beer awaiting them on the doorstep. 'That'll be Bon,' said Irene, who was six months pregnant. 'He'll be back.'

He did come back, and he got stuck into the grog as Nick

fired up a barbie. He talked to Nick about music — Nick was an aspiring musician himself, a blues buff. Bon told him about the solo album he wanted to make (Silver also confirms he wanted to make a solo album).

MARY WALTON: 'Bon was just fine, he was Bon as he always was. He was drinking a real lot. Too much probably. And really wasn't eating that well. But that was just because he was partying. He was, by that stage ... you know, I can imagine Bon getting lonely, getting bored with it all, and really just wanting to settle down, because that was the sort of guy that he was too.'

Bon picked up after Christmas and headed west; first stop, Adelaide, where he stayed with Bruce Howe. Band commitments required him back in Britain by the middle of January. They were set to record a new album, and Bon was already toying with a few ideas.

BRUCE HOWE: 'Bon wasn't particularly happy when I last saw him. He was talking about permanent relationships, having children, stuff like that. He looked dreadful. He seemed to sense, the closer you get to the top, you've still got the same personal life, and that's when he started, for the first time, to have this philosophical conversation with me. You could see, he'd been overseas, it was all starting to get really big, and he was still ... where do you go? You either have a family, or you chase endless relationships with women that make you feel good, but don't really make you feel good, and the more popular you get, the more money you make, the more you question if it's you people really love or whatever. It was almost like he was admiring the fact that I'd stayed behind. I said, Well, I think I'm as happy as you are, I'd love to be doing what you're doing, but I can't trade off what I've got here.

'We were talking about love. Bon always had this trouble with the word love. That day he drank a full 40 oz bottle of Johnnie Walker. He got really out of it. He was talking about how I'd stayed in Adelaide, and had a wife and son, and he was saying how he could never do that, and then we started talking about love, and I said, It's only a word, and he said he felt like he could never commit himself totally to one person. He wanted to know why?'

From Adelaide, Bon went to Perth, to see his folks.

ISA: 'That time he was home, that's when he told me, This one I'm working on now is going to be it. They were going to hit the top this time. So that must have been that music that was written; they called it *Back in black*. They had to give it a name, you see, but Ron, I think, did all the words.

'Oh, he used to open the fridge in the morning, and I had to bite my tongue, because I don't like drink. But it was his way of living, I couldnae...'

CHICK: 'You'd go into any of the rooms in the house and you'd find an empty bottle.'

ISA: 'He wanted to buy us a house. But we already had the duplex we were in. I said, Ron, we don't need it. He did take us out one day and we went around looking at a bit of ground, to build a house. But it fell through or something.

'And then he went away again. I said, Ron, you ought to make a will. He said, I'm not going to die.

'He said, I don't need to make a will, I'm not going to die.'

Although Bon returned to Australia over summer 1979/80, he did not make any public appearances. This is his last performance on Australian soil, an impromptu one, at a party for AC/DC at the Cremorne Strata Inn in Sydney, February 5, 1979. Left to right: drummer Ray Arnott, Angus, Malcolm, Bon, and George Young on bass.

fifteen
february, 1980

bon arrived back in London in the new year — 1980. He had just over a month to live.

Before anything else, he found a flat in Victoria, not far from Buckingham Palace. It was a nice place, in a block called Ashley Court; small, but nice. Silver lent him a few things to help set up house. He liked it neat and tidy.

He then went off with the band to Cannes for the annual Midem music industry convention. AC/DC collected a swag of precious metal records. France awarded them two golds — one each for *If you want blood* and *Highway to hell* — Canada gave them a gold, and Britain, a gold and silver for *Highway to hell*.

Returning to London, there was little on the calendar to

interrupt time designated to writing songs for the new album. Bon was very excited about that, constantly scribbling on scraps of paper and in little blue exercise books that he carried around. The band still had to honour ticket holders to the two gigs that were cancelled on the last tour, the Newcastle Mayfair and the Southampton Gaumont, which were re-scheduled for January 25 and 27 respectively. A 'Top of the Pops' appearance was also being organised, to promote the current single 'Touch too much'. And Angus's wedding, to his Dutch girlfriend Ellen, was on. But that was all.

A great deal of this time Bon spent with a Japanese girl he met known as Anna 'Baba', who moved in with him. Anna was a friend of Ian Jeffery's Japanese wife Suzie. They had been at boarding school together in London in 1976. Anna went back to Japan to complete her education and as soon as she was able she returned to London, which she loved so much. 'The best time in my life it could be. Indeed it was. The best thing and the worst thing did happen to me there then.'

Anna got in contact with her friend Suzie as soon as she arrived back in London. On January 27, she was invited over to the Jefferys' for Sunday dinner, and afterwards, maybe they'd go to Southampton to see AC/DC.

ANNA: 'Had a Sunday dinner with Bon and Jefferys and ridden in the bus to Southampton with them. When their show starts, I mean, when the singer turn up the stage with shiny smile and rhythm, I knew I was naturally in it. After the music over, all the audience gone and the roadies fixing all the instruments on the stage. Busy. Bon stands there with con-tented smile. How did you like the show? It was beautiful.

'Back to London, highway to the town. By the time bus stopped around his flat, I've seen him being quite high with a bottle of booze in his hand. Being drunk but not so quietly and gentle. And his back going home alone, unsteady on his feet.'

The next morning, Bon phoned Suzie to ask her to ask Anna if she'd like to come over to his flat and cook him a Japanese meal. Anna obliged. Bon wooed her 'like the sweetest gentleman'.

After going with him to the BBC to tape the band's 'Top of

the Pops' appearance — 'Touch too much' which would tran-
spire to be so prophetic — Anna spent her first night with Bon.
'Waking up in the morning with him playing Billy Preston. "Be
dressed," he says, "We go to your place and get a couple of
things." Got a cab to Finsbury where I stayed then, but the way
back, not a couple but all my belongings were with us.'

Mick Cocks had by then moved into a flat in Kensington
with Joe Furey. 'I ran into Bon in Victoria; I went to a gig there
one night, and after the gig I just bumped into him. He said,
Come back for a drink, so I said, Okay. He was into saki,
because his girl was Japanese. We'd just be sitting on the
couch, and she'd come out with this warm saki in a pot, and
we'd get rat-arsed. And then she'd cook, it'd just arrive so
we'd eat.

'She couldn't speak English. Bon was teaching her a bit, and
he was learning a bit of Japanese. She was more like the
mothering type. She was a sweet girl. Bon liked her. I think he
was experimenting. But it was fairly obvious she wasn't going
to satisfy any of his deeper needs.

'Drugs were rampant at the time, but I know drugs were
not a problem for Bon. It was alcohol, it was a social thing. I'm
not saying Bon didn't have the odd toot here or there,
everyone did, but he was busy writing the new album. He
was really positive. He wanted to experiment with his lyrics,
and some of his lyrics, he was always reading them to me,
over the phone, and I was encouraging him.'

JOE FUREY: 'He was constantly having to simplify stuff to fit
in with the Youngs' format of the band. Lots of stuff he just
didn't even bother showing to them. Like, that line, She had
the body of Venus with arms — that would have gone
straight over their heads. Like, Who's this Venus, some chick
without arms?'

SILVER: 'Probably for quite a while after we broke up, I still
cashed his cheques for him. It was probably only a matter of a
couple of months he'd been doing that sort of stuff for himself.

'Getting that flat was a big thing for him. He was kind of
really proud of that. I lent him a lot of stuff, because he didn't
have anything, you know. But he was quite pleased with
himself.

'He was probably a bit more tired in that last while. I think his health just started deteriorating very early in his life.'

ANNA: 'Just the way things seemed to rush us. Going to Albert Hall, London Zoo, horse riding he'd teach me how, and to the Hyde Park to listen to the Sunday speeches there, and this summer, just drive through Europe by bike without map. How wonderful! And more and more Bon suggest: We go there too. Never made it.

'I realised, in those days, that when we're taking hands, he often take fast hold of my hand like he's saying something doing that. Something not for our bright future but something so hopeless. May be in a tormented hell.'

Bon was drinking heavily, as Anna testifies: 'Waking late in the morning, start with a glass of Scotch and music'. He was listening to Eric Clapton's *Slowhand*, John Lennon's 'Imagine', the Pretenders' first album, which had just come out, and Tchaikovsky.

Suddenly though, something snapped inside Bon. He told Anna she would have to leave. He said he had to start working. Anna was devastated. Bon had told Ian Jeffery that Anna was distracting him. Suzie explained to Anna that she was smothering Bon.

ANNA: 'So next morning, before he wakes up, very quietly I packed my suitcase and left to the shop on the street, just to get some fresh milk as it's running out and he always liked it in the morning.'

Anna rang Suzie from the public phone in the shop, to ask if she could stay there that night.

ANNA: 'She says, Okay, but Bon just phoned and said you're gone. Going back to the flat, and just taking time opening the door as it's heavy, hard to unlock always. And there was Bon's back at the record player, playing "Wonderful tonight", my favourite song on *Slowhand*.

'Where are you going? Bon seeing my suitcase packed. Just trying to get close to the moon, I answered. Who's gonna cook for me if you go? Bon said. And the plans for coming days. This Sunday, he wants to invite his friends from Paris, the Trust, for Japanese food party.

'Till then, I said to myself, I'd be with him here just till then.

And another day busy being happy... He said, It's been the best for a while, like he's angry with it.'

Trust came to dinner on Sunday. Mick Cocks was there too.

ANNA: 'It was like the Last Supper. Had lots fun. Just Bon seemed that he didn't want me to smoke though. Why?'

The next day was Monday, the 18th, Bon's last. He left the flat first, in the early afternoon. Anna got dressed after about an hour, and left too. She bumped into Bon on the way out. 'My bank is closed,' he said. 'I'm hungry.'

'Do you want me to cook something?' she asked.

ANNA: 'Quick cooking of Japanese soup and fish cake. Doing dishes, I turn back and saw him giving me such a sad look as if he's the one who's hurt separating tonight but me. Dishes done, he calls my name, says, Thank You. Too formal, we've never been like this. And, See you, he said firmly.'

Anna went over to the Jefferys' in Maida Vale.

ANNA: 'Ian came back, said nothing. Plug, the roadie who's staying there, came back later, said that Bon didn't come to the studio. About 11 o'clock at night, he phoned and says: How are you doing?

'Fine.'

'Just checking if you are okay.'

'Fine, I'm fine. How are you?'

'Just sitting on my own. Drinking And writing lyrics. I didn't go to studio today, maybe tomorrow. (That means I can't see you tomorrow either?) Do you have a blanket?'

'No, I'm sleeping in the sink. No, I have a blanket. And you? Do you have a blanket?'

'I have too many for one.'

'I don't think so.'

'Well, I just wanted to check if you were okay. Is Ian there?'

'And he spoke to Ian and the night fell. Wrapped up in a blanket that Plug left on the couch. In the middle of the night or before dawn, I woke up and saw this white light coming through the door. Pain in the abdomen but it went through to the window next second and back to sleep unaware. Maybe I was dreaming.'

Next day, in the afternoon, Anna went shopping with

Suzie. But all her strength had left her. The city seemed dusty and unreal. Back at Maida Vale, when Ian came home, he said Bon hadn't shown up at the studio again. When Plug came back later, he was irritated. 'Where the fuck's Bon?' he demanded.

ANNA: 'Suzie suggest to phone him at the flat. Afraid. Say no. But can't face this. Decided to ring him up at 12.00 a.m. Up to 12.00, I'll wait for him. No phone rings. Time goes slowly. And finally at 12.00, when I put my hand to the phone, I jumped back for fear. The phone started to ring. Suzie nod. So I pick it up. Is Ian there? Not that dear voice husky but the biting businesslike manner. I handed the phone to Suzie and left the room.

'After a while, I heard some sort of screaming. I walked into the room. And there Suzie is sitting with Ian having his arm around her and crying.

'For some tragedy she was crying. I fell down on my knees, asked, Is it Bon? She took my hand and nod. Her face furrowed by tears. Has Bon died? I asked again.

'Soon, many people walked in the sitting room. They all look tamely. But no one aware that a petal of cyclamen, Ian gave to Suzie on Valentine's Day, fell down without sound.'

sixteen
touch too
much

the news first appeared in the London *Evening Standard* on Wednesday, 20th. By Thursday morning it was in all the papers, under inevitable headlines like ROCK STAR DRINKS HIMSELF TO DEATH. The same story was repeated in all of them: Bon had died in a car parked outside a friend's flat in South London sometime on Tuesday. Left to sleep off a drunk on Monday night, or rather in the early hours of Tuesday morning, Bon's friend, identified as Alistair Kinnear, a bass guitarist, came down on Tuesday evening to find him unconscious. He was pronounced dead on arrival at nearby Kings College Hospital. Police said there were no suspicious circumstances.

The *Evening Standard*'s John Stevens located Kinnear, who

Overleaf: Bruce Howe: 'Bon was fatalistic because he took risks, with drugs, it's true'. Irene: 'Impulsive is the best word. He liked being outrageous'.

subsequently went to ground, and has stayed there ever since. Stevens wrote:

> Speaking from his third floor flat in Overhill Road, East Dulwich, a distraught Mr Kinnear described the drinking bout which led to the Australian star's death.
>
> 'I met up with Bon to go to the Music Machine, but he was pretty drunk when I picked him up.
>
> 'When we got there, he was drinking four whiskys straight in a glass at a time...
>
> 'I just could not move him so I covered him with a blanket and left him a note to tell him how to get up to my flat in case he woke up.
>
> 'I went to sleep then and it was later in the evening when I went out to the car and I knew something was wrong immediately.'

These same few quotes formed the basis of every report run around the world. They would start to seem inadequate as the shock sank in.

Bon was at home early in the evening on the night he died, trying to work, drinking. His mind was wandering. Midevening he called Silver. He had never gotten over her. Silver, by then, was a full-scale heroin dealer. Joe Furey was still heavily involved with her. He was there when Bon rang.

SILVER: 'Bon phoned up, he wanted to go and see someone, I think, at Dingwalls, just check 'em out, and he didn't want to go by himself. I didn't feel like going, but Alistair was around, just visiting, and I said, Oh, Alistair's here, I'll see if he wants to go. So Alistair and Bon went. I didn't hear from Bon again. I got two more calls from Alistair.'

Alistair Kinnear was a would-be musician, although he may have been nothing more than a ligger and a drug slut.

Silver says, 'I know that that night Bon wouldn't have had any drugs, 'cos Alistair wouldn't have given him drugs to save his life', and though that might ordinarily seem unlikely, the eventual autopsy bore out the claim, finding no trace of drugs in Bon's body. 'One of the problems,' Silver asserted, 'was that Bon gave Alistair alcohol!'

Alistair drove to Bon's to pick him up around midnight, and the pair went not to Dingwalls, which would have been closed by then, but to the Music Machine, a dive in Camden Town which at least stayed open late. After several rounds, they left the club, and Alistair drove Bon home to Ashley Court. Bon passed out on the way.

According to Silver, when they got to Ashley Court, Kinnear couldn't move Bon. He roused him, but Bon couldn't, or wouldn't, move. Thinking he could usher him inside if he cleared a path, Kinnear took Bon's keys and opened the flat, leaving the door ajar. The building's front door, however, presented Kinnear with something of a problem, and although he managed to open it, he subsequently locked himself out. If this story too seems at all unlikely, it can be corroborated by a note the caretaker at Ashley Court left ostensibly for Bon and Anna the following day. Anna picked it up a few days after that. It read: 'On morning duties on arrival on 4th floor found door of Flat 15 open, all lights and radios on. Also found one set of keys to flat, on mat inside of front door. Awaited someone to come, and having heard nothing, reported matter to managing agents.'

Stranded on the street, with Bon virtually on his back, and uncustomarily pissed, Alistair phoned Silver, wondering what to do.

SILVER: 'I said, Well, why don't you take him back to your place. Got him back to his place, and by then, Bon had completely blacked out. By then it was probably three in the morning or something.'

JOE FUREY: 'Alistair rang again, about three in the morning, saying Bon was passed out in the car, what could he do about it? It was three flights up or something to his flat. Alistair wasn't the sort of guy who was built to throw someone over his shoulder.'

SILVER: 'He said, What'll I do? And this had happened many, many, many times, so I just said, Just take some blankets down to him. Bon had never been to this place, it was in South London, and so I said, Leave a note for him, saying which flat's yours, so when he comes to, he can come up. And of course, he didn't come up, and then Alistair woke up, with a hell of a hangover, which he wasn't used to, and thought, Oh, he must have found his own way home. Then when he went down to the car ...'

When Kinnear found Bon at 7.45 on Tuesday evening, Bon was probably already dead. Certainly, he was dead on arrival when Kinnear got him to nearby Kings College Hospital.

Kinnear gave the hospital Silver's name and number, as the closest he could think of to Bon's next of kin. The hospital called Silver.

SILVER: 'I went down there with Joe. Joe had worked in hospitals. They didn't tell me he was dead. They told me he was there, and it was serious, would I come down. When we got there, we got shown into a little room, I mean, English hospitals are pretty bloody basic. So it was a bit of a surprise being put in this little room. And then they brought us a cup of tea, and Joe said, Look, this isn't right. They don't do this, he must be dead, they're going to send a doctor in to tell us.'

JOE: 'The body was already identified, he had ID on him.'

SILVER: 'I just freaked right out. I mean, I didn't sort of get hysterical or anything. I just shut down. I gave them Mensch's number.'

JOE: 'After that point, the machine took over, all of a sudden they were interested. It was inexperience; they were like, We've got to control the media, otherwise it might affect our career, we're on the verge of ... It wasn't like, Hang on, Bon's just died, we'll worry about anything else later. I'm not saying any of that came from Malcolm or Angus. But this was the way the new management was handling it.

'I mean, it was devastating, at the time, but the real hurt came in the way it was all handled by the management.'

Although she can't actually remember doing so, it had to be Silver, in shock, who phoned Angus. Angus later told *Sounds*, 'Peter, our manager, got to the hospital as soon as he could to find out exactly what had happened and identify him, because everyone was in doubt at the time. I immediately phoned Malcolm 'cos at the time I thought maybe she had got the wrong idea, you know, thought it was him. And Ian, our tour manager, said it couldn't be him 'cos he'd gone to bed early that night. Anyway, the girl gave me the hospital number, but they wouldn't give any information until the family had been contacted. Anyhow, Malcolm rang Bon's parents 'cos we didn't want them to be just sitting there and suddenly it comes on the TV news, you know.'

Ian Jeffery, who went with Peter Mensch to the hospital, identified the body. He was struck by the fact that Bon's neck was twisted, and showed bruising. However, it was accepted then — with an autopsy yet to be performed — that Bon had choked on his own vomit.

ISA: 'It was the day after my birthday, on the 18th, we got the phone call on the Wednesday. I nearly tore my hair out.'

CHICK: 'We'd been over to the club for senior citizens...'

ISA: '... and the phone was ringing when we came in the door, couldnae get in quick enough, and I heard the voice, and I said, Oh, Ron, and it wasnae Ron, it was either Angus or Malcolm. It wasnae Ron at all, he used to phone me...'

CHICK: 'He always used to phone home.'

ISA: 'He used to give us a ring wherever he was. We got a shock.'

Isa rang Irene, in Melbourne. Irene had spoken to Bon only a few days earlier, when he rang her and told her he wanted to set something up for her; and she had just been talking about him then, on the phone to Mary, about how he had a Japanese girlfriend, and they were laughing together, Well, he's had every other nationality...

Irene rang Vince in Sydney.

The news then hit Australia. Even the cynical tabloids, underneath the sensational headlines, seemed genuinely shocked and saddened. 'When Bon Scott died in London yesterday,' the Sydney *Telegraph*'s Roger Crosthwaite said, 'a little piece of Australian rock history ended.'

There was, indeed, almost a sense of national mourning.

PETER HEAD: 'I was playing in a piano bar in Alice Springs. My wife rang and told me, I was half way through a show, playing to about 20 people I guess, quite a few Aboriginals. So I just went out and said, I'm sorry, I can't go on. The audience was shocked too, they just got up and left.'

Pat Bowring reported in the Melbourne *Sun*: 'No funeral arrangements have been made (yet) and the offices of EMI Records in Perth, where his parents live, are handling the flood of flowers and other tributes pouring in from Bon's friends and fans'.

Ted Albert wrote to Chick and Isa:

We have just heard the tragic news and are completely stunned. I would like to try and express to you both, and to Derek and Graham, our feelings for you at this time, and to send you the deepest sympathy from all of us.

We have lost a really good friend. There are not many people in the entertainment world, unfortunately, who you could call a friend, though the public often are made to think differently, but Bon was one of the real exceptions — a genuine person with a generous nature and a real wish to make others happy — a gentleman in the truest sense.

His only interests were his family, his music and living. He was not one, as so many of us are, to always be dreaming of better days and hoping for better things. He was a realist who lived for the present and was quite happy to live each day for itself and to be content with his lot. He gave absolutely everything he had to his music and the living of life — and you cannot ask for more than that.

Unlike many who pass through life without leaving any trace, Bon has left behind a heritage through his music, records and films, that will be for the benefit of others for many years to come. Only today we learned that the boys latest album had sold one million copies in the USA alone, which to me represents a million people whose lives have been enriched by Bon's work.

I can't tell you how saddened we are by our loss, but we know that this can in no way compare with your own loss, and we want you to know that our thoughts are with you at this time.

GRAEME SCOTT: 'I was in Bali. There was a telegram for me. Funny thing was, I was on the ship in Hong Kong, at Christmas, and when you go there, there's these guys, they set up shop, in the alleyways, and I bought a cassette of *Highway to hell*, and there was no picture of Ron on the cover. And then a couple of months later, he died. It was strange.'

The autopsy was held on Friday, February 22. The verdict was 'Death By Misadventure — Acute Alcoholic Poisoning'.

The Coroner, Sir Montague Levine, said Bon was 'the captain of his own destiny', concluding that 'this young man of great talent was a consistent and heavy drinker who died from acute alcoholic poisoning after consuming a very large quantity of alcohol'.

PERRY COOPER: 'You know what I think it was? I think it was just a bad night. Like John Belushi. We had John Belushi on the label too, and he used to come in, and he'd have his bag of cocaine, but I never knew John to inject himself, and so when I heard how he died, I've gotta tell you, it just had to be one of those unforeseen things that happen, maybe he was depressed or something, maybe this girl was leading him on... The same thing happened with Bon. It was just a bad night.'

Bon was alone when he died. It was a cold, bleak night, as an icy wind whipped across the bald hills of Dulwich. Locked inside Alistair Kinnear's Renault, Bon shivered and jerked under a thin blanket.

Under the weight of the accumulated ardour of more than 15 long years on the road, in a conspiracy of circumstances, Bon's ailing system finally gave way; he hadn't eaten, and he was drunk. It was freezing cold. His heart was heavy, his head light. The world outside was harsh. Unable to find a comfortable position, curled around the gearstick, his neck cricked. The bile rose up in his stomach and blocked his asthmatic windpipe. He would be a free man in the morning.

ISA: 'When they did the autopsy, I thought, Oh God, don't tell me there's going to be something else.'

JOE: 'That's what they were supposed to find. It would have been directed at finding that. That huge Fleet Street system would have been paying people to find something.'

The fact that not even Fleet Street could find a scandal surely suggests there wasn't one. Still, Australian *Rolling*

Stone's London correspondent Bruce Elder reported, 'AC/DC's manager Peter Mensch did his best to play the whole story down'. For that very reason perhaps, conspiracy theories soon sprang up, fuelled by the dual suspicions — both seemingly well founded — that some people wanted Bon out of AC/DC, and that he mixed in heavy drug circles. A story went around that Bon's flat was turned upside down the night he died. And though that is partially true — Bon's flat was mysteriously rifled through, but a couple of days after his death — there is ultimately no evidence to suggest any foul play in the actual event of his death.

SILVER: 'There was a lot of weird shit after he died. The flat was closed off, and that's probably the sort of thing that would send people off on conspiracy theories, because it suggests there's something to hide, and there's nothing to hide.

'I rang up and said, Look, can I go around to the flat and get my stuff, because I'd lent Bon a lot of stuff. Forget it. Mensch was friendly, polite and pseudo-helpful right up until the time Bon died, and after that, I was no longer relevant. The other thing was, Bon wanted to be buried in Kirriemuir.'

Anna too was shut out, even if she was still staying at the Jefferys' place, the virtual eye of the storm.

JOE: 'She was ringing us, and her English wasn't that good, saying, Do you know what they're doing? She was in a totally foreign environment, her key in the whole situation was Bon, so imagine how she would have felt. She was really distraught. Also, you know that if Bon was there and that was going on, he would have got fairly pissed off! That generated a lot of hate towards Mensch.'

Anna was desperate to know what happened that night, what might have been going through Bon's head. It was more likely Bon was thinking about Silver, or even Irene — certainly, he called Coral in LA, but all he got was her answering machine — but Anna didn't know that. She phoned Alistair. 'When I saw him at the flat, he was already so drunk,' he told her. After they'd been to the Music Machine, he said, 'I took him to the flat but you weren't there'.

ANNA: 'I couldn't have kept Alistair on the phone so long as he sounded depressed, shocked and so weak.'

Anna thought Bon's feelings may have been reflected in something he wrote that night. All she had to go on otherwise were some lines he had written earlier and shown her, which she learnt off by heart, as follows:

I'm enjoying myself while
I could be writing a song
that's the end
They're bye bye
Everybody knows
Everybody accepts
Everybody knows
Let them talk about you
As they think about me

The only other documentary evidence of Bon's frame of mind around that time has surfaced in the form of a single scrap of paper, on which is written a few lines. It would not do to read too much into a verse nominally titled 'Hairy Kerry', but given both Bon's predilection for things Japanese, and his penchant for word-plays, it is tempting. 'Hairy Kerry' read:

Who's gonna clean it up
Someone's gotta clean it up
Is nothing sacred?

Anna went around to Ashley Court hoping she might find Bon's notebooks. But the flat was closed. She did bump into Mr Burke, the caretaker. It was then that he gave her the note he'd written on Tuesday, which had gone uncollected. He also told Anna that on the Wednesday, 'two big men' came by and got into the flat. He protested, he said, but they went on about their business, picking through things.

Even Graeme Scott can confirm this, seemingly, and strangely, unconcerned. 'When he died, some people went around, and took a few things. Someone had not broken in, but just gone there, and took what they wanted.'

Anna could only presume the 'two big men' were Ian and Jake, another AC/DC roadie, who had brought her suitcase, and other chattels, around for her. When she asked after some other things that were in the flat, sentimental items particularly, Ian told her, 'Everything is packed and taken to the office to send to Perth to his parents'.

JOE: 'All of a sudden, they're telling us we have no right to get into his flat. It was like, Whaddya mean, you didn't drop by a week ago to see if he had anything in the fridge. It comes back to management, and they are playing it far too hardball.

'At the level AC/DC were operating, with the financial infrastructure Leber & Krebs put around them when they came in, there was always the feeling... you see, most people working at that level have a percy, who would just take care of his house, that sort of thing, and make sure he didn't end up somewhere where he forgot to go home. It's pretty standard for management, record companies, to put those people on. So you'd have the situation covered.

'Bon wasn't that chronic. He had that sense of satisfaction about him, as I said, but physically, he wasn't that well. So from a rock'n'roll perspective, it was negligence. You take care of people better than that. Because that's the way the system works. It was a conspiracy of neglect more than anything else.'

After the autopsy, Bon's body was flown out to Australia to be cremated by his family. Anna eventually went back to Japan, but she was haunted by Bon, the questions she never found answers to. On the first anniversary of Bon's death, she went to Perth, to visit his grave, to pay her respects to his parents, and hopefully to see his notebooks, which his parents should have had, since Ian Jeffery told her everything was to be sent to them.

But all Chick and Isa got was a suitcase containing a few items of clothing and a couple of personal effects. Nothing else. No papers. Or musical instruments, records, photo albums — nothing.

Bon was cremated in Fremantle, on Friday, February 29, his ashes buried the following day. He lies in the Fremantle Cemetery's Memorial Garden, shaded from the restless dusty sun under tall gums.

Memorial notices had run in papers all around Australia in the preceding days, placed by friends, family and fans. The funeral notice itself appeared in the *West Australian* on the Thursday:

Scott: The [public] funeral of the late Mr Ronald Belford (Bon) Scott is appointed to arrive at the Crematorium Chapel NEXT SATURDAY MORNING for a Uniting Church Service at 11.00 o'clock.

'Bon's parents were obviously in a bit of shock about it,' Angus told *Sounds*, 'and they had people from our record company in Australia there with them to look after all the details, but they never got the word about what really happened until we flew out there.

'The funeral itself was more or less quiet, though there were a lot of kids outside, you know. It was better being quiet, because it could have been very bad if a lot of people had just converged there.'

Bon's friends felt left out. Alberts' Fifa Riccobono went to Perth to organise everything, and the result, in typical style, was overprotective. Not that the funeral wasn't open, just that arms weren't. Mary Walton only learned about it because Isa kept Irene informed, who in turn kept Mary informed. Irene couldn't make it because she was just about to go into labour. Vince too was tied up. Mary tried to ring Isa to say she was coming, but Fifa wouldn't let her talk to her. Even Isa admonished Fifa, 'But she's an old friend'.

The funeral went unreported even by the local media. A handful of fans congregated harmlessly outside the church. There were no television cameras, newspaper reporters, not even rock journalists.

MARY WALTON: 'I was surprised by that. And that there was no one there from the music business. Maybe that was because it seemed like it was a private affair, maybe because it was Perth, I don't know.'

The band arrived in limousines. Unschooled in the social graces, Malcolm and Angus didn't know how they were supposed to behave. They were pleased to see a familiar face in Mary.

Maria was there with her family. So were all the Hendersons. Vince's parents. Brian Gannon, Bruce Abbott, those who'd stayed behind. Ted Ward.

MARY: 'Everyone was just in shock more than anything else — I know I was — no one really showed much emotion. So everyone just sort of stuck together.'

Still nervous, Malcolm had to ask Fifa if it was alright for Mary to ride in the limo with them after the service.

MARY: 'We went to the parents' place afterwards, and then I went with the boys back to their hotel. I went out sailing with Phil in the afternoon, then had dinner at the hotel, then caught the last flight back to Melbourne. That was it.'

Phil and Cliff went on to Melbourne too, while Malcolm and Angus flew straight back to London. Pressure was already mounting to get back on track. After the breakthrough made by *Highway to hell*, a huge amount of expectation now surrounded AC/DC, and Bon Scott or no Bon Scott, the machine couldn't just stop.

Then a few days later, a strange, eerie thing happened: everyone got cards from Bon. Christmas cards. He hadn't put enough postage on them. For the recipients all around the world, it was a touching postscript to his final sendoff, a reminder of one reason why they held him so dear in the first place — Bon always made an effort.

The obituaries, testimonials and tributes hit the music press, all echoing the same sentiments — that Bon was a great bloke, a great talent, but tragically, yet 'another victim of rock's deadly grind'. In *RAM*, alongside its four-page coverstory obituary by Vince, the names 'Harry & George' appeared undersigned to a full-page testament which read simply, 'A great singer, a great lyricist, a great friend, one of a kind. We'll miss you.'

Vince wrote: 'How or why you died, Bon, I don't give a damn. I only know and care that it was too soon.'

MOLLY MELDRUM: 'Bon dying hit me like John Lennon dying. People say to me today, How can you still have the enthusiasm? Well, it's been our lives. If Bon was alive today, he'd have the same enthusiasm he always had. If you have to react to it like, Oh, I've got to get up and do this, go to the recording studio — that's when it's time to pack it in. It's got nothing to do with age — you just love it.'

Fittingly, the man who replaced Bon in AC/DC, Brian Johnson, paid him a tribute which was not only full of humility, but also cut through the bullshit. 'That poor boy was loved by thousands of people worldwide,' he said. 'When we did a warm-up gig in Holland, this kid came up to me with a tattoo of Bon on his arm and said, This bloke was my hero, but now he's gone, I wish you all the luck in the world. I just stood there shaking. I mean, what can you say when people are prepared to put their faith in you like that? Since then, I feel like I've been singing for that kid and so many others like him.

'I think Bon Scott had a bit of genius. It annoys me that nobody recognised that before. He used to sing great words, write great words. He had a little twist in everything he said. He had such a distinctive voice as well. Oh great, when the man died they were starting to say, Yeah, the man was a genius. That was too late, too late.'

ISA: 'Angus always used to say, It should never have happened. We used to say too, If only he'd done this, if only he'd done that. But you only said that long after he'd gone. Why didn't somebody watch him? But you couldn't watch him. He went his own way, and nobody could stop him.

'If only someone got onto him and made him dry out somewhere, that's all I say.'

GRAEME SCOTT: 'I always thought he was meant to die when he did. A lot of times earlier, he could have died.'

Unable to articulate his grief more appropriately, Malcolm took a swing at Mick Cocks one night when he bumped into him.

MICK COCKS: 'That was when they were looking for scapegoats. He put everybody off side — Angry, everybody.

'It was a moment of sadness for everybody, so it was just stupid. Normally, I would fight back, but under those circumstances, I didn't. I thought, This is not right. A lack of respect. I don't mind celebrating somebody's death; I don't have negative thoughts about Bon in terms of, Oh, he was hard done by,

or that he missed out on this or that, or that he was emotionally not together, or that he was drunk. To me, that means
nothing. To me, he lived and died the way he wanted to.

'We were friends. I just took it as everybody not being sure
how to react, I mean, sometimes it's nice to be able to blame
somebody. And maybe they felt a little guilty, maybe they felt
they should have been paying a bit more attention to what he
was doing. But I don't think that's true either, I think it was
just one of those things that can't be helped.

'Bon was his own man, and one thing you couldn't do was
tell him what to do.'

JOE FUREY: 'I thought it was nice that he got right to the top.
Chronologically, it might look like the top came with *Back in
black*, but he was aware that that was happening. It's like
letting go, you maybe feel the sense that the angels are calling
and you look back and think, I've done it, I don't need to keep
fighting. The body's not enjoying this anymore. That's the
way I like to see it. He'd done it and he was called.'

Of course, the question always remains, What if? There's no
doubt that Bon was really only just hitting his stride as a
writer. He was capable of so much more, and indeed, he was
talking about a solo album. But such musings, now, are
hypothetical and pointless, if not presumptuous. The legacy
Bon left is rich enough as it is.

AC/DC, it's true, went on to greater success. But Bon never
defined success in terms of numbers. He wasn't so naive as to
deny it — because it put money, however filtered down, into
his pocket — but what was as equally important to Bon as
people buying his records was that they were listening to
them, getting off on it.

Bon's life and work were inevitably intertwined, but it wasn't
as if he had trouble distinguishing between art and reality. It
was more a matter of whether or not, besieged by the pervasive
loneliness of life on the road, he chose to know. Because in the
end, he was painfully aware of what was important and what
wasn't. In that, Bon was like most of us, a spiritual battler who
grappled with the bigger questions, and was simply befuddled
by them. He just wanted to do the right thing.

Larger than life in his own time, Bon, in death, became an icon. That's how most of us remember him — the public figure. His friends remember him according to their individual catalogue of memories. Bon chose his own way of life and he lived it to the full, realising most of his dreams. This was one of his successes.

That he is remembered so fondly by all who knew him, almost without exception, as a person of sincerity and great generosity of spirit, and of humour, is another success.

But if the commercial success AC/DC finally found was, to Bon, in itself empty. If he found he still had the same personal problems, it was not so much of a failure that he was unable to resolve them, because that's the nature of life: it doesn't necessarily provide a novelist's neat, apocryphal ending.

Surpassing fleeting fame, Bon's soul became public property as he assumed, finally, immortality.

It is cold comfort for the loved ones left behind.

epilogue

molly was spouting on 'Countdown' that Stevie Wright would replace Bon. It was an obvious conclusion to jump to, but Alberts quickly stood on it. 'We don't know where he got that from,' a spokesperson said, 'but there's absolutely no truth in the rumour. Stevie's got his own thing to do, and AC/DC have theirs.' Stevie's 'thing' was his heroin addiction, which had effectively seen him frozen out of Alberts altogether.

Molly himself was attacked for having bad taste in even raising the issue of a replacement. 'That's just absurd,' he snapped back. 'I've known Bon for 12 years, longer than most of these other people who found it tasteless, and I know he wouldn't have minded. Life goes on; if I dropped dead, I'd expect "Countdown" to announce a replacement immediately and keep going.'

As soon as Malcolm and Angus returned to London from the funeral, they had, indeed, 'got straight back to work on the songs [they] were writing at the time it happened'.

CERTIFIED COPY OF AN ENTRY
Pursuant to the Births and Deaths Registration Act 1953

DEATH	Entry No. 74

Registration district	Lambeth	
Sub-district	Lambeth	Administrative area
		London Borough of Lambeth

1. Date and place of death
Dead on arrival on Nineteenth February 1980
Kings College Hospital, Denmark Hill

2. Name and surname
Ronald Belford SCOTT

3. Sex Male

4. Maiden surname of woman who has married —

5. Date and place of birth
9th July 1946
Forfar, Scotland

6. Occupation and usual address
Musician
15 Ashley Court, Morford Crescent, Westminster

7. (a) Name and surname of informant | **(b) Qualification**
Certificate received from M B Levine, Assistant Deputy Coroner for Inner South London. Inquest held on 22.2.80

(c) Usual address —

8. Cause of death

Acute alcoholic poisoning

Death by Misadventure

9. I certify that the particulars given by me above are true to the best of my knowledge and belief.

....

Signature of informant

10. Date of registration	**11. Signature of registrar**
Twenty-second February 1980	C R Harris Registrar

Certified to be a true copy of an entry in a register in my custody.

.... CA Thorpe .... Deputy Registrar 22nd February 1980 Date

IR 68132

It was amazing, given the band's deep suspicion of the press, that as Dave Lewis put it in the *Sounds* feature called 'The show must go on', published on March 29, 'the ever-articulate Angus allowed himself to become the band's spokesman at a time when many others would sulkily shun the glare of publicity'. But Peter Mensch wanted the assurance out that AC/DC would not fold, and were, in fact, auditioning new singers even then.

Bon meant little to Mensch personally; his primary concern was simply that the band's momentum wasn't allowed to abate. And this next album, everybody, Bon included, believed, was going to be the one. For Malcolm and Angus, their supreme ambition was a bulwark against their grief.

'We got a little rehearsal studio and songwriting became our therapy,' Angus said in another interview. 'Then our manager kept pestering us about what we all dreaded: don't you guys want a new singer? We kept putting it off...'

Alberts said, 'Nine names have already approached them for the job, although of course I can't say who they are. It will be quite a gap to fill, but the band will be auditioning lead singers almost immediately.'

Speculation was rife. *Melody Maker* ran with the Stevie Wright rumour; *NME* and *Juke* suggested it would be one Allen Fryer.

Fryer was George's choice, erstwhile front man with a small-time Adelaide band called Fat Lip. Hailing from Elizabeth, he was another Gorbals boy, a mate of Jimmy Barnes and John Swann. But with the way everything was going, George's opinion was carrying less and less weight. (Fryer himself would go on, ironically, to sing alongside Mark Evans in an eighties heavy metal band managed by Michael Browning, called Heaven.)

AC/DC, such as it was, was holed up in a rehearsal studio in Pimlico, and it was under the watchful eyes, and ears, of Peter Mensch, Mutt Lange and Atlantic Records, that hopefuls flexed their vocal chords.

The gig would go, of course, to Brian Johnson, who at the time was working in a garage back in his hometown of Newcastle, on Tyneside, after abandoning the musical career he dreamed of from the first time he saw local hero Eric Burdon in the early sixties. His band Geordie enjoyed a couple of minor hits in the early seventies, but by the latter half of the decade, their run was over.

The story goes that an AC/DC fan in Chicago sent Peter Mensch a tape of a Geordie album, and Mensch was immediately interested. Geordie was an undistinguished sort of hard rock outfit, but Johnson possessed a pair of lungs of the sort of proportions required by AC/DC. He was located, he squeezed an audition into his 'busy' schedule, and he was hired.

Meanwhile, in the Newcastle north of Sydney, Dave Evans, AC/DC's original singer, sat unawares by phone, dressed head-to-toe in leather and studs waiting for a call which would never come.

Bon was one of a kind and the band knew he could never be replaced as such; besides, Angus was now the star attraction, the front man. Any singer would just have to fall in behind him. And just bellow. Which is what Brian Johnson did, and still does.

The next best thing to a Scot is well likely a Geordie and indeed, Johnson was just the sort of character AC/DC were looking for — down to earth, self-deprecating and with a salty sense of humour. Johnson, in turn, was old and wise enough to know not to overstep his mark.

Johnson was officially accepted by the band even before the end of March, barely four weeks after Bon was buried. The band claimed Bon would have wanted it that way, and they were right. To have come this far and not gone on with it, would have been a betrayal of all Bon's efforts. Bon wouldn't have sat around feeling sorry for himself. The ultimate irony, of course, is that Johnson's shrieking style is essentially as unintelligible as Bon's — which was the main problem the Americans had with Bon — but helped by superior technology, Johnson has served AC/DC admirably.

Johnson would never equal Bon's songwriting ability, but certainly, he would become AC/DC's most eloquent spokesman.

The band spent the first two weeks of April rehearsing with

Johnson and Mutt Lange in London, and then set sail for the Bahamas, where they were booked into the Compass Point Studios in Nassau.

In the same way they'd claimed they didn't want a Bon clone, the band also claimed they weren't interested in 'grave-robbing' any of Bon's final song ideas. But it may well be that there was an unavoidable spilling over of some of Bon's ideas into *Back in black*. Anna Baba believes that Bon's notebooks contained ideas that wound up on the album. 'Rock'n'roll ain't noise pollution' for one, she claims, was a title he was toying with, inspired by the time when the caretaker at Ashley Court complained about loud music late at night. And Ian Jeffery, one of the 'two big men' who cleaned out Bon's flat, has openly admitted he has a 'folder of lyrics of 15 songs' written by Bon.

But if some of Bon's ideas were used, and if that's not unreasonable since Malcolm especially provided him with more than a few lyric ideas or themes in his time, at least he might have been awarded a credit — which he wasn't.

Interest in AC/DC was at a premium in anticipation of the release of *Back in black*. The *Music Week* (UK) top 75 singles dated July 9 contained no less than four AC/DC 'oldies' — 'Whole lotta Rosie' (at number 38), 'High voltage' (number 48), 'Dirty deeds' (number 54) and 'Long way to the top' (number 55). When the album was released at the end of July, less than six months after Bon's death, it became an instant, world-wide smash.

It may have an ambient sound which is somewhat cold, and it may lack the full roundedness of *Let there be rock* or *Highway to hell*, the songs themselves lacking the sinewy texture Bon was responsible for, but certainly *Back in black* stands as a penultimate distillation of the unique musical voice of AC/DC. Some songs may beg the question of Bon's involvement, but others are quite clearly not his work. *Back in black* abounds in lyric cliches, and though Bon was never averse to using a good cliche, he always did so with his own twist applied to it.

The punters didn't mind either way. In Britain, the album went straight to number one. In the United States, although it 'only' went to number four, it lingered in the top ten for over five months. In Australia, it went to number two, held out from the top spot only by the Police's *Zenyatta Mondatta*. By the end of the year, the band would have earned 27 platinum or gold album awards in eight countries.

By now, *Back in black* has sold over ten million copies worldwide, making it, alongside Def Leppard's *Hysteria*, the equal biggest selling 'heavy metal' album of all time. It was AC/DC's crowning achievement, which irrevocably established the band as simply one of the biggest in the world. As a result, the band's back catalogue — the six albums Bon made — has never been out of print, and continues to sell to this day.

JOE: 'Again, a lot of the animosity at the time of his death, people just wanted to convey to his parents just how successful he was. Wanting to say, Do you realise now, you are going to become rich. There were people that wanted to make sure that that was passed on, didn't get lost in the vaults.'

Alberts sent Chick and Isa to Singapore for a holiday after all the fuss had died down. They were delighted with that.

GRAEME: 'Our accountant told us, it would probably last two years, but it's still going. We can't really say anything, because it's between the Youngs and the Scotts. AC/DC and us.'

It's unfortunate that Bon failed to arrange anything for Irene, as he so clearly wanted to do, when his estate by now must be worth millions of dollars. Irene stood by Bon through his lowest ebb, and it's testimony to her strength of character that she hasn't become embittered by the fact that she's ended up with nothing.

Irene was pregnant with a baby boy when Bon died, and she went on to have another one. She lives happily to this day, or like anybody, as happy as you can be, with all the troubles you can have. But happy at best.

Silver got busted, in London, not long after Bon died. It was a bad bust. She'd lost her passport, and she had virtually nothing to fall back on, so she went down hard. Bon invested a lot of emotion in Silver, and even though she eventually came good — got clean, and now, a responsible single mother, is a contributing member of the community — she was probably just the wrong woman for him, at the wrong time. The sort of domestic dream Bon harboured for them both could never have come true.

AC/DC hit the road for the first time without Bon, with Brian Johnson, in August, after testing the water in Holland and Belgium. They toured America for two months, then Britain through into November, and then in December finally returned to Australia to tour for the first time since *Dirty deeds done dirt cheap*. That was only four years earlier, but it seemed like a lifetime. It was a lifetime.

Bon's death was deeply felt in Australia. BON LIVES! graffiti was spreading fast. But an audience as generous of spirit as Bon himself equally embraced his replacement. 'A Triumphant Return' it was called. The Sydney gig at the Showground was rained out two nights in succession, but when it did go on, with Swanee and the Angels supporting, 30,000 kids got exactly what they wanted. The memory of Bon presided over the event.

A party was held backstage after the show. Everybody was there. Mark Evans was there, George and Harry, the entire Young clan, Ted Mulry, Ted Albert, Peter Mensch, Sherbet, Angry Anderson, Pat Pickett, Lobby Loyde — everybody except Angus, who slipped away. The band was presented with forty platinum, gold and silver albums.

A sour note was struck when an unidentified woman in the crowd yelled out for the original members of the band, but AC/DC discard their past as it suits them. She may well also have called for Michael Browning; he was going about his business elsewhere in the city, discarded by AC/DC after he'd served his purpose.

'All I can really say is that Bon is still around and watching,' Brian Johnson said. 'I can't tell you anymore because it's all so personal, but at night in my hotel room I had proof that he was there in some form. I know that he approves of what the new line-up is trying to do. He didn't want the band to split up or go into a long period of mourning. He wanted us to build on the spirit he left behind.'

Demand for AC/DC grew to such a point in America that

Atlantic finally relented and in May, 1981, released the initially rejected *Dirty deeds* album. Five years old, it soared to number three, where it sat for four weeks. The entire back catalogue then peppered the charts; by the end of the year, the band was awarded another haul of precious metal. By now, both *Dirty deeds* and *Highway to hell* have sold over three million copies each in America alone.

Even then though, there was still one height AC/DC hadn't yet scaled — to the very top of the American charts. They wouldn't have long to wait.

By December 1981, with the follow-up to *Back in black, For those about to rock*, AC/DC claimed its first ever US number one. *For those about to rock* might not have stayed there long — in fact, it was the first new AC/DC album that didn't outsell its predecessor — but the thing was, it got there. There wasn't much left now that AC/DC hadn't achieved.

And indeed, if as they say, the only way to go from the top is down, then it was down that AC/DC went. They would bounce back before the decade was out, but the mideighties was as testing a time as any for AC/DC.

After touring for most of 1982 on the back of *For those about to rock*, the band went into hibernation. A break was long overdue after seven or more years on the road. But when the band reemerged in August, 1983, with the album *Flick of the switch*, they found they weren't able to just pick up where they'd left off.

The production credit the album bore, to Malcolm and Angus themselves, was merely the tip of the iceberg of a purging the pair had effected throughout the entire band and its infrastructure. It's a classic syndrome: the successful campaigner who fears his own troops. But Malcolm and Angus never trusted anyone anyway. They sacked practically everybody: Mutt Lange, who had artistically engineered their breakthrough; drummer Phil Rudd; Peter Mensch, who had himself usurped Michael Browning; even de-facto official photographer Robert Ellis was ousted. The replacement of Rudd by Englishman Simon Wright meant that there wasn't an Australian-born member left in the band.

It was only the larger disaster of *Fly on the wall*, the 1985 follow-up to *Flick of the switch*, that prompted Malcolm and Angus to rethink their dictatorship. When Stephen King, long an AC/DC fan, invited the band to contribute some material to the soundtrack of the film *Maximum overdrive*, Malcolm and Angus recalled George and Harry. The result, 'Who made who,' was a 1986 turntable hit which served notice that AC/DC were on the comeback trail.

With George and Harry behind the controls again, the next album, 1988's *Blow up your video*, completed the return. The single 'Heatseeker' was the band's first bona fide, albeit minor, hit since 'You shook me all night long'. The album was further helped along, ironically, by a set of videos which saw AC/DC finally catch up, for better or worse, with MTV.

The next album, 1990's *The razor's edge* — on which George started work again, only, again, to be sacked, replaced by Canadian Bruce Fairbairn — consolidated AC/DC's come-back. The band was now entrenched as a rock'n'roll institution, like the Stones, or Tina Turner or Bruce Springsteen — a living piece of rock'n'roll history. Successive generations of kids will keep coming to see them just so they can say they saw them, which is the basis on which the Stones today function. And just like the Stones, nobody, for all AC/DC's imitators, does AC/DC better than AC/DC.

Still, when the band more recently contemplated sacking Brian Johnson — for whatever reason, not that they've ever needed one — they ultimately thought better of it. Not even AC/DC, they feared, could survive losing its singer for the second time.

George and Harry have never again reproduced the sort of magic they were capable of in the seventies, and today Alberts lives largely on the back of AC/DC and its other former glories. The Midas touch with which George steered the company deserted him not long after AC/DC took their first step outside the nest. The Angels left the label to sign to Epic in America. Rose Tattoo became an increasingly erratic proposition, and acts like John Paul Young and the Ted Mulry Gang simply faded away.

Alberts eventually moved out of Kangaroo House, studios and all, into a new building on Sydney's leafy north shore. It was the end of an era. George and Harry found themselves out of time in the eighties, out of touch, producing almost nothing except their own Flash & the Pan material.

Ted Albert himself had just bought into a promising stage musical called *Strictly ballroom* when, in 1990, he died of cancer. *Strictly ballroom*, as a film, of course, went on to phenomenal success — and propelled John Paul Young back into the charts, with a remixed version of 'Love is in the air' from the soundtrack — but Ted's death saw a dark cloud descend upon Alberts, such as it stood, and it hasn't lifted.

Of course, AC/DC could never be the same after Bon died. Not since the first rush of hits off *Back in black* have they produced anything to equal all the earlier classics, and indeed, it's part of the band's characteristic paranoia, that they are thought lesser of now. But like a vintage bluesman, AC/DC deserve the respect and success they enjoy. The energy and commitment AC/DC have is the least the punters should expect from any rock'n'roll band. But AC/DC have always been distinguished by their lack of pretension and their sense of humour, and these are qualities they cling to.

Bon was contemptuous of the critics that so misunderstood AC/DC, but as it became clear not only that AC/DC weren't going to go away, but what they'd started, their critical reputation improved, to the point where they now stand as a touchstone, and Bon himself is recognised as one of the great lost oracles.

To have called AC/DC heavy metal in the seventies was as inaccurate as it is to call them heavy metal today. To start with, they've never looked like a heavy metal band. 'To me,' Malcolm once said, forgetting AC/DC's glam origins, 'it's disgusting to see men prancing around with make-up on and hairspray wafting around them.' AC/DC never were and still aren't anything more or less than a straight rock'n'roll band, and straight rock'n'roll bands are the best kind of rock'n'roll bands. Where the confusion arises, today, is due to the enormous influence they've had. Heavy metal as it now stands, alongside grunge — which are two sides of the same coin — both unquestioningly accept AC/DC as a fundamental antecedent. The headbangers loved AC/DC from the very first, because like Led Zeppelin, they could be embraced as a heavy metal band, if one that transcended the genre — AC/DC were a rock'n'roll band that just happened to be heavy enough for metal.

Before grunge, there was thrash, and before thrash, hardcore, and before hardcore, punk. AC/DC didn't fit the punk stereotype, but it was as early as hardcore that they were recognised, and their influence felt. By the time thrash emerged, AC/DC's influence was pervasive.

AC/DC was a band that cut its own swathe, and it was Bon that gave AC/DC the character and spirit that they've only ever been able to approximate since he died.

It was a mystique that Bon lent AC/DC, even with all his flesh and blood and guts reality, which is now what the band lacks. Angus still parades in the school uniform he should have grown out of years ago, a cartoon character who comes off stage and admits it's a role he plays. The band has become two-dimensional. They're no less pudgy-faced and red-eyed — obviously, honestly human — which is admirable when one of the great failings of so many rock bands is patent, showbusiness phoniness; but they seem to run on autopilot.

Bon provided the spark — sweet inspiration! — that ignited the fire, that elevated Malcolm and Angus above mere guitar-smiths churning out riff after riff in a rote fashion.

But Malcolm and Angus patched up the band as best they could, and carried on. What else could they do?

biographies

TED ALBERT: The chief of J Albert & Son, the music publishing company that became a record label in its own right and was home to an extended family in the seventies, which was headed by the Vanda/Young production team and included not only AC/DC but also John Paul Young and the Ted Mulry Gang. Ted Albert died of a heart attack in 1990.

'UNCLE' JOHN AYERS: Harmonica player in Fraternity. Upon their demise, he formed Mickey Finn, an R&B outfit that would become an Adelaide institution.

ANNA BABA: Lived with Bon in London for the last few weeks he was alive. After he died, she returned to her Japanese homeland and went to work in medical publishing.

ROB BAILEY: The original bassist in AC/DC. He was sacked after cutting the first album with the band. Today, he is involved in new age music.

CORAL BROWNING: Michael Browning's sister, who worked for him and AC/DC in London, and then America, up until Peter Mensch took over management of the band in mid-1979. She went on to work for Virgin Music in Los Angeles.

MICHAEL BROWNING: Managed AC/DC between the end of 1975 and mid-1979. His experience included running clubs, such as Sebastians and then the Hard Rock Cafe, and managing Doug Parkinson and then Billy Thorpe and the Aztecs, Australia's biggest band in the early seventies. Sacked by AC/DC, he returned to Australia and set up Deluxe Records, which gave INXS, among other bands, its first recording deal. He went on to manage bands himself; the most successful, in the late eighties, being Noiseworks. Today, he heads his own company, Australian Talent International.

PHIL CARSON: General manager of Atlantic Records in London in 1976, he was responsible for signing AC/DC to the label. Now based in Los Angeles, where he heads Victory Music, he was reluctant to be interviewed for this book.

HELEN CARTER: A girlfriend of Bon's in Sydney in 1975/76. She went on to become a musician herself, initially as bassist-songwriter with Do-Re-Mi, who enjoyed such hits as 'Man overboard' in the eighties.

MICK COCKS: Rhythm guitarist in Rose Tattoo, a band Bon himself brought to the attention of Alberts. Leaving the Tatts in 1979, Mick landed in London, where he saw a lot of Bon before his death. He subsequently returned to Australia and rejoined the Tatts, then left again, only to rejoin again as the band reformed.

PERRY COOPER: New at Atlantic Records' head office in New York in 1977 when AC/DC had just joined the label, and as director of special projects, he became one of the band's first champions there. He went out on the road with them often, and always roomed with Bon. He still works at Atlantic.

JOHN DARCY: A roadie for the Valentines in 1969, he remained friends with Bon for years after. He went on to work with numerous other bands before getting out of the business, and today he lives with his family in the hills outside Melbourne.

MAL EASTICK: Lead guitarist in Adelaide band Stars, who supported AC/DC on their controversial return Australian tour in 1976. Today, he plays the blues.

MARK EVANS: Bass player in AC/DC between 1975 and 1977. He went on to play with a number of other bands, such as Finch and Heaven, before retiring from the stage gracefully and taking work in a music shop, which only interrupts his golfing schedule. After some ten years, he recently won an out-of-court settlement with Alberts over unpaid royalties.

JOHN FREEMAN: The drummer in Fraternity. He went on to play alongside Uncle and Bruce Howe in Adelaide R&B institution Mickey Finn, and today performs as an acoustic delta blues guitarist.

JOE FUREY: Met Bon and Silver Smith in Sydney in the summer of 1977/78 and, living in London thereafter and working for UFO, remained friends with them both.

CHRIS GILBEY: Worked at Alberts as a promotions man and later general manager between 1973 and 1977. He has gone on to become one of the single most powerful figures in the Australian music industry, with interests in many of its facets.

RICHARD GRIFFITHS: AC/DC's first booking agent in Britain. Today, he is chief executive officer with Epic Records in New York.

PETER HEAD (nee BEAGLEY): As keyboardist for Headband, he was a contemporary and friend of Bon's in Adelaide in the early seventies. Under the Mount Lofty Rangers aegis, he cut a number of unreleased demos with Bon in 1974.

MAUREEN HENDERSON: Lived around the corner from the Scotts in Fremantle when Bon was growing up. She taught Bon to kiss.

HAMISH HENRY: A wealthy Adelaide patron of the arts who acted as benefactor to Fraternity, and managed the band. He later went back to the family business, but then up and moved to Queensland, where he is now a successful manufacturer of children's playground equipment.

BRUCE HOWE: The leader of Fraternity, he steered the band on after Bon joined AC/DC, with Jimmy Barnes singing in his place, but it was short-lived. He went on then to rejoin Uncle in Mickey Finn, an R&B outfit which later also numbered John Freeman. He was summoned by Jimmy Barnes to join his band after Cold Chisel split, but soon returned to Adelaide, and today he still lives on the Peninsula, just down the road from the Largs Pier Hotel, and plays with the Mega Boys.

DAVE JARRETT: A promotions man for WEA Records in London in the late seventies, whose brief included AC/DC. Today, he lives in Adelaide and heads The Rock Pool, a resource centre for musicians.

IAN JEFFERY: AC/DC's tour manager for many years, from 1977 until the mideighties, he later went back to work for Peter Mensch, with Metallica. He lives in Japan, and eluded being interviewed for this book.

ALISTAIR KINNEAR: He was with Bon on the night he died. He could not be located.

HERM KOVAC: Played drums in the Ted Mulry Gang. Today, he runs Ramrod Recording Studios in Sydney.

DENNIS LAUGHLIN: The original lead singer in Sherbet, he was AC/DC's first, short-lived manager. Today, he manages a hi-fi store in Geelong.

VINCE LOVEGROVE: Met Bon in Perth in the early sixties, and with him formed the Valentines. They remained friends and they both found themselves living in Adelaide in the early seventies, Vince working as a journalist and later an agent, in which capacity he was instrumental in Bon's joining AC/DC. He went on briefly to manage Cold Chisel before moving into television as a producer, and then back to rock'n'roll, as manager of the Divinyls. In the mideighties, he discovered his second wife Suzie, and thus also son Troy, had AIDS, and devoted himself to nursing them — they have both subsequently died — and documenting the experience through films and a book in the hope of raising awareness and understanding of the disease.

IAN 'MOLLY' MELDRUM: He is, well, Molly, media personality, creator of 'Countdown', 'the oldest teenager in Australia', whose enthusiasm for rock'n'roll and particularly Australian rock'n'roll shows no signs of abating. He is barred from the St Kilda Football Club.

PETER MENSCH: As part of the New York management company Leber & Krebs, he usurped Michael Browning's position as manager of AC/DC in 1979. He was himself subsequently sacked, but since his other charges have included Def Leppard and Metallica, he has remained successful. He declined to be interviewed for this book.

WYN MILSON: Played guitar alongside Bon in his first ever band, the Spektors. He went on with Bon to join the Valentines, and after that, became a live sound engineer, a job he still performs at the highest level.

TED MULRY: The leader of the Gang, a hitmaker for Alberts throughout the seventies. Today, he plays the clubs, and still writes material.

PAT PICKETT: A wicked friend of Bon's who managed to attach himself to both Fraternity and AC/DC. In doing so, he learnt the ropes as a roadie and today enjoys almost legendary status himself as one of that game's elder statesmen.

PHIL RUDD: The drummer in AC/DC between 1976 and 1983. Today, he runs a recording studio in New Zealand. He politely declined to be interviewed for this book.

CHICK & ISA SCOTT: Bon's parents. Today, they live in modest surrounds in Perth.

GRAEME SCOTT: Bon's youngest brother, he left home to go to sea in the late sixties, and dropped in and out of Bon's life according to where either of them was around the world at any one time. He eventually settled in Thailand, where, with his Thai wife, he ran a bar.

SAM SEE: Guitarist/keyboardist in Fraternity, after he'd formed Sherbet and left the Flying Circus, and before he rejoined the Circus. He went on to play all around the traps, before recently taking up musical directorship of Channel 7's 'Tonight Live'.

MARIA SHORT: Bon's first real steady girlfriend, whom he lived with on and off, in both Perth and Melbourne between 1965 and 1968, and with whom he always kept in touch. Today, she lives in Perth with her family, and is highly successful in the rag trade.

SILVER (nee MARGARET) SMITH: She and Bon lived together in London during 1976 and 77, although they continued to see each other right up until Bon died. She eventually returned to Adelaide, and today, has a mortgage on a small bungalow with a large garden, which she shares with her son and two German Shepherds. She has been drug and alcohol free since 1986.

PAM SWAIN: Met Bon in 1979 when she was working for the then 2JJ, and enjoyed a brief fling with him. Today, she works for ABC-TV.

IRENE THORNTON: Bon's wife. They were married, in Adelaide, in 1972. They separated in 1974, when Bon joined AC/DC, and divorced finally in 1978, though they remained friends always.

HARRY VANDA: Formerly of the Easybeats, he is the passive partner to George Young in the production team that shaped the success of not only AC/DC but also William Shakespeare, John Paul Young, Rose Tattoo, the Angels and, their own recording persona, Flash & the Pan. He refused to be interviewed for this book.

MARY WALTON (nee WASYLYK, now RENSHAW): A dear friend of Bon's, she met him initially in the sixties, when the Valentines were based in Melbourne. Then a budding fashion designer, she went on to open her own boutique. Today, she still works in the same business, and lives with her kids in Melbourne.

ANGUS YOUNG: Lead guitarist in AC/DC, he refused to be interviewed for this book. The author did, however, interview him for a *RAM* cover story in 1990.

GEORGE YOUNG: Formerly of the Easybeats, he was the sixth member of AC/DC, the producer who guided the band from the very first. He refused to be interviewed for this book.

MALCOLM YOUNG: Rhythm guitarist, he formed AC/DC in 1973. He refused to be interviewed for this book.

british & australian discography

(Entries appear in chronological order of first release; all releases Australian except where indented as 'UK'; where any one release, including reissues, duplicates another except for date, no separate entry is included)

valentines

SINGLES

Every Day I Have To Cry (Alexander)/I Can't Dance With You (Marriott/Lane)
(Clarion MCK-1773, May, '67)

She Said (Wright/Young)/To Know You Is To Love You (Spector)
(Clarion, August, '67)

Why Me/I Can Hear The Raindrops (Lovegrove/Ward)
(Clarion MCK-2167, February, '68)

Peculiar Hole In The Sky (Vanda/Young)/Love Makes Sweet Music (Ayers)
(Clarion MCK-2441, June, '68)

My Old Man's A Groovy Old Man (Vanda/Young)/Ebeneezer (Prince/Taylor)
(Philips BF-427, March, '69)

Nick Nack Paddy Whack (trad. arr. Valentines)/Getting Better (Scott/Milson)
(Philips BF-444, August, '69)

Juliette (Milson/Ward/Scott)/Hoochie Coochie Billy (Lovegrove/Ward/Milson)
(Philips BF-469, March, '70)

fraternity

SINGLES

Why Did It Have To Be Me (Ashdown/Stewart)/Questions (Hayward)
(Sweet Peach SP-105, September, '70. Did not feature Bon)

Seasons Of Change (Robinson/Johns)/Sommerville (Howe/See)
(Sweet Peach SP-113, May, '71)

The Race, Part 1/The Race, Part 2 (Ashdown/Stewart)
(Sweet Peach SP-116, October, '71)

If You Got It (Fraternity)/Raglan's Folly (Jurd/Scott)/You Have A God (M. Jurd/C. Jurd)
(Raven 0601, October, '71)

Welfare Boogie (Fraternity)/Annabelle (Jurd/Bisset)
(RCA 102038, March, '72)

ALBUMS

Livestock (Sweet Peach SP-12005, 1971)
Livestock (Bisset/Jurd)/Sommerville/Raglan's Folly/Cool Spot/Grand Canyon Suite/Jupiter's Landscape/You Have A God/It

Flaming Galah (RCA SL-102038, April, '72)
Welfare Boogie/Annabelle/Seasons Of Change/If You Got It/You Have A God/Hemming's Farm/Raglan's Folly/Getting Off (Jurd)/Sommerville RIP/Canyon Suite

ac/dc

(All Australian releases on Alberts, through EMI; UK, as indicated, Atlantic. All songs Young/Scott/Young except where indicated)

SINGLES

Baby, Please Don't Go (Williams)/Love Song
(AP-10700, March, '75)

High Voltage/Soul Stripper (Young/Young)
(AP-10829, June, '75)

Long Way To The Top/Can I Sit Next To You, Girl? (Young/ Young)
(AP-10990, December, '75; UK, K-10745, April, '76)

TNT/Rocker
(AP-11070, March, '76)

Jailbreak/Fling Thing
(AP-11135, June, '76; UK, K-10805, August, '76)

Dirty Deeds Done Dirt Cheap/Rock in Peace
(AP-11265, October, '76)

Love At First Feel/Problem Child
(AP-11340, January, '77)

   Dirty Deeds Done Dirt Cheap/Big Balls/The Jack
   (UK, K-10899, January, '77)

Dog Eat Dog/Carry Me Home
(AP-11403, March, '77)

   Let There Be Rock/Problem Child
   (UK, K-11018, September, '77)

Let There Be Rock, Part 1/Part 2
(AP-11548, October, '77)

   Rock'n'Roll Damnation/Sin City
   (UK, K-11142T (10″), May, '77)

Rock'n'Roll Damnation/Cold Hearted Man
(AP-11754, June, '78)

   Whole Lotta Rosie (live)/Hell Ain't A Bad Place To Be (live)
   (UK, K-11207T (10″), October, '78)

Whole Lotta Rosie/Dog Eat Dog
(AP-11832, November, '78)

Highway To Hell/If You Want Blood
(AP-104, August, '79)

   Girl's Got Rhythm/Get It Hot
   (UK, K-11406, November, '79)

Touch Too Much/Livewire (live)/Shot Down in Flames (live)
(UK, K-11435, January, '80)

High Voltage (live)/Livewire (live)
(UK, HM-1, June, '80)

EP

**Girl's Got Rhythm/If You Want Blood/Hell Ain't A Bad Place
To Be (live)/Rock'n'Roll Damnation**
(UK, K-11406E, November, '79)

ALBUMS

High Voltage (APLP-009, February, '75)
**Baby, Please Don't Go (Williams)/She's Got Balls/Little Lover/
Stick Around/Soul Stripper (Young/Young)/You Ain't Got A
Hold On Me/Love Song/Show Business**

TNT (APLPA-016, February, '76)
**Long Way To The Top/Rock'n'Roll Singer/The Jack/Live Wire/
TNT/Rocker/Can I Sit Next To You, Girl? (Young/Young)/High
Voltage/School Days (Berry)**

High Voltage (UK, K-50257, May, '76)
**Long Way To The Top/Rock'n'Roll Singer/The Jack/Livewire/
TNT/Can I Sit Next To You, Girl? (Young/Young)/Little Lover/
She's Got Balls/High Voltage**

Dirty Deeds Done Dirt Cheap (APLP-020, October, '76)
**Dirty Deeds Done Dirt Cheap/Ain't No Fun (Waiting Around
To Be A Millionaire)/There's Gonna Be Some Rockin'/Problem
Child/Squealer/Big Balls/Rock In Peace/Ride On/Jailbreak**

Dirty Deeds Done Dirt Cheap (UK, K-50323, December, '76)
**Dirty Deeds Done Dirt Cheap/Love At First Feel/Big Balls/
Rocker/Problem Child/There's Gonna Be Some Rockin'/Ain't
No Fun (Waiting Around To Be A Millionaire)/Ride On/
Squealer**

Let There Be Rock (APLP-022, April '77; UK, K-50366, October, '77)
**Go Down/Dog Eat Dog/Let There Be Rock/Bad Boy Boogie/
Overdose/Crabsody in Blue/Hell Ain't A Bad Place To Be/
Whole Lotta Rosie**

12 Of The Best (APLP-029, unreleased)
**Long Way To the Top/High Voltage/Problem Child/TNT/Whole
Lotta Rosie/Let There Be Rock/Jailbreak/Dirty Deeds Done
Dirt Cheap/She's Got The Jack/Dog Eat Dog/She's Got Balls/
Baby, Please Don't Go**

Powerage (UK, K-50483, April, '78; APLP-030, June, '78)
**Rock'n'Roll Damnation/Down Payment Blues/Gimme A Bullet/
Riff Raff/Sin City/Next To The Moon/Gone Shootin'/Up To My
Neck In You/Kicked In The Teeth**

If You Want Blood (UK, K-50532, October, '78; APLP-034, November,
'78)
**Riff Raff/Hell Ain't A Bad Place To Be/Bad Boy Boogie/The
Jack/Problem Child/Whole Lotta Rosie/Rock'n'Roll
Damnation/High Voltage/Let There Be Rock/Rocker**

Highay To Hell (UK, K-50628, July, '79; APLP-040, October, '79)
**Highway To Hell/Girl's Got Rhythm/Walk All Over You/Touch
Too Much/Beating Around the Bush/Shot Down in Flames/Get
It Hot/If You Want Blood/Love Hungry Man/Night Prowler**

retrospectives

THE SPEKTORS: *Bon Scott with the Spektors* (UK, See For Miles,
SEACD-6)
On My Mind/Yesterday/Gloria/Vince Lovegrove interview

THE VALENTINES: *The Valentines* (Clarion, CLR-501)
**To Know You Is To Love You/She Said/Everyday I Have To Cry/
I Can't Dance With You/Peculiar Hole In The Sky/Love Makes
Sweet Music/I Can Hear The Raindrops/Why Me?/Sooky Sooky
(Covay)**

THE VALENTINES/FRATERNITY: *Bon Scott – Seasons of Change,
1968–72 (Raven, RVLP-33)*
**Getting Better/Ebeneezer/Hoochie Coochie Billy/My Old Man's
A Groovy Old Man/Nick Nack Paddy Whack/Juliette/Bon Scott
Interview with David Day, 5KA/Annabelle/Welfare Boogie/
Hemming's Farm/Sommerville RIP/Getting Off/If You Got It/
Seasons Of Change**